RESISTING MARGINALIZATION
Unemployment Experience and Social Policy in the European Union

Edited by
DUNCAN GALLIE

D1486315

OXFORD
UNIVERSITY PRESS

*This book has been printed digitally and produced in a standard specification
in order to ensure its continuing availability*

OXFORD
UNIVERSITY PRESS

Great Clarendon Street, Oxford OX2 6DP

Oxford University Press is a department of the University of Oxford.
It furthers the University's objective of excellence in research, scholarship,
and education by publishing worldwide in

Oxford New York

Auckland Bangkok Buenos Aires Cape Town Chennai
Dar es Salaam Delhi Hong Kong Istanbul Karachi Kolkata
Kuala Lumpur Madrid Melbourne Mexico City Mumbai Nairobi
São Paulo Shanghai Taipei Tokyo Toronto

Oxford is a registered trade mark of Oxford University Press
in the UK and in certain other countries

Published in the United States
by Oxford University Press Inc., New York

© the several contributors 2004

ISBN 0-19-927184-4

Cover design: Rowie Christopher

RESISTING MARGINALIZATION

ACKNOWLEDGEMENTS

The chapters of this book are based upon a series of research programmes funded by DG Research under the Fourth and Fifth Framework Programmes. These were brought together within a 'project cluster' focussing on 'Unemployment, Work and Welfare', which provided an opportunity to compare findings and discuss the mutual implications of the results of the different programmes. The structure and themes of the book reflect the work of the cluster.

Our thanks to Fadila Boughanemi who was the Scientific Officer at DG Research responsible for the cluster, in particular for her assistance with the organisation of the Workshop on 'Social Exclusion, Activation and Welfare' in Brussels in October 2002, which provided a valuable opportunity to discuss the provisional conclusions of the cluster with EU policy makers.

Chapter 2 uses data drawn from the European Community Household Survey (ECHP), made available by Eurostat, as well as a special survey of the employed and the unemployed in member states of the European Union, commissioned by DG V in 1996 and subsequently released as part of the Eurobarometer series (Eurobarometer, 44.3). Chapter 5 was written as part of the EUROMOD project, financed by *Targeted Socio-Economic Research* programme of the European Commission (CT97-3060). The authors are grateful to Eurostat for access to the European Community Household Panel (ECHP, Wave 2 and 3); for the permission, as described in the agreement between the Office National de Statistique and the EUROMOD project members, to access microdata from the French 'Family Budget' (BdF) survey 1994–95; and for access to the UK Family Expenditure Survey (FES), which was made available by the Office for National Statistics (ONS) through the Data Archive. Material from the FES is Crown Copyright and is used by permission. The authors also thank Sonia Bhalotra, Maria Laura Di Tomasso, Hans Hansen, Holly Sutherland, and Terry Ward as well as seminar participants at the LSE (STICERD) and in Athens, Barcelona, Brussels, Rio de Janeiro, the United Nations, the World Bank and Cambridge for helpful comments. Additional personal acknowledgements can be found in specific chapters.

Neither the funders of the programmes nor the data providers mentioned above bear any responsibility for the analyses or interpretations presented here. An equivalent disclaimer applies to the other data sources and their respective providers. The views expressed in the book as well as any errors are the authors' responsibility.

We are grateful to the Policy Press for granting permission to Ivar Lodemel to replicate two figures for Chapter 8.

Our thanks to Alison Bateman and Ying Zhou, of Nuffield College, and to the staff at Oxford University Press for their assistance in the preparation of the book.

CONTENTS

ABBREVIATIONS

AFDC	Aid for Families with Dependant Children
ALMP	active labour market policies
BdF	Family Budget
BEPGs	Broad Economic Policy Guidelines
ECJ	European Court of Justice
EES	European Employment Strategy
EUROMOD	European tax-benefit model
IEA	International Association for the Evaluation of Educational Achievement
ISCED	International Standard Classification of Education
JSA	Job seeker's allowance
OECD	Organization for Economic Cooperation and Development
OMC	open method of coordination
PAP	Personalized action project
PARE	Part of the re-employment assistance scheme
RMI	Revenue minimum d'insertion
SAA	Social Assistance Act
SCELI	Social change and economic life initiative
SGP	Stability and Growth
TANF	temporary assistance for needy families
TIMSS	Third International Mathematics and Science Study
TSER	Targeted Socio Economic Research
UB	Unemployment benefit
YEA	Youth Employment Act
YUSEDER	Youth Unemployment and Social Exclusion

LIST OF CONTRIBUTORS

Iain Begg is a Visiting Professor at the European Institute, London School of Economics.

Duncan Gallie is an Official Fellow of Nuffield College and Professor of Sociology at the University of Oxford.

Torild Hammer is Senior Research Fellow at NOVA, Norwegian Social Research, Oslo.

Herwig Immervoll is an Honorary Research Associate of the Microsimulation Unit, Department of Applied Economics, University of Cambridge and Research Fellow at the European Centre for Social Welfare Policy and Research.

Thomas Kieselbach is Professor and Head of the Institute for the Psychology of Work, Unemployment and Health (IPG) of the University of Bremen.

Ivar Lødemel is Senior Research Fellow at Oslo University College, Norway.

Steven McIntosh is Research Officer at the Centre for Economic Performance, London School of Economics.

Iver Hornemann Møller is Director of Research of the Centre for Social Integration and Differentiation in Copenhagen and Professor at the University of Coimbra, Portugal.

Marie-Laure Morin is Director of Research in the CNRS, Laboratoire Interdisciplinaire de Recherches sur les Ressources Humaines et de l'Emploi (LIRHE), Université de Toulouse 1 and adviser at the Cour de Cassation.

Cathal O'Donoghue is a Lecturer in the Department of Economics at the National University of Ireland, Galway.

Serge Paugam is Director of Research in the CNRS and Professor of Sociology at the Ecole des Hautes Etudes en Sciences Sociales, Paris.

B. Reynes is Maitre de conferences de droit privé and Director of the Laboratoire Interdisciplinaire de Recherches sur les Ressources Humaines et de l'Emploi (LIRHE), Université de Toulouse 1.

Helen Russell is Research Officer at the Economic and Social Research Institute, Dublin.

Francine Tessier is Ingénieur de Recherche in the CNRS, Laboratoire Interdisciplinaire de Recherches sur les Ressources Humaines et de l'Emploi (LIRHE), Université de Toulouse 1.

Rik van Berkel is a Lecturer and Researcher at the Department of General Social Sciences, Faculty of Social Sciences, Utrecht University, Netherlands.

C. Vicens is Ingénieur d'Etudes at the Laboratoire Interdisciplinaire de Recherches sur les Ressources Humaines et de l'Emploi (LIRHE), Université de Toulouse 1.

CHAPTER 1

Unemployment, Marginalization Risks, and Welfare Policy

DUNCAN GALLIE

Recent years have seen a rapid growth of comparative research into unemployment. In particular, this has focused on two issues: the factors that determine the risks of marginalization resulting from unemployment and the growth of new social activation policies designed to reintegrate the unemployed. These have been largely treated as separate spheres of research. Yet they have important implications for each other. Policies designed to facilitate reintegration into the labour market involve crucial assumptions about the mechanisms that lead to the marginalization of the unemployed. Policies are likely to be successful only insofar as they are based on a well-grounded understanding of the underlying sources of labour market vulnerability and the barriers that prevent people from re-entering employment. The objective of this book is to bring the results of recent research into the processes underlying marginalization together with research into the new policy initiatives. How far do such policies address the factors that have been shown to be the crucial determinants of entrapment?

The chapters draw upon a number of research projects funded by the European Union under the Fourth and Fifth Framework Programmes. They each involved large-scale multi-country research groups that were able to provide in-depth expertise on the countries involved. Taken together they offer at least two major strengths.

First, the range of countries covered by the studies provides particularly good leverage for assessing some of the key arguments that have been developed. Theories of entrapment are frequently of a universal character, implying that similar factors will be responsible for tendencies for marginalization in different countries. By comparing experiences of, and responses to, unemployment in countries with different cultural and structural characteristics, these research projects make it possible to examine the validity of such assumptions and the likelihood that any specific policy solution will have general applicability.

Second, the projects differed in disciplinary orientation: depending on the programme, the research teams consisted predominantly of economists, jurists, social-psychologists, sociologists, or social policy analysts. This was reflected in considerable differences in the methodological approaches adopted, which included the analysis of large-scale surveys, the use of micro-simulation modelling, small-scale in-depth qualitative interviews, and institutional analysis. In their substantive interests, there are many points of intersection of the different research programmes, such that similar issues were illuminated using quite diverse methods. Given the known deficiencies of any particular methodological approach, the convergence or divergence of conclusions from studies of a rather different type provides us with perhaps our best guide to the robustness of knowledge.

In introducing the two broad themes of the book, we begin by examining the intellectual and policy debates that form the context within which the research programmes were developed and then turn to examine the specific contributions of the studies.

Unemployment and Marginalization

Our central focus is on marginalization in terms of the labour market, that is, with the processes that lead to people confronting severe difficulty in entering or re-entering employment. There is no simple threshold at which this takes place, rather it must be conceptualized as involving movement along a dimension of job acquisition difficulty that culminates in entrapment in permanent worklessness. We can broadly distinguish between three theoretical perspectives that have offered contrasting accounts of this process. These are respectively, the social exclusion, the motivational deficiency, and the skills deficiency perspectives.

Social Exclusion

The social exclusion perspective is characterized by an emphasis on resource deprivation as the critical factor creating vulnerability to marginalization. The concept itself is notoriously slippery. Starting life in French sociology as a term designed to emphasize the importance for marginalization of weak social networks, its application became increasingly diffuse as it moved into the mainstream discourse of EU social policy. At its most general, it referred to a situation of multiple deprivation, in which a combination of structural disadvantages led to a vicious circle of progressive marginalization. An important point of departure for researchers has been the conceptualization developed by Kronauer (1998), which emphasized six key dimensions of social exclusion: labour market, economic, institutional, relational, cultural, and spatial exclusion. As Kieselbach points out in Chapter 3, research shows that three factors are particularly important with respect to psychological distress and the difficulty of re-employment, namely length of unemployment, economic deprivation, and social isolation.

Chapters 2 and 3 examine how far unemployment is empirically associated with economic deprivation and social isolation. The research programmes they draw upon were based on rather different methodologies (quantitative in one case, qualitative in the other). They were also different in the coverage of the unemployed: Chapter 2 draws on survey evidence for all adults of working age, while Chapter 3 focuses on the situation of young adults aged 20–24. Despite these differences, the conclusions they reach are remarkably similar. There is no simple, deterministic link between unemployment and the other dimensions of social exclusion. Rather, the impact of unemployment varies substantially between societies as a result of major institutional and cultural differences, in particular in the welfare and family systems.

In its emphasis on economic deprivation, the social exclusion perspective built upon the long-standing concern with the implications of unemployment for poverty. The early literature on unemployment was carried out in contexts where loss of work tended to be associated with very high risks of impoverishment. This was the case both with respect to the interwar studies, where there was virtually no welfare provision, and in the major postwar British studies, where welfare support for the unemployed was of a minimal type. Did unemployment have similar effects across the wider range of contemporary EU countries?

The cross-national comparisons confirm that in most countries unemployment brings a higher risk of poverty. But at the same time, the extent to which this is the case varies substantially between countries. As is shown by Chapter 2, this is confirmed both by relative poverty measures and by measures of self-reported financial hardship.

Taking the relative measure, the proportions ranged from only 18 per cent of the unemployed in poverty in Denmark to 43 per cent in the United Kingdom. The differences reflected to a considerable extent the operation of the welfare system, with generous social transfers in Denmark lifting a much higher proportion of the unemployed out of poverty than the more restricted social transfer system in the United Kingdom. With respect to self-reported financial hardship, it is clear that the level of economic development in a country was also of major importance. While the unemployed were again most protected in Denmark, financial hardship was particularly marked in the Southern European countries and in Ireland, as well as in the United Kingdom.

The social exclusion literature (and indeed earlier studies that focused on the implications of unemployment for social relations) assumed that unemployment inherently undermined people's ties with the local community and heightened tensions within the family, thereby increasing risks of family dissolution. However, comparative research has revealed major differences between countries in the extent to which unemployment is associated with social isolation. As shown in both Chapters 2 and 3, the risks of unemployment leading to social isolation are low in the Southern countries. This is due to the fact that the unemployed in these countries are more frequently integrated into a family environment (particularly that of the parental family) and have patterns of local sociability that are both stronger and more informal in type, with lower entry costs.

The most important factor underlying country differences in social isolation were prevailing patterns of household formation. The Central and Northern countries of the European Union have a high prevalence of single-person households and a tendency for young adults to leave the parental home at a relatively early age. In the Southern European countries on the other hand the family remains a pivotal institution, with extensive normative responsibilities for looking after the well-being of young adult children, and indeed, of providing for them within the parental home.

The risks of experiencing the multiple deprivation of lack of work, economic deprivation, and social isolation varied considerably depending upon the country in which a person became unemployed. In the Northern countries, the unemployed were protected by the fact that they were less likely to experience poverty; in the Southern countries, by the strength of family ties and social networks. It was the unemployed in countries such as the United Kingdom, France, and Germany that were most likely to be affected by the type of multiple deprivation postulated by the social exclusion perspective. The welfare system provided a lower level of financial protection than was to be found in the Northern countries, and, at the same time, people were without the strong social support that characterized the Southern countries.

While social-structural conditions in the Southern countries provided protection from the more immediate social and psychological costs of unemployment, they were not unproblematic. In Chapter 3, Kieselbach makes use of qualitative interviews to explore in greater depth the way unemployment is experienced in these countries. To begin with, while underlining the importance of the Southern family pattern for social support and immediate psychological well-being, he draws attention to longer-term psychological costs. Support comes at the price of dependency, often in the specific form of the prolonged residence of young adults with their parents. Over time, such dependency may generate its own tensions within the family, arising from a sense of restricted autonomy or clashes in lifestyle. Most crucially, it may inhibit longer-term maturation processes, which are usually conceived in terms of people's ability to organize their lives independently.

Another factor that affects the life experiences of many of the unemployed in the Southern countries is the prevalence of casual work in the informal economy (a situation which contrasts sharply with its minimal importance in the Northern and Central EU countries). In the Southern countries about 80 per cent of the long-term unemployed interviewed had been involved in informal work, compared with 30 per cent in Germany and a very small proportion in Sweden and Belgium. Such informal work is not necessarily distinct from the issue of greater family dependency, since it may involve work in small-scale family enterprises. Again Kieselbach underlines the ambiguities of such casual work from a social exclusion perspective. It provides some income to offset the virtual absence of state welfare support. But at the same time, it often places people in unregulated work situations where working conditions are poor (and potentially dangerous); it rarely provides real opportunities for skill development and it may actually enhance entrapment in a precarious sector of the labour market by making it difficult for people to seek the type of work that would provide better long-term opportunities.

While the comparative research results underline the variability of the severity of the experience of unemployment in different countries, and the need to take into account the mediating effects of specific cultural and institutional patterns, this does not provide direct evidence about the validity of the causal dynamics that underlie social exclusion theory. The theory postulates a vicious circle in which unemployment generates increased poverty and social isolation, which in turn entrap people in a situation of labour market marginality. It can be seen in Chapter 2 that analyses using longitudinal data provide only partial support for the argument. Unemployment certainly increased poverty risks in most countries (although as has been seen to very different degrees) and poverty in turn proved to be a highly significant factor associated with difficulty in returning to employment. However, there was no evidence of a similar process with respect to social isolation. Unemployment did not in itself lead to greater social isolation; nor was there any evidence that those who were more socially isolated found it more difficult to find work again. In short, the evidence is consistent with the view that there can be powerful vicious circle-effects that lead to marginalization, but these are almost entirely with respect to the mutually reinforcing effects of unemployment and poverty.

Motivational Deficiency

In contrast to writers from the social exclusion perspective, for whom the causes of marginalization were primarily a result of resource deprivation, a second influential group of analysts have pointed to the importance of the attitudes of the unemployed themselves. Unemployed people, it is suggested, tend to be less committed to employment than others: their inability to obtain a job reflects a lack of effort in searching for work and unreasonable demands about the quality of jobs they are prepared to accept. From this perspective, the unemployed are, to a significant degree, to be seen as responsible for their own marginalization.

There are, broadly speaking, two versions of the motivational deficiency argument. The first sees it largely as a cultural phenomenon. In some cases, most clearly in 'underclass' theses, the roots of low employment commitment are traced back to failures in early socialization. Whether because of family breakdown or being brought up in problem areas of residence, such people were never required to assimilate a conventional work ethic in their early formative years. However, other cultural factors have also been associated with lower work motivation. It has been suggested that women may be less committed to work than men, since they have alternative role identities as wives and mothers responsible for domestic work. The young have also been viewed as a group with potentially lower commitment to employment, since they are emerging from a distinctive youth lifestyle and have lived previously dependent on their parents.

The second version of the motivational deficiency thesis focuses primarily on the impact of financial incentives. Motivation is regarded as relatively malleable and changes in financial incentives are thought to produce corresponding changes in employment commitment. The underlying assumption is that people tend to regard work as a disutility. They would prefer to remain unemployed and receive benefits if the financial rewards of work are not significantly above their income out of work. The provision of financial support to the unemployed is held to reduce the value that people attach to having paid work, raise the level of the wage at which they would be prepared to accept a job, and reduce the intensity of their job search. The more generous the welfare provision and the closer it replaces the income that a person would receive in work, the more negative its impact on the work attitudes of the unemployed.

Cultural Variations in Work Motivation?
A primary issue with such arguments is whether there is sound empirical evidence that employment commitment is lower among unemployed people than among others. Sociological studies have attempted to directly measure employment commitment through attitudinal questions in representative surveys. Research on the adult unemployed casts considerable doubt on the assumption of a lower cultural commitment to employment among the unemployed. Work motivation is at least as high among unemployed as among employed adults (Gallie and Vogler, 1993; Gallie et al., 1994; Gallie and Alm, 2000). There is also no evidence that the unemployed in countries with more generous welfare systems, such as the Scandinavian countries, had lower commitment than those in countries where benefit provision was much lower. Indeed employment commitment was particularly high in countries such as the Netherlands, Sweden, and Denmark, which provided exceptionally high protection of living standards (Gallie and Alm, 2000).

Social–psychological theory and research provides insight into why employment commitment should be high among unemployed adults. As Kieselbach emphasizes in Chapter 3, the consistent finding of psychological research is that the unemployed have higher levels of psychological stress than those at work; there is very little evidence of any significant category of the 'happy unemployed'. Moreover, longitudinal research indicates that this negative effect of unemployment on psychological well-being is causal. Having a job provides an important set of psychological stabilizers that make work vital to people quite independent of pay. These include opportunities for control, skill use, externally generated goals, variety, opportunity for interpersonal contact, and social status in the community (Warr, 1987). For those with substantial work experience, the loss of an environment that provides this type of support for self-identity sharply undermines personal well-being. There are then strong motivational grounds, irrespective of financial incentives, for the unemployed to want employment.

Much of this post-war unemployment research, however, was based upon studies of the experience of unemployed men. There has been much less investigation of whether the employment commitment of the unemployed differs between men and women. Arguably the existence of a legitimate domestic role for women may compensate for the absence of the 'latent functions' of unemployment emphasized in the psychological literature, reducing the motivation to find work.

In Chapter 4, Hammer and Russell address this issue, focusing on young adults who had experienced at least 3 months of unemployment. They draw on new comparative data from large representative samples of young adults with experience of unemployment in three Northern European countries (Finland, Norway, and Sweden), a Central (Germany), and a Southern European country (Spain). The countries were chosen to explore factors that might mediate the gender effect, in particular whether gender differences might be affected by the level of unemployment and by the type of welfare regime. It is possible that high levels of unemployment might strengthen a breadwinner culture and the view that priority should be given to getting men back into work. In contrast, the existence of a welfare system that was institutionally supportive of women's employment, for instance through the provision of good childcare support, might be expected to reduce the gender commitment gap. This could be partly due to the norm-setting role of welfare institutions and partly to their effects in reducing the strain for women arising from the combination of work and family responsibilities.

A first point to note is that there was evidence in each of the countries of lower work motivation among the young adults who had remained unemployed compared to those who had managed to re-enter employment. Although the cross-sectional nature of their study means that conclusions about causality must be regarded as highly provisional, this may indicate that, in contrast to the adult unemployed, motivational factors do play a role in the entrapment of young adults (whether as prior selection factors or as outcomes of unemployment experience). Young adults are typically involved in a cultural transition between a dependent lifestyle heavily focused on education and an independent lifestyle that is usually primarily supported by work. They would have experienced relatively little in-work socialization. The experience of unemployment may have a particularly important role in this phase of the life cycle in affecting the development of work values.

Apart from the case of Norway, there was no evidence, however, that young women were less committed than men when unemployed. Moreover, the country comparisons showed that gender differences were not accentuated by high levels of unemployment or reduced by welfare systems that supported female labour market participation. Unemployed women's employment commitment was as high as that of men in both of the high unemployment countries—Finland and Spain. Young unemployed women's commitment in the 'male breadwinner' welfare regimes of Germany and Spain was similar to that in Sweden and higher than that in Finland, which had welfare institutions that were much more supportive of female employment. But, although the type of welfare regime did not affect commitment, it did affect the labour market outcomes of unemployed people. In particular, young mothers who experienced unemployment in Germany and Spain were more likely to withdraw from the labour market, irrespective of their level of commitment, reflecting the low level of support such regimes provided for working mothers.

While the research underlines the overall similarity in the employment commitment of young unemployed men and women, it also demonstrates the high degree of diversity in each country in the work values of young unemployed women. In particular, there was considerable variation in their employment commitment depending on their family situation. Unemployed women who had a partner or a child showed significantly lower levels of work commitment (the converse of the effect among men, for whom family responsibilities were associated with higher commitment). This could not be accounted for either by vulnerability to financial deprivation or by the implications of family responsibilities for the ease with which people coped with unemployment. The authors suggest that the experience of unemployment may reinforce more traditional role identities among specific groups, contributing to the formation of a dualistic pattern of work attitudes among women.

Financial Incentives and Work Motivation

The economics literature has focused primarily on the implications of financial incentives for work motivation, in particular on the potential negative consequences of unemployment benefit systems. The central argument is that where welfare support provides a high replacement rate, such that there is limited difference between income in and out of work, the unemployed will have lower motivation to find a job. Welfare systems that provide relatively generous benefits that help maintain the living standards of the unemployed, it is suggested, tend to undermine the motivation to work and thereby lead to longer durations of unemployment. Research in this perspective does not rely on direct measures of commitment, but rather infers commitment from the length of time that it takes people to find work.

Despite its influence on welfare policy in a number of countries, the evidence for replacement rate effects is less than satisfactory. The United Kingdom is perhaps the country in the EU that has placed the greatest policy emphasis on the need to ensure that there are strong financial incentives for the unemployed to seek work. Yet research in this country into the effects of replacement rates on the duration of time spent unemployed is remarkably inconclusive (Nickell, 1979; Narendranathan and Stewart, 1993; Arulampalam and Stewart, 1995). There are major technical difficulties in defining and measuring replacement rates that have to be surmounted in such research and some of the variation in results may reflect different choices on how to handle these (Atkinson and Micklewright, 1985). But the overall pattern of results to date suggests that, even if such effects can be found, they are very modest in size. For instance, a recent overview of research in this area concluded that on average the results would point to a 10 per cent increase in the replacement rate extending the duration of unemployment by only $1-1\frac{1}{2}$ weeks (Spiezia, 2000). Moreover, British research indicates that these effects are evident only in the first 5–6 months of unemployment (Narendranathan and Stewart, 1993). This is scarcely strong grounds for thinking that financial disincentives linked to the unemployment benefit system are responsible for entrapment in long-term unemployment.

A significant problem for research into these questions is the need for much better strategies of measurement of replacement rates. This is particularly the case with respect to cross-national comparisons. This issue is addressed by Immervoll and O'Donoghue in Chapter 5, which assesses the appropriateness of different strategies for estimating replacement rates and shows how simulation models can provide more rigorous comparative measures between countries. It draws upon the methodology of the European Tax-Benefit Model (EUROMOD) project which was concerned with developing an integrated European simulation model for assessing change in tax and benefit policies.

The logic of a financial disincentives argument would appear to refer to the way people respond to the extent to which the standard of living they were accustomed to (or are likely to be able to obtain) in work is preserved or eroded when unemployed. But studies of replacement rates most frequently focus upon the relationship between (usually gross) unemployment benefits and employment income. In terms of people's experience of changes in their standard of living, it is the overall household income rather than their personal income that is likely to be the crucial factor. Thus, adequate estimates of the effects of transitions from unemployment to work (or vice versa) have to take into account a wide range of inter-related factors that can vary with changes in employment status. Differential tax treatment of earned income and benefits may mean that net replacement rates, taking account of tax, and contribution payments, are substantially higher than estimates based upon gross income. The loss of earned income may trigger off eligibility rights to a range of other benefits (either for the person who has directly lost their job or for another household member). Moreover, a major factor affecting overall household income will be the extent of earnings brought in by other household members.

The research focused on a comparison of replacement rates in Denmark, France, Spain, and the United Kingdom. These were chosen as examples of four different types of 'welfare state regime'. Denmark represents a 'universal' regime; France a 'conservative', Spain a 'Southern', and the United Kingdom a 'liberal' welfare state regime. The results reveal the particularly harsh effects of unemployment in the United Kingdom. Taking those currently unemployed, about 52 per cent of the Danes, 53 per cent of the French, and 47 per cent of the Spanish had replacement ratios of 80 per cent or more compared to only 22 per cent of the unemployed in the United Kingdom. In each country only a minority of people were in a situation where they were likely to be as well off or better off financially out of work. This was the case for only 1.0 per cent of the unemployed in the United Kingdom, 15 per cent of the Spanish, and 18 per cent of the French and Danish unemployed.

Unemployed women had higher replacement rates than unemployed men in each of the countries, with the absolute difference being greatest in Denmark and Spain. This was not because women had access to more generous unemployment benefits. Rather, their labour market opportunities were such that their earnings potential tended to be inferior to that of other household members (and, as a result, their earnings made less difference to the household's financial situation than earnings of male household members). In all of the countries, replacement rates were also higher for younger people (those aged 25 or less) than for older employees.

The research also examined the way that income in and out of work was composed, thereby showing the factors that accounted for variations in replacement rates. The results posed a serious question mark over the view that the level of benefits was the most crucial determinant of the financial incentives for work. A major factor affecting the likelihood of having a high in-work replacement rate was the presence of other earners in the household. With the possible exception of France, spouses' and other household members' earnings were more important components of income than benefits for those with high replacement rates. This helps to account for the inter-group differences mentioned earlier. Women's replacement rates were higher partly because they tended to have low earnings when in work, but also because they had a higher probability of living with partners with higher earnings. The relatively favourable replacement rates of young people reflected the fact that they frequently were living with their parents.

In short, the research establishes that the financial situation of the unemployed varied substantially between countries, with living standards best protected in Denmark and France and least well in the United Kingdom. However, despite the variations in welfare regime, the great majority of the unemployed in each country were less well-off than they would have been in work. This calls into question any simple assumption that there is a lack of financial incentives for people to obtain work. Where replacement rates were high, this was in general more likely to be a result of the incomes of other members of the household than of benefits per se. The welfare theory of disincentives assumes a far more dominant role of benefits in determining living standards for those out of work that would appear to be warranted by the evidence.

Such comparative evidence on replacement rates raises the issue of whether it is plausible that the variations to be found can account for much of the country differences in risks of entrapment in unemployment. Denmark can in many ways be taken as a critical case of a country in which the financial incentives to work were particularly low. It is a country which has had high compensation rates, which provide support for unemployed adults for a relatively extended period. In terms of household income, as is shown by Chapter 5, living standards were protected particularly well, especially in the case of women. Indeed, it had a particularly high proportion of people who were actually better off out-of-work than in-work. Research on the Danish unemployed has suggested that there may be a within-country effect of the replacement rate on risks of unemployment entrapment for men, although not for women (Pedersen and Smith, 2001). Yet if one takes rates of long-term unemployment as an indicator of risks of marginalization, Denmark was well below the EU average through the 1990s and indeed, well below either Spain or the United Kingdom, where unemployment was associated with much sharper falls in living standards. In 2000, the proportion of the unemployed who were long-term unemployed was 20 per cent in Denmark, compared with 46.9 per cent in the European Union as a whole, 47.6 per cent in Spain, and 28 per cent in the United Kingdom (OECD 2002). It is clear that countries with high replacement rates do not necessarily have high levels of labour market marginalization.

Skill Deficiency

The third approach to marginalization focuses on the vulnerability that arises as a result of skill deficiency in a rapidly changing labour market. Early postwar unemployment studies consistently noted that unemployment risks were not randomly spread across the workforce, but were concentrated on particular categories of the workforce. In particular, those in semi-skilled and unskilled manual work were considerably more likely to be unemployed, and especially long-term unemployed, than non-manual workers (White, 1983; Daniel, 1990). This pointed to the lack of adequate skills as an important determinant of unemployment risks. However, as such studies noted, previous occupational class was a very imperfect indicator of skills as such, since a significant proportion of unemployed people had experienced downward mobility from more skilled work prior to becoming unemployed. A focus on 'manual occupations' is also not well-adapted to the evolving industrial structure since there may be significant numbers of low-skilled non-manual employees in service sector work.

A convincing assessment of the significance of skill disadvantage depends upon having a well-validated measure of low-skill. The selection of specific measures of skill may have important implications for the conclusions reached, yet the choice of one or another definition of low-skill has rarely been supported by rigorous assessment of the way it relates to the types of competencies that are likely to be important on the labour market. In Chapter 6, Steven McIntosh first considers how best to define the category of low skill for comparative analyses, taking account of recent developments in the measurement of specific competencies, and then provides an inter-country comparison of the relative disadvantage of the low-skilled.

The objective was to seek out a measure of skill that was available in a wide range of comparative data sets, and that could allow for an assessment of change over time, and then test its validity by reference to more rigorous measures of competence. Educational attainment has been one of the most frequently used indicators and, although educational structures are highly diverse between countries, a comparative framework is available through the International Standard Classification of Education (ISCED). How far did the measures of lower educational attainment, in particular that of a person having only lower secondary education or less (ISCED 2 or lower), reflect low levels of skill in terms that would be generally recognized as relevant to job performance?

An important development of recent years has been the initiation of comparative studies of mathematical and literacy competencies. With respect to mathematical skills, the researchers were able to build upon the Third International Mathematics and Science Study (TIMSS), which provided an indicator of what could be regarded as the most basic competencies likely to be required in an employment setting. The results provided strong confirmation of the view that those with an educational attainment of ISCED Level 2 or below did have very low levels of mathematical competence. In France, only half of thirty basic questions were predicted to be answered correctly by 90 per cent or more of students, while in other countries the proportions were even lower. For their measure of literacy skills, the researchers drew on the results of the International Adult Literacy Survey (IALS). The level of literacy that is commonly regarded as below the minimum required of most new employees is IALS Level 2. The analysis showed that two-thirds of the low-skilled in terms of the ISCED definition were at IALS Level 2 or lower and, indeed, 73 per cent of those at this literacy level fell into the low-skilled ISCED categories. In short, in terms of both mathematical and literacy ability, a definition of the low-skilled in terms of the lowest ISCED categories appeared to be well-founded.

A comparison of the unemployment rates of those with less than upper secondary education with those of people of upper secondary or tertiary education reveals a very general pattern of disadvantage for the low-skilled across the EU countries. In every country other than Portugal, the risk of unemployment was higher for those with lower secondary or less education compared to those with upper secondary education. And in all countries, the disadvantage of the low-skilled was markedly worse when compared to those with tertiary education. At the same time, there were substantial differences in the extent of this low-skill effect. It was greatest in Ireland and the United Kingdom in comparison with those with upper secondary education, and in Belgium, the United Kingdom, and Ireland in comparison to those in tertiary education. In contrast, it was much less marked in both cases in the Southern European countries—Italy, Portugal, and Spain.

Has the vulnerability of the low-skilled been increasing over time? A comparison of unemployment risks between the mid-1980s and the mid-1990s in the Netherlands, France, Sweden, the United Kingdom, and Portugal shows fluctuation over time but no consistent direction of change. However, the 1990s saw a rise in several countries in the relative risks that the low-skilled would be non-active. At least in part, this is likely to have reflected constrained withdrawal from the labour market and in some countries the reclassification of the unemployed as suffering from disability. Measured in terms of the employment rate, the situation of the low-skilled has been in sharp decline.

There has been a sustained debate about the relative importance of trade competition and technological change in accounting for the erosion of low-skilled jobs. For some it has been the growth of international competition from developing countries that has undercut such jobs in the advanced societies and has led to a shift in favour of higher-skilled forms of production. For others it has been primarily the rapid spread of new technologies that has automated many areas of work traditionally carried out by the low-skilled, while creating a demand for higher skilled technical expertise. The research reported in Chapter 6 suggests that technological change was a much more important factor than trade competition in eroding low-skilled work, particularly with respect to the least skilled workers of all.

What is likely to be the future for the demand for low-skilled workers? Could it be that trends in the growth of service industries may compensate for the erosion of less-skilled work in agriculture and the manufacturing sector? The analysis of the implications of sectoral change between 1985 and 1995 for low-skilled work in France, the Netherlands, Portugal, Sweden, and the United Kingdom suggests that this is unlikely. It confirmed the sharp decline of low-skilled labour in the agricultural, industrial, and construction sectors that previously had been major employers of this type of worker. Only Portugal showed relatively stable employment of the low-skilled in these sectors. While the evolution of the position of the low-skilled was more favourable in the service sector, job opportunities for the low-skilled remained approximately constant over the period 1985–95. Overall, the combination of a sharp reduction of low-skilled jobs in agriculture, industry, and construction and net stability in the service sector implied a marked and ongoing contraction of low-skilled employment.

Policy Responses to Marginalization

Policy interventions to reduce the risks of marginalization for those affected by economic restructuring can come into play both prior to, and after, the loss of work. The former could be termed 'preventative' responses, the latter 'curative'. The principal example of the former is the development of regulative controls over the handling of redundancies (particularly collective redundancies), with a view to preventing people becoming unemployed in the first place and ensuring that they are equipped with the skills to find alternative employment. 'Curative' responses have traditionally consisted of measures designed to provide financial support for the unemployed, *inter alia*, to provide the time and resources for efficient job search. The last decade has seen substantial changes in both types of policy response, at least in terms of formal policy formulations, and an important objective of recent research has been to assess the way such changes have been implemented and their efficacy in reducing risks of marginalization.

The Regulation of Collective Redundancies

The effectiveness of collective redundancy provisions represents a critical case in that these are the most elaborate employment protection regulations available to any sector of the workforce. They are available to only a minority (and therefore concern only a minority of those that become unemployed) because they are tied to specific criteria such as the size of the company or the number of people affected by the redundancy. However, they set the norms for what is to be regarded as best practice; they are 'exemplary measures'. They are the arena for experiments with new types of protection and integration mechanisms. If employees covered by these measures have inadequate protection, then, *a fortiori*, other sectors of the work force must be very much more exposed. Their importance has been recognized by the fact that they have become the object of European regulation—through the European Directives of 1975 and 1998.

In Chapter 7, Marie-Laure Morin and her colleagues examine cross-cultural variations in the formal rules governing collective redundancies and then examine how different systems operate in practice. The researchers compared the nature of the regulations in four countries—France, Germany, Italy, and Spain. At a formal level there are marked differences in the regulative systems. On the basis of a detailed comparison of the legal provisions, three ideal typical models of protection were distinguished: the 'employer liability' model (most closely approximated by France); the 'dialectic model' (approximated by Germany and Italy) and finally the 'administrative intervention' model (to which Spain is closest).

These types or models reflect differences in the functional roles of the three key actors—the employer, the employee representatives, and the administrative authority. In an 'employer liability' system, the responsibility for ensuring adequate protection for employees is placed primarily on the employer (subject to the framework of legal guidelines and judicial control). In a 'dialectic system', responsibility is shared between the employer and the representatives of the person- nel, with clear requirements for consultation and agreement between partners if the redundancy provisions are to be acceptable. Finally, in the third system of 'administrative intervention', major responsibili- ty for protection is placed on the public authorities, who have the right of *prior* authorization before any redundancy measures can be taken. The third of these systems, the authors argue, is in the process of disappearing. Prior administrative authorization was dropped in France in 1986, and even in Spain it relates primarily to control of the grounds for invoking collective redundancy procedures. The core issue then is that of the relative merits of the 'employer liability' and 'dialectic models'.

A notable point about the 'employer liability' model is that the obliga- tions of the employer at the time of a collective redundancy are much more strictly defined by the regulations than in the case of the 'dialectic model'. For instance, in France the acceptable motives for introducing collective redundancies were highly restrictive (and have been made steadily more restrictive by judicial interpretation). Explicitly excluded were motives linked to discipline, age, professional aptitude, and any arguments based on the desire to make additional profits or economies in the interests of competitiveness. In the 'dialectic system', as exemplified by Germany, there was much less attempt to provide detailed specification of the grounds for collective redundancy, rather these were covered by the more general formula of 'urgent necessities' confronting the enterprise, such as economic difficulty or technical change. There were similar differences in requirements with respect to preventative action. In France, the employer was required to demonstrate that a serious effort had been made to find alternative jobs within the company. For firms with more than fifty employees, French legislation required that employers present a 'social plan' with measures to avoid or reduce dismissals. In contrast, in Germany the contents of the social plan were more weakly specified, with the terms to be agreed by the social partners through negotiation. Finally, the regulative provisions in France were much more specific about the measures that had to be taken to assist those who were actually made redundant (for instance, in the obligation to propose to individuals a reorientation agreement).

In principle then, different country regulative systems offered sharply contrasting procedures for protecting employees affected by redundancy initiatives. To examine how these worked in practice, the researchers carried out case studies in a total of thirty firms in the four countries. The striking conclusion they reached was that, despite the major institutional differences, the process of redundancy was remarkably similar between the countries.

This was particularly evident in the outcomes in terms of the types of people who were finally selected for redundancy. One of the key purposes of collective redundancy regulations was to provide protection for those who were likely to be in a relatively weak position in the labour market if they lost their jobs. This was particularly emphasized in German law, which gave priority of protection based on length of service, age, and family responsibilities. Yet in practice, in all systems, it was the most vulnerable who were affected: older workers, those with low skills, and those with long service—precisely the type of people who were likely to find it most difficult to find another job.

Why should this have been the case? The authors point to the sub-version of the formal process through the individualization of the redundancy process. There was a potential conflict between the concern for social protection and the interests of companies to retain their most skilled staff. This led employers in both countries to seek to bypass the regulations, for instance through repeated redundancy measures that fell below the size threshold for collective redundancy procedures. But even when the procedures were respected, for instance, passing through the control of the Works Councils in Germany, the same process of subversion was apparent, with the adoption of early retirement measures that were targeted on older workers. This reflected a relatively high level of consensus between the different parties on financial compensation and early retirement as the preferred way of handling redundancy.

Even in the last decade, this subversion of the formal redundancy process posed considerable costs on older people who wanted to remain in the labour market, since they experienced particularly high levels of unemployment and job precarity. But, in the future, its implications are likely to be even more severe. Given the concern about the costs of pension schemes in aging societies, the early retirement option is likely to be increasingly discouraged, leaving a larger proportion of those made redundant struggling for employment.

There have been, however, significant developments in redundancy practices within both France and Germany which have sought to improve the level of labour market protection. A major source of vulnerability, as was seen in the previous section, is skill deficiency and this is likely to be particularly problematic among older workers whose technical knowledge may be highly outdated given the rapidity of technological change. A central issue then is how to provide better mechanisms for skill maintenance and development among older workers. French law has taken an interesting initiative in this respect by the creation of an obligation on employers to ensure that workers are able to adapt to the evolution of their jobs. Initially resulting from judicial interpretation, this obligation was given legal status by the Loi Aubry in January 2000. It has the benefit of depriving the employer of the possibility of dismissing for inaptitude to work, unless employer training had been offered. The assumption is that, within reasonable limits, employers should find alternative jobs even if this means incurring additional training costs. French experiments were also interesting in their emphasis on an individually tailored support programme for those made redundant, a system that is likely to be more sensitive to the specific problems that older workers might have and to provide remedial training.

A second experiment described in Chapter 7 that deserves close attention is the effort in Germany to preserve employee contractual status for those made redundant. It is clear from the powerful effect of duration of unemployment on the difficulty of re-finding work that unemployment status has a stigmatic effect and is used as a selection criterion by employers. By far the most effective time to give help to those about to be made redundant is prior to the moment of formal redundancy. This underlies the German schemes for assisting reorientation during the redundancy notice period and for transferring such employees to fixed-term contracts with companies specialized in retraining and job placement.

Overall, the researchers highlight the severe deficiencies of the prevalent institutional forms of protection and see a need for a substantial renewal and extension of collective redundancy procedures to provide greater long-term security for older and less-skilled employees. Such recent experiments provide useful pointers as to the direction such reforms should take.

Activation Policies

The most striking developments in policy initiatives to reduce the risks of marginalization have been with respect to 'curative' responses, or the measures taken once people have entered prolonged unemployment. The last decade saw in many countries a movement away from so-called 'passive' policies, concerned with the protection of the living standards of the unemployed, to 'activation' policies designed to reinforce and assist job acquisition.

There were examples of 'activation' provisions in some countries well before the 1990s. For instance, the Federal Social Assistance Act (SAA) introduced in Germany in 1961 made discretionary powers of workfare part of German social assistance legislation. But these were to lie largely dormant until later decades. With the introduction of the RMI (Revenu minimum d'insertion) in 1988, France had introduced provisions for assistance to be accompanied by 'social insertion' contracts designed to improve employability, although it is clear that implementation was patchy and varied heavily depending on the local authority.

It was not until the 1990s that activation policies came to the forefront as an articulated and relatively generalized effort of policy reform. The effective start of the movement can be found in the Danish Youth Allowance Scheme of 1990, which required 18–19-year olds who claimed social assistance to participate in activation in return for benefits; the Norwegian Social Services Act, 1991 and the Dutch Youth Employment Act (YEA) of 1992. German activation policies became more operational after 1993, when local authorities were required by Federal Law to sanction recipients who did not alter their behaviour after a threat of sanctions issued by a social worker. The development of such policies in the United Kingdom is usually dated from the introduction of the job seeker's allowance (JSA) in 1996 and to the 1998 Jobseeker's Employment Act, which introduced the New Deal for Young People.

A controversial issue has been how far the European experiments involved the implementation of US style 'workfare' principles or were of a distinctive type. This is addressed by Ivar Lodemel in Chapter 8. On the basis of a detailed examination of the policies in six countries, he concludes that, although Norway came close to a workfare model, in the majority of European countries studied (Denmark, France, Germany, the Netherlands, and the United Kingdom), the schemes differed from the pure workfare model in a number of important ways. To begin with, 'work-for-benefits' was only one of the alternatives that people were offered. Usually, the schemes also provided opportunities for employment in subsidized jobs (where the person received a normal wage), for temporary contracts in publicly created jobs, for some type of training or education, and in some cases for other non-work activities such as voluntary work. The schemes also tended to differ from a pure workfare model in that it was rarely the case that people would lose all of their financial support for non-compliance. In general the conclusions suggest that the European schemes come closer to 'activityfare' than to 'workfare' in the conventional sense.

However, there were important differences between countries in the emphasis of schemes. The Danish, Dutch, and the British (New Deal) schemes reflected a greater priority to social integration and human resource development, while Norwegian activation policy was more concerned with labour market discipline and job placement. These differences could be seen in the nature of the options available within the programmes. While in Denmark and Britain there were explicit education options (albeit rather different in their ambitions), in Norway the Social Services Act of 1991 did not contain any reference to training and it is clear that this was not an important aspect in the way the scheme was implemented at local level.

Schemes also differed in terms of whether they were almost exclusively targeting the 'able-bodied' unemployed or were also concerned with an attempt to enhance the integration of the most marginalized, who might need considerable assistance (psychological or physical) before they were able to handle even basic work routines. This was partly reflected in the range of options offered—in particular, whether educational courses, voluntary work, and social activities for those furthest from the labour market were available. The Danish and Dutch schemes had gone furthest in seeking to provide some form of activation for those with very weak employability.

Finally, the jobs offered by schemes varied substantially in terms of the formal rights attached to them. They could, for instance, grant trainee status rather than a normal work contract, so that they were outside the scope of general labour market law. Arguably (compare the discussion of collective redundancy measures in Chapter 7) the contractual status of a job is important not only in terms of the security it brings but also because it affects the way the job is seen by future employers and their views about the desirability of employing its holder. In both France and Germany there was a movement in the 1990s to increase the contractual regularity of job offers under activation schemes (for instance the *Emplois Jeunes* programme in France and the *Help Towards Work* schemes in Germany).

A wide range of EU countries, then, took the initiative of introducing activation measures in the second half of the 1990s. But how successful were these in enhancing social inclusion? Were some forms of activation more successful in ensuring social inclusion than others? This issue is taken up by Rik van Berkel in Chapter 9, drawing upon evidence from studies carried out in Denmark, Belgium, the Netherlands, Portugal, and Spain. The research team distinguished between five key domains; work, consumption, sociability, culture, and politics (in the broad sense of the term) and explored how broadly activation encouraged social insertion.

The research led to three principal conclusions. The first was that those on activation measures did appear to be protected from severe forms of social exclusion, and generally considered that activation had improved their situation. The second was that for many it was a restricted form of social inclusion, particularly with respect to the quality of jobs. Finally, the researchers argue that, if activation programmes are to avoid producing their own exclusionary dynamic, they need to look to types of social activation that do not involve formal employment or even direct measures of preparation for participation in the labour market.

While many countries lack adequate evaluation studies, the available evidence indicates that the efficacy of such schemes in securing regular employment was very limited (a point we return to later). The programmes tended to increase people's income and hence their ability to participate in consumption (an effect that varied by country), but there were at best only very modest improvements in other indicators of inclusion. The programmes did appear, however, to have significant psychological benefits. A majority experienced their participation in such schemes as progress in relation to unemployment. For instance, 70 per cent of the Belgian and 61 per cent of the

Danish activated respondents reported increased self-esteem and self-respect. They were also associated with increased social integration, with people experiencing enlarged social networks and an improvement in their social life. As a result, those on such schemes felt more confident and self-assertive and considered that their lives had become more useful and interesting.

Such judgements, involving comparison with the situation of being unemployed, did not necessarily mean that people were content with their experiences of the programmes. In practice there were considerable variations in satisfaction by type of programme. Generally, it was the programmes that provided training and skill development opportunities that were most appreciated. In contrast, those in long-term subsidized jobs were more likely to feel trapped in a separate sector of the labour market that provided few opportunities for returning to regular work. Those in such jobs felt that they were still seen as having an inferior status to regular workers and only a minority felt that recognition from their social environment had increased as a result of participation in subsidized work. There was a risk, then, that people became trapped in activation, either through being unable to escape from what were regarded as pseudo-jobs with few opportunities for either financial or skill improvement or through experiencing recurrent cycling between different programmes. While activation, then, may have increased inclusion relative to the experience of unemployment, it remained at best 'partial inclusion'.

The research also pointed to the risk that activation programmes may themselves harden lines of social exclusion. The definition of 'target groups' at the same time implies that there are people who are less able to be helped; it creates a residual group of the unemployed who are not able or willing to be activated. Paradoxically, the wider the reach of the programmes and the more they seek to include marginalized groups, the more acute the status problems of those who are left out (or who drop out) are likely to become. Those not included in such schemes are likely to be viewed as inherently non-employable, thereby incurring a particularly high risk of social exclusion. Activation policies then generate progressively more difficult challenges for themselves and require constant experimentation with new ways of assisting those in the most difficult situations. In order to do so, they are likely to have to move away from a preoccupation with rapid job acquisition and focus instead upon forms of activity that will gradually build up people's capacities for handling their environment.

Sources of Policy Change

One of the striking features of the introduction of activation policies was how rapidly they spread across different EU societies in the second half of the 1990s. There are different factors that might potentially account for this. It might for instance have been due to the ideological dominance of the United States in an era when globalization was transforming the reach and speed of information dissemination or it might have reflected developments specific to the countries of the European Union. Lodemel takes up these issues in Chapter 8. He is sceptical of the view that the critical factor was ideological contagion from the United States, given that the specific policies adopted by the European countries were very different in type from the experiments in the United States. At best such dissemination might have accounted for the popularity of broad notions such as the need for reciprocity between rights and obligations. Given that the policies of the European countries placed a much stronger emphasis on human capital development (even in a country as reputedly close to US thinking as the United Kingdom), the source of the ideas underlying them had to be sought elsewhere.

Yet it is clear that activation policies were not just the product of specific political party orientations within the European countries. They were introduced by parties both of the right and of the left. They also could not be accounted for as some natural development from prior policy inheritance, since this differed substantially between countries and, in certain cases, the nature of such policies involved a marked rupture with previous traditions.

Both Lodemel (in Chapter 8) and Begg (in Chapter 10) suggest that the European Union may have played an important role in encouraging the spread of common ideas about activation across the Member States. Begg places this within the wider context of the evolving nature of social policy formation in the European Union. In formal terms, the scope for EU intervention was highly restricted by the fact that social policy was regarded as a matter for national governments and was outside the scope of collective decision-making through qualified majority agreement. It was only where social policy could be viewed as an integral part of competition policy (for instance, with respect to the health and safety of work conditions) that this principle could be breached, leading to the formulation of directives with significant regulative power.

The development that provided a mechanism for an extension of EU influence with respect to activation was a more informal one.

It followed the move to develop a European Employment Strategy (ESS), after the Amsterdam Treaty in 1997. As well as fixing broad objectives with respect to both employability and adaptability that accorded well with the principles of activation, the new strategy led to the implementation of a new procedure for guiding policy formation. This was the so-called 'open method of coordination (OMC)', in which the representatives of Member States agreed on common guidelines and monitored progress towards meeting them, but left the choice of detailed policies to national governments. This increased the moral pressure on countries to take effective action, while reducing the defensiveness that arose with attempts to directly expand EU competence. Arguably this type of consensual approach had the effect of significantly increasing the circulation of information about different national experiments, while making national governments more open to learning from the experience of others.

There seems widespread agreement that these new procedures were remarkably effective in the latter 1990s in diffusing ideas and inspiring new policy developments. After the Nice summit of 2000, the model was extended to guide the development of policies for promoting social inclusion (NAPincs). However, their longer-term sustainability as a route for social policy reform is a matter of debate. As Begg points out, the legitimacy of policy-making through the OMC is questionable. Important constraints on policy are developed outside the sphere of national political institutions, but without significant controls at European level. At the same time, the very fact that it is a 'soft' form of policy coordination may make it difficult to introduce rigorous monitoring and provides few levers for enforcement. The pressures for compliance in the system lie primarily in the risk of public 'shaming' rather than in the existence of any material sanctions. Finally, the dependence on consensual decision-making means that it is relatively easy for individual countries to block a reform dynamic, limiting the process to measures that represent the lowest common denominator.

Marginalization Risks and Welfare Policy

How effective were these new policy developments in addressing the underlying sources of marginalization risks? In the case of innovations in collective redundancy procedures, it is clear that, even the most sophisticated protective systems currently prevalent were inadequate in providing labour market protection for the most vulnerable.

The most recent experiments still involve very limited groups of employees and there is little sound evidence for assessing them. However, the most ambitious policy reform in recent years with respect to unemployment has been the shift towards activation policies, and the consequent reduction in reliance on 'passive' policies of financial protection. Here there is more research evidence available, although as will be seen, it still leaves many questions unanswered.

The Limits of Activation

The evidence discussed in the previous sections suggests that activation policies may have an important effect in mitigating the severity of the impact of unemployment. Their emphasis on sustaining work motivation is consistent with the evidence in Chapter 4 that employment commitment may be more fragile for young adults who experience long-term unemployment, although it should be noted that this does not appear to be a significant issue for the wider population of the unemployed. Such programmes, as seen in Chapter 8, also improve people's sense of personal well-being and reduce the psychological distress associated with unemployment. They appear to enhance social integration, although this is a significant problem only in certain countries and does not appear to be directly linked to employment chances.

However, there are grounds for doubting the efficacy of such programmes in achieving their principle objective with respect to the reduction of marginalization risks, namely providing people with a path to regular and sustainable employment. This is evident from the fact that, in general, only a minority of participants exit the programmes and enter into regular employment. For instance, taking those who left between 1998 and 2002 from one of the most ambitious programmes—the UK New Deal for Young People, on average only about 39 per cent were known to have left to an immediate destination of unsubsidized employment, and only 36 per cent had entered sustained employment (defined as an unsubsidized job from which the participant did not return to the programme within 13 weeks).[1] The type of scheme or option people entered affected their employment chances (Bonjour et al., 2001). Schemes based on

---

[1] Data for Great Britain (Department for Work and Pensions, 2003). The destinations of a substantial proportion of leavers (*c.* 29 per cent) were unknown and it is probable that at least some of them moved into jobs, so the success rate of the scheme may have been somewhat higher than this.

employment in a regular workplace are substantially more effective than those that place people in artificially created jobs or provide training disassociated from workplace experience.[2] After 18 months of entering the programme, 50 per cent of those on the subsidized employment option were in employment, compared to only 27 per cent of those that had taken the 'education and training option', a difference in the average level of employment that remained substantial (18 percentage points) even when individual characteristics were controlled. But it remains the case that, even for those on the most successful options, employment chances were not high.

This still leaves open the issue of whether the schemes *improved* the chances of those involved and it is here that there is a particularly severe lack of reliable research. A comparative research programme into the aggregate impact of active labour market policies in five countries (France, Germany, the Netherlands, Spain, and Sweden) in the 1990s produced mixed results (de Koning and Mosley, 2001). There was some evidence that the resources devoted to such programmes measured by expenditure (and in some cases the number of participants) had a positive impact on the outflow from unemployment to employment, but the effect was relatively small (Anxo et al., 2001; de Koning and Arents, 2001) and it was only in Germany that some impact was found on the level of long-term unemployment (Schmid et al., 2001).

Individual-based studies of the most recent types of activation policies are relatively rare and pose difficult technical problems.[3] An investigation of the outcomes of the UK New Deal for Young People estimates that the programme caused an increase of about 5 percentage points (relative to the pre-programme baseline of 26 percentage points) in the probability that young men who had been unemployed for 6 months would get a job in the following 4 months (Blundell, 2001; Blundell et al., 2001). This overall estimate of employment success was very similar to that derived from a study of Swedish programmes in the 1990s, which found that the decision

[2] This is consistent with findings from other countries (O'Connell, 2002; Siancsi, 2002).
[3] This is in part because they raise very tricky issues of research design. In the past, labour market researchers have tended to rely on detailed comparison between those who participate in programmes and those who do not, to establish whether the schemes produced better results than would have occurred if they had not been in place. But, given the very general coverage of the new programmes, there is no fully comparable control group available for assessing the outcomes for similar people who did not pass through a scheme.

to participate in a programme rather than stay longer in open unemployment increased long-term employment probabilities by 5 percentage points (Sianesi, 2002).

There is currently little information on the longer-term implications of different types of activation scheme. Official measures of success in job acquisition tend to be based on relatively short periods in employment, with little information about the quality of the job in terms of longer-term opportunities for skill development and career progression. They certainly do not provide measures of social inclusion as usually understood. More sophisticated research widens the time window, although it is rare for participants to be traced for longer than two years. Without such longer-term data, it is difficult to know whether the programmes are doing more than converting long-term unemployment into recurrent unemployment or into cycling between different types of programme. One of the few studies that was able to track participants for an extended period (5–6 years), using register data, found that programmes in Sweden both raised employment chances and the probability that people would enter a process of cycling between alternating spells of unemployment benefit and programme participation (Sianesi, 2002).[4]

Financial Support: A 'Passive' or 'Active' Policy?

The implementation of activation schemes was often presented as a transition from 'passive' measures (financial support) to 'active' measures (facilitating job acquisition). The language was not neutral: the former were associated with notions of benefit dependency and low work motivation, while the latter were associated with the development of self-sufficiency and employment commitment. Leaning on an economic theory in which unemployment was understood no longer as due to a deficiency in demand management but as reflecting a 'natural rate' of unemployment that was affected *inter alia* by the level of unemployment compensation, governments sought to introduce benefit reduction measures that would reduce financial disincentives to work.

However, as has been seen, research results on the impact of benefit replacement rates are inconsistent; those effects that have been found are in general relatively small and they are evident primarily

---

[4] Sianesi attributes this to the fact that such programmes not only provide skill enhancement but the economic disincentive of re-entitlement to unemployment benefit.

for those in the early months of unemployment rather than for the long-term unemployed. Cross-national differences in welfare generosity do not correspond to the predicted variations in employment commitment. A national programme of research on the Swedish unemployed found that receipt of the relatively generous insurance benefit in that country had no effect on work motivation, while risks of long-term unemployment were related more strongly to resource limitations and local labour market conditions than to motivation (Aberg, 2001). The research reported in Chapter 4 finds that, where work motivation was lower among young women, this was due to family rather than to financial experiences. Overall, it seems unlikely that the effect of benefit levels on work motivation is a major factor underlying the process of marginalization.

The relatively limited impact of higher benefit levels on unemployment durations is not perhaps surprising. In contrast to the simpler version of incentives theory frequently adopted by policy-makers, job search theory had postulated more complex effects of benefit levels, whereby higher benefits could have quite different motivational implications for different types of unemployed people (Mortensen, 1977; Holmlund, 1998).[5] Moreover, as was seen in Chapter 5, welfare benefits are only one factor (and not the most important) in determining replacement rates in terms of household income, which is likely to be the most important influence on people's experience of change in their living standards. Finally, any tendency for more generous welfare provision to extend the duration of job search has to be taken together with the evidence that the acute lack of resources experienced by those in poverty is also a significant obstacle to obtaining a job (Chapter 2). This may be due to the effect of poverty in reducing people's access to information, undermining their self-confidence, and sapping their physical health.

The evidence is consistent that economic deprivation is a major, indeed the most important, source of psychological distress for the unemployed (Whelan et al., 1991; Gallie, 1999). In the light of the evident welfare problems associated with low levels of benefit, there has been a growing interest in the possibility of altering the

---

[5] In particular, higher time-limited social insurance could create a stronger motive for finding work for those who had either lost eligibility or were nearing the end of eligibility since they would have greater interest in re-qualifying for adequate social protection. Since the longer-term unemployed were most likely to be in the situation of benefiting from this so-called 'entitlement' effect, it was far from clear that higher insurance benefits would be a major factor in encouraging marginalization.

structure of incentives by increasing in-work benefits rather than reducing the level of out-of-work benefit. An example of this is the introduction in the United Kingdom of Working Families Tax Credit. But such measures are also not unproblematic. There may be substantial problems of take-up, reflecting in part worries about the stigma that may result from a system of benefit support that passes via the employer and in part beliefs that there is something inherently improper about taking benefit when one has a job. There is a concern that in-work means tested benefits may limit skill progression in work for those that do receive them, by reducing the incentives for training and promotion.[6] Finally, such evidence as currently exists suggests that their effects on the employment of the key target groups were only very modestly positive for single parents and negative for women with employed partners (Blundell, 2001).

An assumption in 'incentives' research is that an effect of relative financial security on the time taken to get a job is due to its consequences in reducing work motivation. But in the early months of unemployment, extended job search may also reflect a concern to achieve a good match between the individual's skills and the job. Consistent with this, a UK study has found that those who took longer finding work tended to be more stable in their jobs afterwards (Boheim and Taylor, 2000). If the slightly extended durations of unemployment associated with higher replacement rates reflect to any significant degree more careful job search, they are a rather inappropriate indicator of deficient work motivation.

Further, the argument has been made that higher financial protection may provide an important condition for risk-adverse unemployed people to train in new specialized skills, with beneficial consequences for both job quality and output (Acemoglu and Shimer, 1999). Similarly, higher benefit levels may make people more willing to accept short-term jobs and job mobility, despite lower job security. If this is the case, then a relatively generous welfare system could be seen as an 'active' rather than a 'passive' measure. This combination of mobility and high protection underlies interest in the notion of 'flexicurity', a labour market pattern often associated with Denmark. Clearly policies with respect to benefits need to take account not only of the (relatively weak) evidence for their effects on work incentives, but also of their potential positive implications for welfare, job matching, and skill formation.

[6] This effect will depend upon whether or not such benefits are time-limited.

Skill Deficiency and the Quality of Work

The risk factor that emerged most consistently from the different research programmes presented in this book was skill deficiency.[7] This implies that the quality of policy responses must be judged ultimately in terms of how far they help to raise the level of initial skills and provide a mechanism for the renewal of skills across people's working lives. It is clear that neither the different types of activation programme that have spread in European countries in recent years nor the efforts that have been made to adjust financial incentives in order to ensure that 'work pays' provide much of an answer to the underlying problems of skill formation.

Research has revealed how deeply rooted many of these problems are, with their origins traceable to early experiences in the family and at school. There is marked inter-generational inheritance of disadvantage. It is now well-established that occupational attainment is heavily class stratified, with people's opportunities strongly affected by the occupational class position of their parents (Erikson and Goldthorpe, 1992). The most significant mediating factor is probably the effect of parental class position on children's educational attainment (Blossfeld and Shavit, 1993; Erikson and Goldthorpe, 2002). Moreover, those brought up in families in poverty or where the parents experience unemployment have significantly poorer educational and labour market chances (Ermisch et al., 2002; Hobcraft, 2003). Research also has pointed to the heavy toll family instability has on children's chances, with children from families where the relationship between parents has dissolved, or from lone parent families, experiencing greater disadvantage in terms of both low qualifications and unemployment risks (Ermisch and Francesconi, 1997; Francesconi and Ermisch, 1998; Ermisch et al., 2002). It is clear that an attack on longer-term sources of marginalization has to begin with substantial investment in helping vulnerable young people in the pre-school and school contexts (Esping-Andersen, 2002). This has implications for welfare benefit policies: a sharp reduction in the living standards of the unemployed may have serious consequences for the next generation.

While the nature of a person's early social milieu significantly affects their later qualification levels and hence their risk of marginalization, these effects are not deterministic. Later experiences can make it possible for people to escape from situations of early labour

---

[7] See also Nickel (2003).

market disadvantage (Hobcraft, 2003). Skill disadvantage, however, is particularly persistent, since low-skilled jobs offer few opportunities for skill development. The pattern is remarkably consistent across countries: it is those who are in more highly skilled jobs that typically get chosen by their employers for further training. This may be reinforced by higher motivation for learning among those who are better educated and in higher occupations, in part reflecting more positive past experiences and greater self-confidence. Taking the European Union as a whole, both in 1996 and in 2000, more than half of those in managerial and professional occupations had received employer training in the previous 5 years, whereas this was the case for only one in five of those in elementary occupations. Moreover, the relative position of those in elementary occupations grew worse over the period (Gallie and Paugam, 2003). Overall, initial labour market disadvantage is strongly reinforced in the course of people's working lives by the poor employment conditions associated with jobs of low skill level, which typically provide few opportunities for updating skills over time. The rapidly changing nature of skills in the advanced economies accentuates the risk of marginalization of those who do not have access to regular training opportunities.

The relatively short periods of training given in most activation schemes are unlikely to have major effects in reversing years of neglect of skill development and the consequent erosion of basic learning abilities. This would require a policy programme in which the provision of ongoing opportunities for skill development is viewed as an essential aspect of socially responsible employment.[8] It would need a large-scale programme to improve the quality of jobs of the low-skilled, to ensure that people are equipped to adapt to technological change and have the skills needed to survive in the labour market in times of economic difficulty. There are grounds for thinking that policy in this area can be efficacious. Some of the 'Northern' European countries have experimented with ways of improving work organization, task quality, and training opportunities and the evidence would suggest that these have had a positive impact on the prevailing character of work conditions (Gustavsen et al., 1996; Gallie, 2003). In most countries, however, welfare policy concerned with marginalization and policies relating to the quality of working

---

[8] For a more extended discussion of what this might involve in practice, see Gallie (2002).

conditions are treated as quite separate spheres. The development of more effective policies against the longer-term factors underlying risks of marginalization requires dismantling the traditional boundaries between 'social' and 'employment' policy, so that the quality of working life can be made central to a broader conception of welfare policy.

CHAPTER 2

Unemployment, Poverty, and Social Isolation: An Assessment of the Current State of Social Exclusion Theory

Duncan Gallie and Serge Paugam

Social exclusion theory has provided the major alternative account of labour market marginalization to that of the economic theory of financial disincentives deriving from welfare provision. In the latter, unemployment is viewed as the result of a motivational deficit, which is linked to a system of welfare benefits that reduces the value that people attach to work. In contrast, social exclusion theory emphasizes the importance of structural constraints on the unemployed. Unemployment generates a downward spiral through its effects on poverty and social isolation, which in turn reinforce the risk of long-term unemployment. One of the appeals of social exclusion theory was that it appeared to bring together a wide array of previously disconnected research findings. We argue that more recent research does confirm its emphasis on the importance of multiple deprivation for the experience of unemployment. However, it fails to provide support for some of its key tenets about dynamic processes and is more consistent with the much older emphasis on poverty as the critical factor behind labour market marginalization.[1]

[1] The chapter draws substantially on the findings of 'Employment Precarity, Unemployment and Social Exclusion' research programme funded by DG Research under the Fourth Framework Programme (Gallie and Paugam, 2000; Gallie et al., 2003).

Theories of Social Exclusion

Despite much conceptual diversity (Room, 1995; S
Paugam, 1996*b*), there is a common component to mos
of social exclusion that refers to a situation of multiple disau
tages in terms of labour market marginalization, poverty, and social
isolation. These different dimensions of social exclusion are seen as
mutually reinforcing, as constituting a vicious circle that leads to a
progressive deterioration in people's labour market situation (Wilson,
1987; Paugam, 1996*a*; Kronauer, 1998).

The process is generally held to begin with loss of employment.
Lack of employment tends to lead to severe cuts in living standards
and increases the risk that people will experience poverty. This in
turn imposes major resource constraints on job search and therefore
helps to trap people into prolonged unemployment. At the same time
low income makes it more difficult for people to participate in social
activities. The lack of resources and the stigmatic effect of unemployment lead to a reduction of people's social ties and growing
social isolation. As the duration of unemployment grows, there is
likely to be increasing tension over finances in the household and
hence an increased risk of marital breakdown and the dissolution of
partnerships. At the same time, lack of money makes it difficult for
people to maintain previous patterns of sociability with friends in the
community, given the importance of exchange in the maintenance of
social relationships. Increased social isolation in turn may reinforce
labour market marginalization by cutting people off from regular
information about employment opportunities.

There can be little doubt that such a model has the attraction of
bringing together into a more systematic framework, diverse
research results about the social consequences of unemployment.
From the 1980s, a number of studies challenged the view that the
creation of the welfare state had largely eliminated the financial dep-
rivations associated with unemployment. Instead they revealed that
unemployment continued to have severe economic penalties
(Moylan et al., 1984; Heady and Smyth, 1989; Hauser et al., 2000),
which in turn had major implications for psychological distress
(Whelan et al., 1991).

At the same time, several studies underlined the way in which
unemployment made social relations more fragile both within the
household and with respect to the wider community. In-depth qualitative research suggested that unemployment was associated with
strongly accentuated tensions within the family (Bakke, 1940*a*; Fagin

and Little, 1984; McKee and Bell, 1985, 1986) while there was also some quantitative evidence that it was directly conducive to higher risks of marital dissolution (Lampard, 1993). The most influential analysis of the impact of unemployment on community relations was the interwar study of Marienthal (Jahoda et al., 1933), which drew a bleak picture of the withdrawal of the unemployed from even free community activities. More recent research in France (Paugam, 1991) underlined the negative effects of the stigma attached to unemployment (particularly as a result of people's interactions with local social services) for their identities and their ability to relate to other people. The importance of the rupture of social networks for the experience of unemployment could be understood in the light of psychological studies that have pointed to the central role of social support in mediating the severity of the psychological effects of unemployment (Warr, 1987).

There was then a significant amount of evidence from earlier studies of the inter-relationships between unemployment and financial deprivation on the one hand and unemployment and social isolation on the other. However, this evidence was fragmentary in that it was derived from a limited number of national contexts and it typically inferred dynamic processes from cross-sectional data. The last decade, however, has seen a major expansion both of comparative research on the experience of unemployment and of studies that provide a longitudinal perspective on the careers of the unemployed. These have made it possible to address three issues of central importance in the evaluation of the theory of social exclusion. The first is the generality of the associations between unemployment and poverty and social isolation. Are these broadly similar across the European societies or are they heavily contingent upon specific institutional structures or cultural traditions? The second is how far multiple deprivation affects people's experience of unemployment, particularly with respect to psychological well-being. Is it the case that social isolation has effects on the level of psychological distress experienced by the unemployed over and above those of poverty? And the third is whether the argument that there is a vicious circle underlying labour market marginalization can be confirmed by longitudinal data.

Commonality or Diversity in the Social Consequences of Unemployment

The social exclusion model implies that the social consequences of unemployment are deterministic in type and therefore will be broadly similar in different societies. But it could be argued that the risk of loss of employment leading to social exclusion will be contingent on macro-structural differences in the way societies are organized both with respect to the distribution (and redistribution) of income and with respect to culturally determined patterns of household formation and sociability. For instance, there are major structural differences at the institutional level between welfare systems, even in the restricted context of the European Union (Esping-Andersen, 1990). There is at least cross-sectional evidence that these imply considerable differences in poverty risks for the unemployed in different countries (Hauser et al., 2000). If this is the case, processes of social exclusion will not be general processes that occur with job-loss but will depend upon the particular nature of institutional arrangements in specific societies. Similarly, the extent to which unemployment is associated with social isolation may depend on the norms governing the organization of the family and its responsibilities for members in need, which vary between societies. There may also be substantial cross-cultural differences in patterns of sociability; for instance, unemployed people in some societies may have much easier access to local social support because the costs involved in participating in the most common forms of leisure activity may be lower.

Poverty

The advent of the European Community Household Panel has given us the first truly comparable figures for poverty among the unemployed in the different EU countries. Table 2.1 shows the proportions of unemployed in 1996 that were below 60 per cent of median equivalized household income. In each of the eleven countries for which we have adequate data, unemployment consistently raised the risk of being in poverty. But, at the same time, there were very marked differences between countries. For instance in Denmark only 18 per cent of the unemployed were in poverty, while rates were also relatively low in the Netherlands and Ireland (32 and 28 per cent, respectively). In contrast in the United Kingdom the proportion of the unemployed with less than 60 per cent of median income was as high as 43 per cent. Two of the Southern countries—Italy and Spain— also had high proportions of the unemployed in poverty. While the evidence does indicate a systematic effect of unemployment in increasing the risks of poverty, the extent of the problem varies a great deal from one country to another.

Table 2.1 *Poverty rates (<60% of median equivalized household income) 1996*

	All aged 18–65	Unemployed
Belgium	9.1	33.9
Denmark	7.0	17.8
France	12.0	39.0
Germany	7.3	30.2
Greece	16.1	32.1
Ireland	10.3	27.8
Italy	13.4	36.3
Netherlands	9.8	32.1
Portugal	18.8	25.3
Spain	16.8	37.1
United Kingdom	9.6	42.8

Note: Figures given are cell percentages.

Source: European Community Household Panel, 1996.

It could be objected that such poverty measures may give little indication of the real risk of suffering from financial hardship, as they are relative measures which will have different implications for living standards depending on the general affluence of the society. Two different techniques have been adopted to address this. The first is to create a measure of material or lifestyle deprivation based on whether or not people possess a range of normal household items. The second is to take account of people's subjective views on their situation, using questions that address the difficulty they face in making ends meet. When these measures are compared at the individual level, the 'income poor' are considerably more likely to report financial hardship than the non-poor (57 per cent compared with 20 per cent). At the same time, it is evident that 'income poverty' is far from synonymous with experienced financial deprivation. While the measure of material deprivation is highly correlated with self-reported financial difficulty (0.56), the relation of these two measures with income poverty is considerably weaker (0.28 and 0.35), respectively. The discrepancy between the measures varies between countries. Income poverty is least closely related to self-reported hardship in Denmark and Ireland, and most closely in Germany, the Netherlands, the United Kingdom, Italy, and Spain.

But if we take the measure of self-reported hardship instead of income poverty, the same general conclusions emerge about the

Table 2.2 *Percentage reporting great difficulty or difficulty making ends meet, 1994*

	All aged 18–65	Unemployed	Ratio unemp/all
Belgium	8.3	32.6	3.9
Denmark	10.6	26.6	2.5
France	16.3	41.0	2.5
Germany	6.5	26.7	4.1
Greece	51.0	72.6	1.4
Ireland	19.8	55.4	2.8
Italy	16.9	44.8	2.7
Netherlands	7.8	30.6	3.9
Portugal	34.6	53.1	1.5
Spain	33.8	56.1	1.7
United Kingdom	11.9	45.0	3.8

Note: Figures given are cell percentages.

Source: European Community Household Panel, 1994.

consequences of unemployment. Table 2.2 compares the proportions reporting great difficulty or difficulty among the unemployed with those for all people of working age. In all countries, the unemployed are much more likely to experience financial difficulty. But again there are very substantial differences between countries in the difference that unemployment makes. The interpretation of this depends crucially upon whether one considers the absolute level or the differential between the unemployed and the general population. In absolute terms, the experience of financial hardship is most prevalent among the unemployed in Greece, Spain, Portugal, Ireland, the United Kingdom, and Italy. It is least common in Denmark, Germany, and the Netherlands. However, the relative disadvantage of the unemployed is least great in the Southern countries (Greece, Portugal, and Spain) where the levels of hardship are exceptionally high both for the general population of working age and for the unemployed. In contrast, the unemployment differential is particularly high in Germany, Belgium, the Netherlands, and the United Kingdom.

In short, country factors mediate in a very significant way the extent to which unemployment is associated with either relative income poverty or the experience of financial hardship. Analyses indicate that income poverty is very strongly related to specific government policies with respect to social transfers (Nolan et al., 2000). For instance, comparing figures for the 1990s of those who would have been poor if there had been no social transfers with the proportions in poverty after transfers, nearly 90 per cent of the pre-transfer poor were lifted out of poverty by transfers in Denmark, whereas this was the case for only 19 per cent of the pre-transfer poor in the United Kingdom. The exceptionally low level of income poverty in Denmark reflected then the generosity of its 'universalistic' welfare system, while the high level of income poverty in the United Kingdom was related to the minimal principle of protection of its 'liberal' welfare system. In contrast, it seems likely that the level of experienced financial hardship is strongly conditioned by the general level of economic development of the society, which affects the resources available to both those in work and the unemployed.

Social Isolation

With respect to social isolation, it is important to distinguish between three major spheres of sociability: the primary, secondary, and tertiary spheres. The primary sphere involves immediate family and household relations, the secondary concerns interaction with neighbours, friends, and relatives outside the household, and the tertiary relates to participation in organizational and associative life. There is no necessity that the impact of unemployment should be identical in the three spheres. It is at least possible that participation in one sphere may compensate for social isolation in another. For instance, those who live alone may find their sociability in regular contact with friends in the community.

How did unemployment affect these different types of sociability? Table 2.3 compares the pattern for the long-term unemployed with that of people in stable jobs. Minus signs represent a significant negative effect (i.e. reducing sociability), while plus signs indicate a significant positive effect (increasing sociability). The effects are net of a range of controls for age, gender, level of education, household composition, and the existence of problems of vandalism or crime in the local area. Taking first the implications for whether or not people live entirely on their own, there is no consistent pattern between countries. In only four countries do we find that unemployment is associated with greater social isolation (Denmark, Ireland, the Netherlands, and the United Kingdom), in two countries—Greece and Italy—it reduces the chances that people will be living alone and in five countries it makes no difference.

Table 2.3 *Sociability of the long-term unemployed compared to people in stable jobs*

	Primary	Secondary	Tertiary
Belgium	n.s.	n.s.	− − −
Denmark	− − −	+	n.s.
France	n.s.	− − −	−
Germany	n.s.	− −	− − −
Greece	+ +	−	n.s.
Ireland	−	−	− − −
Italy	(+)	+	− − −
Netherlands	− − −	n.s.	− −
Portugal	n.s.	n.s.	n.s.
Spain	n.s.	n.s.	− − −
United Kingdom	− − −	n.s.	− − −

Notes: Results are drawn from a series of separate ordered logistic regressions for each country. The reference is those in stable jobs, with controls for age, gender, level of education, household composition, vandalism, or crime in the area. The French data for meeting with friends are not fully comparable as a different response set was used. Minus signs indicate lower, positive signs higher sociability; (+/−) = $p < 0.10$; +/− = $p < 0.05$; + +/− − = $p < 0.01$; + + +/− − − = $p < 0.001$; n.s. = not significant.

Source: European Community Household Panel, 1994.

A similar picture emerges with respect to secondary sociability. In four countries (France, Germany, Greece, and Ireland) the unemployed are less likely than those in stable jobs to meet friends most days, in two they are more likely, and in five they have the same pattern of sociability as those in stable employment. It is only with respect to tertiary sociability that there is a more consistent pattern. In eight of the eleven countries, the unemployed were less likely than those in secure work to participate in clubs and organizations.

Turning from their relative position to their actual levels of sociability, it is again clear that the degree of social isolation varies very substantially between countries (Table 2.4). In the Southern European countries it was exceptionally rare for an unemployed person to be living on their own, whereas this was considerably more frequent in Denmark, the Netherlands, Germany, and the United Kingdom. Less than 5 per cent of those in the Southern European countries were living on their own, compared with 30 per cent in Denmark and 24 per cent in the Netherlands. Similarly, there were wide variations in the extent to which people were socially isolated

Table 2.4 *Sociability of long-term unemployed*

	% Lives alone	% Meets friends most days	% Participates in club or organization
Belgium	7.9	41.9	18.7
Denmark	30.2	39.3	47.6
France	10.3	55.2*	33.0
Germany	17.2	30.4	29.5
Greece	3.7	55.8	10.4
Ireland	7.1	59.0	21.0
Italy	2.4	62.0	11.8
Netherlands	23.5	31.1	39.0
Portugal	1.1	39.3	9.3
Spain	1.5	67.4	21.6
United Kingdom	15.7	48.4	33.0

Note: European Community Household Panel, 1994.
* The question response scale for France differed from that of other countries.

with respect to friends in the community. At one extreme, 67 per cent of the Spanish unemployed met up with friends most days, whereas this was the case for only 30 per cent of the German unemployed. Finally, participation in clubs or organizations was relatively rare in the Southern European countries, but involved nearly half of the unemployed in Denmark and 39 per cent in the Netherlands.

In short, in contrast to the pattern for poverty, there is no consistent picture of the effects of unemployment on sociability with the exception of tertiary sociability, while the risk of social isolation for unemployed people differed very considerably between countries.

It is important, however, to recognize that measures of the frequency of sociability may underestimate the impact of unemployment on social networks. Arguably, people may continue to meet up with friends as frequently as before, but the qualitative nature of the network may change. In particular, those who are unemployed may come to spend increasing amounts of their time in networks constituted predominantly of other unemployed people. This process of network segregation could have important implications for labour market marginalization. It may be the fact that people are cut off from others in employment, rather than being cut off from any sort of contact, that is crucial for the extent to which they receive information about labour market opportunities. Moreover, where

Table 2.5 *Comparison of employment status of friends between the unemployed and those in work*

Proportion of friends unemployed	In work (%)	Unemployed (%)
All of them	0.8	2.8
Most of them	3.6	19.0
About half of them	5.9	16.7
Some of them	42.0	45.2
None	45.2	12.5
Don't Know	2.5	3.8
Half + unemployed	10.3	38.5
N	7754	4586

Source: Eurobarometer 44.3, 1996.

a person's network consists largely of other unemployed people, they may be less likely to receive either financial or emotional support (an issue to which we return in the next section).

An EU survey carried out in 1996 provides some confirmation that there is a significant degree of network segregation between those in work and the unemployed (Table 2.5). Unemployed people were much more likely to socialize with other unemployed people than were those in paid work. Among the unemployed 39 per cent said that half or more of their friends were unemployed. This was nearly four times higher than the proportion for those in a job (10 per cent). Indeed nearly a quarter (22 per cent) of the unemployed said that most or all of their friends were unemployed. The effect of unemployment in leading to network segregation was virtually identical for men and women.

The Extent and Implications of Multiple Deprivation

The relationship between these different aspects of deprivation is of fundamental importance in any assessment of the risks of social exclusion for unemployed people. Social exclusion refers to a situation where people suffer from the cumulative disadvantages of labour market marginalization, poverty, and social isolation. The different aspects of deprivation are held to be mutually reinforcing over time, leading to a downward spiral in which the individual comes to have neither the economic nor the social resources needed to participate in their society or to retain a sense of social worth. But

Table 2.6   *Percentage of unemployed who are both in poverty
(<50% of the mean) and socially isolated*

	%Poor and living alone	%Poor and no daily contact with friends
Germany	9.9	21.0
Denmark	3.7	2.8
Netherlands	5.7	18.3
Belgium	4.0	13.8
France	4.4	27.7
United Kingdom	9.6	24.6
Ireland	2.8	8.7
Italy	0.6	14.9
Greece	1.3	10.4
Spain	0.7	7.4
Portugal	0.0	14.9

Source: European Community Household Panel, 1994 (Gallie and Paugam, 2000).

how commonly in practice were the unemployed subject to both poverty and social isolation and is there any evidence that the effects of social isolation reduced the well-being of the unemployed over and above the effects of poverty?

Table 2.6 presents a picture of the empirical distribution of cumulative disadvantage involving both financial deprivation and social isolation. It includes both of the types of sociability which could be expected to have a significant affective dimension—primary (involving the household) and secondary (involving close informal links in the community). There is considerable variability between countries in the prevalence of multiple deprivation in both cases. In Denmark only a very small proportion of the unemployed experience the dual deprivation of poverty and social isolation. This is true whichever indicator is taken of social relationships. The Southern countries also show a pattern of low cumulative disadvantage given the virtual absence of unemployed people who are both poor and living on their own. The countries with the highest proportion of people with double deprivation are the United Kingdom, Germany, and France. Nearly 10 per cent of the unemployed in both the United Kingdom and Germany are both poor and living on their own, and more than 20 per cent are both poor and have no daily contacts with friends. In France, there is an exceptionally high proportion (28 per cent) of people who are both poor and have weak informal ties with others in the community.

How does poverty and social isolation affect the well-being of unemployed people? There is now very consistent evidence about the general impact of unemployment on well-being. Psychological studies have consistently shown that unemployment increases psychological distress (Warr, 1987). Moreover, longitudinal studies confirm that this follows job loss (or the insecurity that comes from the announcement of redundancies) and cannot be accounted for by the selection into the ranks of the unemployed of those with poor mental health. Return to employment has also been shown to lead to a marked reduction in distress. A very similar picture emerges from Europe wide studies of the impact of unemployment on life satisfaction (Gallie and Russell, 1998). Comparing the life satisfaction scores of the unemployed and employed over the period 1983–94, in all countries and in all periods the unemployed were markedly less satisfied with their lives than those in employment. In all countries, unemployment lowered life satisfaction for both men and women, although the effect was more marked for men.

A European survey from 1996 provided evidence on psychological distress, using a reduced version of the well-tested General Health Questionnaire (Gallie, 1999). This confirmed that the unemployed suffered from significantly higher levels of psychological distress within the European Union as a whole. The psychological effects of unemployment were virtually as severe for women as for men. Moreover, those who had been unemployed for more than a year had higher distress scores than those unemployed for less than a year. But, although unemployment reduced psychological well-being in all countries, there were considerable variations by country in the difference it made. Its effects were greatest in Germany (both East and West) and in Ireland. In contrast, in all the Southern countries (Italy, Portugal, Spain, and Greece) the severity of the effect of unemployment was lower than average. Distress was also relatively low in the high welfare societies—Denmark, Finland, and Sweden.

But what evidence is there that either the quantitative or qualitative nature of social relationships may exacerbate the problems of the unemployed, in the way suggested by social exclusion theory? The evidence provided in Table 2.7 is consistent with the view that social isolation does play a significant role in accentuating the severity of the experience of unemployment. To begin with it was associated with substantially lower social support, as measured by a series of items asking people whether there was someone they could rely

Table 2.7 *Effects of social isolation on social support, financial deprivation and psychological well-being among the unemployed*

	Model 1 social support		Model 2 financial deprivation		Model 3 psychological well-being	
	Coefficients	Sig.	Coefficients	Sig.	Coefficients	Sig.
Living on own	−0.13	*	0.48	***	0.10	***
No weekly contact	−1.04	***	0.13	n.s.	0.11	***
50%+ of friends unemployed	−0.17	***	0.23	***	0.00	n.s.
Social support			−0.22	***	−0.06	***
Financial deprivation					0.33	***
Model	Ordered logit		Ordered logit		OLS	
N	5099		5096		4973	

Note 1: * = $p < 0.05$, *** = $p < 0.001$, n.s. = not significant.
Note 2: The models control for duration of unemployment, age, sex, class, and country. Model 1 (social support), $\chi^2 = 609.05$ (df 29); model 2 (financial deprivation), $\chi^2 = 641.30$ (df 29); model 3 (psychological well-being), adjusted $R^2 = 0.21$.
Source: Eurobarometer 44.3.

upon in the event of emotional, job search, or financial need.[2] An overall support index was constructed by summing the positive answers with respect to the three types of support, with higher scores indicating greater support. Those who lived on their own and in particular those with no weekly contact with friends had significantly lower levels of support. But it is also notable that, even when these factors had been taken into account, the composition of a person's network was of considerable importance. Networks that consist primarily of other unemployed people are less likely to provide support. There are some plausible mechanisms that may underlie this. Unemployed friends will not be in a position to offer either information about the job market or financial assistance in times of need. It is even doubtful whether they are likely to offer much in the way of

[2] People were asked if there was anyone they could rely on *from outside their household* if they had any of the following problems: if they were feeling depressed, if they needed help finding a job, or if they needed to borrow money to pay an urgent bill, like electricity, gas, rent, or mortgage.

psychological support, since they themselves may well be suffering from higher levels of anxiety and depression. Rather networks are relatively segregated, tending to lock people into their current situation rather than providing a bridge out of it. This may be reinforced by the tendency of those without work to be concentrated in particular local areas (Buck, 1992; Lawless et al., 1998). At the extreme, the situation would be one of collective network exclusion.

The second model of Table 2.7 shows the implications of weak social ties for people's financial vulnerability. Those living on their own and those with a high proportion of unemployed friends were particularly likely to report a high level of difficulty in making ends meet. The importance of the effective supportiveness of the network also comes out very clearly. It must be remembered that one of the constitutive items related directly to, whether or not, a person could rely on someone if they needed to borrow money to pay an urgent bill. Certainly where people did have friends that they could rely on when confronted by these and other crises in their lives, they were significantly protected from financial hardship.

Finally, it can be seen that social isolation had direct implications for the psychological well-being of the unemployed. Higher scores in model 3 reflect greater psychological distress. Both primary and secondary sociability were important. Those who lived on their own and those who did not have at least weekly contact with friends suffered significantly higher levels of distress. The quality of relations was also important. Those who had networks on which they could rely for support had higher levels of psychological well-being. This is consistent with a very substantial literature on the importance of support systems in mediating the psychological impact of life crises (House, 1981). But a final and very important point to note is that, even when the various social isolation and social support variables have been taken into account, financial deprivation has a highly significant impact. Indeed, it emerges as the single most important factor affecting the psychological well-being of the unemployed, with an effect very much stronger than that of any of the social isolation measures.

The Dynamics of Social Exclusion

The 'vicious circle' of social exclusion provides a plausible picture of how the process of marginalization might occur. However, there could be other views about the relationship between the key variables.

One possibility is that cross-sectional associations largely reflect differential processes of selection. With respect to the association between poverty and unemployment, it is conceivable that the fact that the unemployed have high levels of poverty is primarily a reflection of the fact that the poor are more likely to become unemployed. Similar issues arise with respect to the assumed relationship between loss of employment and social isolation. While unemployed people may be more likely to live on their own, the causal sequence can be a matter of debate. While the view that unemployment generates higher levels of conflict in the family and leads to the break up of relationships is certainly plausible, it may also be the case that those who were living on their own at the time of unemployment found it more difficult to acquire a job (say because of reduced sources of information or the lack of financial resources coming from another member of the household). Similarly, self-selection may account for any tendency of the longer-term unemployed to have reduced social networks. Those who become unemployed may be people who had relatively weak friendship networks and low participation in informal associations when they were in work. With respect to associational life, this was certainly the conclusion of an important American study on the unemployed (Schlozman and Verba, 1979).

Any attempt to assess the merits of these different viewpoints is inherently problematic without longitudinal data. The cross-sectional nature of the data that has been available hitherto has made it very difficult to assess causal sequences. While a causal model has generally underpinned research into social exclusion, the evidence that has been deployed has been largely descriptive of the extent of overlap between different types of disadvantages rather than providing direct evidence of the *process* of marginalization. The European Community Household Panel provides the type of longitudinal data needed to assess this, including a range of important control variables. In this final section we consider the evidence for the causal path proposed by the social exclusion thesis. This consists of two distinct phases: first, the consequences of unemployment for people's financial and social situation and second the impact of financial difficulty and the lack of networks for re-employment.

The first phase issue is whether unemployment does precipitate poverty and social isolation. Taking the years 1994–5, we compared the risk of entering into a state of poverty of those who moved from employment to unemployment to that for people who remained in stable employment. Moreover, as they are sometimes considered 'latent' unemployed, those who moved out of employment into non-activity

Table 2.8 *Effects of transitions into unemployment and non-activity on poverty risks*

	Employment to unemployment		Employment to non-activity	
	Coefficients	Sig.	Coefficients	Sig.
Belgium	4.2	**	1.4	n.s.
Denmark	1.0	n.s.	5.4	***
France	4.3	***	2.5	***
Germany	5.1	***	2.2	**
Greece	1.7	(*)	1.5	(*)
Ireland	1.7	n.s.	2.5	***
Italy	4.8	***	1.3	n.s.
Netherlands	2.0	n.s.	1.5	n.s.
Portugal	3.1	***	2.2	**
Spain	2.8	***	1.2	n.s.
United Kingdom	6.2	***	2.7	***

Note 1: Coefficients are a based on a series of separate Logistic Regression models for each country. The models included controls for age, sex, education, presence of dependent children, whether a dependant adult, and size and employment status of others in the household.
Note 2: Note 1. (*) = $p < 0.10$; * = $p < 0.05$; ** = $p < 0.01$; *** = $p < 0.001$; n.s. = not significant.
Source: European Community Household Panel 1994 and 1995.

were also compared with the stably employed. Given the known importance of individual and household characteristics for poverty status, all of the analyses included controls for age, sex, education, and household structure.

As can be seen in Table 2.8, a transition into unemployment did lead to a markedly greater risk of poverty in eight of the eleven countries. The only exceptions were Denmark, the Netherlands, and Ireland. It seems plausible that, in the first two of these countries, the negative effects of unemployment for living standards were strongly mediated by the generous nature of the welfare system. In the majority of countries there is also an effect of transitions into non-activity in raising poverty risks, although with the exception of Denmark and Ireland, the coefficients tend to be lower than for the transition to unemployment. It is notable that the countries where moves to non-activity did not lead to poverty were, apart from the Netherlands, not the same as those that provided good protection in the face of unemployment. In particular, the Southern European countries do better in this respect, with no significant effects in Spain and Italy and only a weak effect in Greece.

While the evidence supports the assumptions of the social exclusion thesis with respect to the link between unemployment and poverty, this is not the case for the relationship between unemployment and social isolation. It was seen earlier that the extent of social isolation among the unemployed varied very substantially between countries, with no consistent evidence that it was associated with higher isolation apart from the case of participation in associational life. The problematic nature of the causal relationship emerges even more strongly from the longitudinal analysis. In no country was there evidence of a significant causal impact of unemployment on whether or not a person lived alone. Similarly, in none of the countries were new entrants to unemployment less likely to meet up regularly with friends. Finally, despite the association in the cross-sectional data between unemployment and lower participation in organizations and clubs, the longitudinal evidence did not support the view that this was generally a result of unemployment itself. The effect of unemployment in reducing participation in associations was only significant for men in Ireland (and in Spain at the 10 per cent level) and for women in Denmark.

This suggests that patterns of sociability must be understood primarily as long-term cultural formations that are unlikely to be affected by short-term changes in people's employment situation. A person becomes unemployed in the context of a specific type of community life, and this may well be of major importance for the way that unemployment affects their well-being. The extent to which the unemployed were likely to experience social isolation was strongly influenced by these distinctive societal patterns of household organization and sociability. In the Southern countries, young unemployed adults were far more likely to be living at home with their parents. But this was not specifically because they were unemployed, but because young people in general in these societies were more likely to live in this way. They were also far more likely to meet regularly with neighbours, friends, and relatives. Again this mainly reflected the fact that the frequency of sociability was much higher in the society at large. In countries such as Denmark and the Netherlands, informal sociability was much rarer for the unemployed and those in work alike, but instead there was more active participation in formal organizations. In Germany, again largely reflecting the more general patterns of sociability, the unemployed had low levels of participation in both informal and formal social life in the community.

Table 2.9 *Effect of poverty and sociability on transitions from unemployment into work 1994–6*

	Poverty	Living alone	Not meeting friends	Not club member
Belgium	— —	n.s.	n.s.	n.s.
Denmark	— — —	n.s.	n.s.	— — —
France	— — —	n.s.	—	n.s.
Germany	— — —	n.s.	n.s.	n.s.
Greece	— — —	n.s.	n.s.	n.s.
Ireland	— — —	—	n.s.	n.s.
Italy	— — —	+++	n.s.	—
Portugal	n.s.	n.s.	n.s.	n.s.
Spain	— — —	+++	— —	(−)
United Kingdom	— — —	—	n.s.	n.s.

Note 1: Results are drawn from a series of separate discrete time models for each country in which the dependent variable was the transition probability of leaving unemployment for a job. For full details of the regressions, see Gallie et al. (2003).
Note 2: Minus signs indicate lower probabilities of obtaining a job, positive signs higher probabilities; $(+/-) = p < 0.10$; $+/- = p < 0.05$; $++/-- = p < 0.01$; $+++/--- = p < 0.001$.
Source: European Communty Household Panel 1994, 1995, and 1996.

The second phase of the social exclusion argument underlines the importance of poverty and social isolation in acting as barriers to re-employment. This was examined by looking at how these factors affected the escape from unemployment of all those who had a spell of unemployment between 1994 and 1996. Again, the individual variables of age, sex, and duration of unemployment were included, together with health given its potentially important influence on people's ability to get a job.

Table 2.9 provides a summary overview of the results of the empirical analyses. It is clear that in most countries poverty had a strong significant effect in making it more difficult to get back to work, just as would be predicted by the social exclusion thesis. The only country in which there was no discernible effect was Portugal, although the size of the coefficient for the effect was also somewhat less great in Greece and Spain. Thus, although as was seen in the first section, the extent of poverty among the unemployed varied very substantially from one country to another, the impact of poverty was very similar across countries.

Turning to the different social isolation variables, the most notable conclusion to be drawn from the results is their very limited impact in most countries on job acquisition chances. Living alone had no effect in six of the ten countries and its effect went in quite different directions among the remainder. It facilitated getting back to work in Italy and Spain but made it more difficult in Ireland and the United Kingdom. Social isolation with respect to friends in the community made no difference to job chances in eight out of the ten countries, although in the two where it did have an effect (France and Spain) this was negative as predicted. Finally, participation in clubs or organizations had no effect in seven of the ten countries, although it did reduce employment chances in Denmark, Italy, and Spain. In general, the emphasis on social isolation as a critical factor in the process of entrapment into a marginalized position in society is not confirmed by the empirical data.

Conclusions

Our starting point was the need to assess the evidence about three assumptions of the social exclusion thesis. The first was that the associations it postulated between unemployment on the one hand and poverty and social isolation on the other were common across societies with rather diverse institutional structures and cultural traditions. The second was that social isolation made a significant difference to the severity of the effect of unemployment over and above the impact of poverty. And the third was that the causal relationships postulated by the vicious circle of exclusion argument were empirically valid.

The evidence suggests that the most illuminating aspect of the social exclusion thesis is its emphasis upon the implications of the cumulative disadvantage of poverty and social isolation for the experience of unemployment. The strongest effect on the psychological well-being of the unemployed was that of financial hardship. Unemployment was associated with higher poverty risks and more severe experiences of financial hardship in all countries, although the proportions affected differed substantially between countries partly as a result of different welfare arrangements. Even taking account of financial hardship, social isolation is also associated with lower access to social support at moments of difficulty, to sharper experiences of financial difficulty and to lower psychological well-being. However, the association between unemployment and different types of social isolation varies substantially between countries. In particular the Southern societies provided a much more supportive social environment for the unemployed, through greater integration into both family life and local community sociability.

The evidence, however, is more qualified about the causal argument underlying the social exclusion thesis. There was support for a vicious circle linking unemployment and poverty. Unemployment did appear to directly lead to higher poverty risks in all countries, albeit to varying degrees. Poverty in turn would appear to be a significant barrier to people obtaining a job. However, there is no confirmation of a similar vicious circle in the case of social isolation. Longitudinal data shows that unemployment led to little change in people's social lives. Rather the extent of social isolation seems to be affected primarily by longer-term cultural patterns of family and community sociability in particular societies. Finally, there is no evidence that social isolation is a significant barrier to job acquisition. While social isolation is undoubtedly an important factor in understanding the distress caused by unemployment, it is poverty that appears to play the key causal role in the process of marginalization.

CHAPTER 3

Psychology of Unemployment and Social Exclusion: Youth Unemployment and the Risk of Social Exclusion

Thomas Kieselbach

The psychological consequences of job-loss and unemployment have played an important role in the scientific investigation of the consequences of unemployment. The research that is described in this chapter has tried to go beyond the classical focus of psychological unemployment research in the last 25 years first by linking the psychological consequences of unemployment to processes of social exclusion and second by examining the significance of differences in national institutional and cultural contexts for vulnerability to exclusion and for the prevalence of specific types of moderators of the psychological consequences of unemployment.

The Psychology of Unemployment

The effects of unemployment can only be understood by taking into account both the social and individual meaning of work. The starting point for any account of social–psychological approaches to the consequences of unemployment must be the work of Marie Jahoda, who, as an author of the Marienthal study in the the early 1930s, was co-responsible for one of the most influential studies in the social sciences (Jahoda et al., 2002). Assuming that work represents the most important connection to reality, Jahoda (1979, 1982) tried to define the latent functions of work—as distinct from the manifest function of earning one's living—in terms of five categories. The primary emphasis was on the significance of structural context. The activity of work incorporates the following psychological dimensions: it imposes a time structure; it compels contacts and shared experiences with others outside the nuclear family; it represents goals and purposes beyond the scope of an individual; it enforces activity; and it provides status and social identity (Jahoda and Rush, 1980).

Fryer and Payne (1984) opened the debate about the importance of individuals' own agency and the personal meanings they attach to work by focusing on people who apparently did not experience negative consequences but coped relatively well with unemployment (the so-called 'proactive unemployed'). Their small but highly influential qualitative study was based on eleven unemployed people, who were pre-selected for their ability to cope well with the experience of job-loss and continuing unemployment. While taking account of the resource side of the individual coping process, the study remained focused on the importance of individual agency. Yet, given the enforced nature of exclusion from paid-work in our societies, an approach based on the latent functions of work was perhaps a more persuasive social psychological account than one concerned predominantly, as in the agency approach, with the active role of the individual.

A new phase in unemployment research was initiated by Peter Warr in the 1980s, culminating in his comprehensive review on 'Work, unemployment and mental health' (1987). This re-addressed the issue of the characteristics of the social environment that are conducive or detrimental to mental health. Warr emphasized a number of factors in this respect: the opportunity for control, the opportunity for skill-use, externally generated goals, variety, environmental clarity, availability of money, physical security (accommodation, food, etc.), opportunity for interpersonal contact, and valued social position.

The unemployed are likely to experience disadvantage with regard to most of these factors. Their opportunity for control is reduced by repeated failure while looking for a job, the impossibility of influencing employers, and dependence on the social welfare bureaucracy. They experience a deterioration in the opportunities for skill use, and a decrease in externally generated goals due to their inability to use their vocational qualifications, the fact that only a minority use their leisure time actively, the low level of external demands, the reduction of the range of goals, and the decreased significance of previously important goals.

Restriction to the family environment and the home, loss of stimulation from the contrast between work and leisure, and reduction in financial possibilities all lead to a reduction in variety. Uncertainty about which behaviour will lead to success in finding a job, and the necessity of presenting oneself in a different light with each application, result in loss of environmental clarity. The clarity of the social environment is further reduced by a style of life 'characterized by short-term thinking' (Biermann, Schmerl, and Ziebell, 1985), as a result of the uncertainty regarding any future plans. The reduction of financial means can lead to deterioration of nutrition and, sometimes, the necessity of moving into a different neighbourhood ('physical security'), which in turn can reduce the level of support from the unemployed person's usual social network.

Interpersonal contacts can increase in number due to more available time, particularly in the case of young unemployed people. For other groups of the unemployed, however, there is a greater risk of self-isolation due to financial restrictions or to a sense of shame. The work ethic in our society tends to devalue the unemployed socially. This situation is often reinforced through individualistic ideologies, such as the 'belief in a just world' (Lerner, 1974, 1980), which imply that each person gets what he or she deserves. In this way the social position of the unemployed is undermined, their claims on society are deprived of legitimacy, and they themselves are rendered incapable of asserting themselves in conflict situations (Kieselbach, 1987). This weakened social position is supplemented by dependence on state institutions, which put those dependent on them in the role of humble petitioners, giving rise to feelings of worthlessness and helplessness.

While research has tended to focus on the general effects of unemployment for psychological well-being, a number of studies have recognized that the strength of these effects can vary. The more systematic introduction of a series of moderators and mediators co-determining the individual effects of unemployment has laid the foundation for research into the differential effects of unemployment (Wacker, 1983). This approach is capable of explaining the personal effects of unemployment in a more nuanced way than is often suggested by the relatively naive assumptions underlying the public discourse. The different forms by which individuals cope with unemployment corresponds to a lack of uniformity among the unemployed themselves in terms of both demographic and psychological features (see Kieselbach, 1991). An analysis of the moderators involved in coping highlights the fact that, just as unemployment itself is no uniform event, no uniform reactions can be predicted about the people directly affected by unemployment.

Two directions have been taken by researchers in the attempt to develop typologies of the various forms of reactions to unemployment. The first was limited to distinguishing between different types of individual response to unemployment. In the influential interwar 'Marienthal Study', Jahoda et al. (2002) distinguished between the following four types of reaction:

- brokenness, subdivided into
  - apathy (defined as the inability to conduct household affairs properly; an indifferent, indolent mood; total lack of planning; high alcohol consumption, begging, stealing);
  - despair (depression, hopelessness, loss of control, abandonment of job search, social comparison with a better past);
- resignation (no more expectations towards life, giving up of planning, no more future orientation, hopelessness, but still with the ability to manage household affairs).
- unbrokenness (highly active, sustaining plans and hopes for the future, continuous attempts to look for work).

A more recent approach, derived from a small empirical study in Northern Ireland, developed a typology orientated to the types of activity that people engaged in when unemployed (Kilpatrick and Trew, 1985). The authors analyzed the usage of time by unemployed men and their respective mental health measured by GHQ mean scores and formulated the following typology:

(1) passive cluster (no or only passive activities like watching TV: lowest scores for mental health);
(2) domestic cluster (most of the time at home devoted to domestic chores: mental health only slightly better than in the passive cluster);
(3) social cluster (social activities with others: mental health less affected by unemployment);
(4) active cluster (active leisure time and work-related activities; mental health least affected by unemployment).

Warr (1989), criticizing any concept of adaptation that merely implies a reduction in psychological morbidity without referring to the extent to which comprehensive individual development is severely hampered by unemployment, distinguishes between 'resigned' and 'constructive' adaptation. In the case of constructive adaptation the person affected develops interests and activities outside the conventional labour market, spends more time on hobbies, extends his social activities and gets involved in voluntary or community organizations, whereas the more widespread form, resigned adaptation, consists of self-isolation and a far-reaching reduction in expectations in many areas of life.

A second approach tried to develop a dynamic theory of individual responses, postulating a specific pattern of change as the unemployment spell lengthened. Bakke (1940*a*) formulated a 'cycle of adaptation' in unemployed families: momentum stability–unstable equilibrium–disorganization–experimental readjustment–permanent readjustment. The sequence shock–optimism–pessimism–fatalism, as described by Harrison (1976), has perhaps become the best known formula. The presumption of any such ideal-typical sequence has been criticized on various grounds, in particular because it lacks an adequate empirical basis and creates a stereotyped picture of the behaviour of unemployed people (Kelvin and Jarrett, 1985). The dominant perspective of psychological unemployment research has focused on the health (more specifically mental health) effects of job-loss and unemployment. This perspective has been considerably broadened in the last decade by a growing interest in processes leading to social exclusion. While a clear general picture of the relationship between unemployment and health emerged from previous research, the question of *key mechanisms* linking unemployment and social exclusion had not been dealt with. When excluding mechanisms are discussed, reference is primarily made to the factors that lead to exclusion from the labour market. The processes linking labour market exclusion with social exclusion have not been given priority until now. Research that would allow insights into the more subtle processes underlying the societal inclusion and exclusion of the young unemployed in society clearly requires the systematic incorporation of both monetary and non-monetary, and objective and subjective factors.

The Psychology of Unemployment and Social Exclusion

While acquiring considerable political salience among EU policy-makers, 'social exclusion' was developed as a predominantly scientific concept within French sociology (Paugam, 1991, 2000), and subsequently elaborated by US and German sociologists (Silver, 1994; Kronauer, 2002). The increasing interest in the topic can be explained by the trends in the labour market, in particular the persistence of higher levels of structural unemployment than had been experienced prior to the 1980s, and an increasing flexibilization and precarity of labour markets. It has been reinforced by the greater policy pressure on people without sufficient coping resources to respond adequately to the changing requirements of the labour market. This reflects changing views about the proper role of the welfare state and an emphasis on activation strategies that seek to place greater responsibility on the individual. An important concern for academic researchers became whether the experience of unemployment may trigger processes of social exclusion that crystallize lines of social stratification, with certain groups of the population coming to be regarded as 'dispensable' and outside the scope for assistance (Vogel, 2000).

While widely used in the political debate about poverty and unemployment in Europe, social exclusion must be considered as an umbrella concept rather than as a precisely operationalized term. Perhaps the most useful elaboration of the concept is that by Kronauer (1998), which is more comprehensive than many others. In contrast to the use of the term in France (or of the concept of underclass in the United States), Kronauer developed his understanding of social exclusion in the light of the current employment crisis which especially affects low qualified manufacturing workers. Sustained high unemployment rates have the consequence that more and more people cannot lead a life which fits the societal standards for material and social well-being. This analysis of the social consequences of unemployment and poverty requires a terminology which takes into consideration both monetary and non-monetary aspects of living, and the characteristics of the individual and the society. This broader understanding has also become increasingly important for analysing the situation of young people facing unemployment (Kieselbach, 1997). Correspondingly, in this research project social exclusion is understood as a dynamic, multidimensional process which incorporates social and economic (monetary and non-monetary) aspects of living, subjective experiences and objective situations, and which depends upon available personal and social resources.

The use of the term social exclusion easily evokes the image of a specific situation which stands in contrast to that of social inclusion. But it is better seen as defining the end point of a dimension characterized by greater or less vulnerability to marginalization. Thus social exclusion can only be understood by focussing not just on what it means to be excluded, but also on those factors enlarging or diminishing the vulnerability of the individual. For this reason, we will principally use the term 'risk of exclusion'. Figure 3.1 depicts

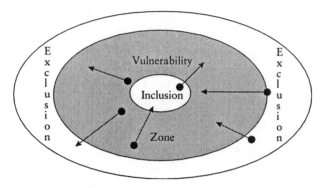

Figure 3.1 *The exclusion–inclusion paradigm.*

this inclusion–exclusion paradigm. The arrows stand for different hypothetical 'movements' of people within this continuum.

1. *Exclusion from the Labour Market,* which describes the situation of facing external barriers to (re-) enter the labour market combined with resignation regarding one's employment chances.
2. The second dimension, *economic exclusion,* is usually referred to as poverty and includes the financial dependency upon the welfare state or a socially unacceptable income, and the loss of the ability to financially support oneself or one's family.
3. *Institutional exclusion* can occur from the educational system (in both schools and further qualification and training institutions), institutions dealing with unemployment and poverty, and public and private service institutions (such as banks and insurance agencies). Besides the lack of support both before and during phases of unemployment, the experience of institutional dependency can lead to feelings of shame and passivity, making the effect of state support counter-productive. The fourth and fifth dimensions are closely linked with each other.
4. *Exclusion through social isolation* describes either withdrawal by other members of the person's social network or their own retreat, leading to a reduction of contacts to only one specific group of people or even to general social isolation.
5. *Cultural exclusion* refers to the inability to live according to the socially accepted norms and values with the possible consequence of an identification with deviant norms and behaviours. Stigmatization and sanctions from the social surroundings are also subsumed within this dimension.

6. *spatial exclusion* which manifests itself in the spatial concentration of people with limited financial means, often coming from a similar social and/or cultural background, and in feelings of isolation due to the lack of an adequate infrastructure within the residential area (e.g. with respect to transport, shops, but also cultural events).

The Research and its Context

The 'Youth Unemployment and Social Exclusion' (YUSEDER)[1] research project focused on the risks of social exclusion among long-term unemployed youth and their implications for psychological well-being. It examined the key mechanisms linking the experience of long-term youth unemployment to various dimensions of social disintegration. In this context, not only the mechanisms exacerbating the stress of unemployment (vulnerability factors) but also the protective mechanisms preventing or reducing the risk of social exclusion have been central to the research (Kieselbach, 2000*a*, *b*; Kieselbach et al., 2001).

The research was carried out in three Northern European countries (Sweden, Belgium, Germany) and in three Southern European countries (Spain, Italy, Greece). At the time of the research, youth unemployment was significantly higher in all partner countries than total unemployment rates except in the case of Germany where—due to the dual education system and the associated longer periods of training—the rate of youth unemployment was similar to that of adult unemployment (see Figure 3.2). However, the German labour market is characterized by a high degree of disparity between the situation of West and East German youth. Young people between the ages of 20 and 24 years are much more severely affected by unemployment in East Germany.

[1] The consortium of the research project has been coordinated by the University of Bremen (Germany): Prof. Dr Thomas Kieselbach (the German team: Gert Beelmann, Andrea Stitzel, Ute Traiser) and included the following national partners: University of Gent (Belgium): Prof. Dr Kees van Heeringen, Wouter Vanderplasschen, Tine Willems, Gwendolyn Portzky; University of Bologna (Italy): Prof. Dr Michele La Rosa, Dr Vando Borghi, Federico Chicchi, Roberto Rizza; Autonomous University of Barcelona (Spain): Prof. Dr Louis Lemkow, Dr Josep Espluga, Josep Baltierrez; Greek Network of Health Promoting Schools and Institute for Child Health, Athens: Katerina Sokou, Demetra Bayetakou, Valentine Papantoniou, Katerina Christofi; University of Karlstad (Sweden): Prof. Dr Bengt Starrin, Erik Forsberg, Marina Kalander Blomqvist, Dr Ulla Rantakeisu.

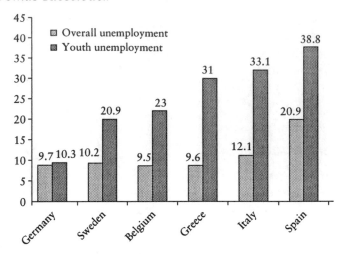

Figure 3.2 *Overall unemployment rates versus youth unemployment rates (>25 years of age) for six European countries in 1997.*
Source: Eurostat, 1998.

There were, however, marked differences between countries in the extent of youth disadvantage. In Belgium, the rates were two to three times higher than the overall rates, with female unemployment rates especially high. An extreme situation can be found in the region Wallonia where over 40 per cent of all females under 25 are unemployed. Parallel to the increase in total unemployment in the early 1990s, in Sweden, youth unemployment increased rapidly and equally strongly for the 16–19 year olds and the 20–24 year olds. After a slight decrease in the mid-1990s, the unemployment rate for both age groups rates was about 15 per cent, twice as high as the overall unemployment rate. But, in sharp contrast to the Belgian situation, in Sweden the rates were higher among men than among women (in 1995: 16.6 versus 14.0 per cent).

The highest levels of youth unemployment were to be found in the Southern countries. In Greece, well over a third of young people between 15 and 19 years of age were unemployed in 1995. Rates among young women were especially high. In 1995, the rate for young women aged 15–24 was 37.7 per cent, compared to 19.4 per cent for men. In Italy, the proportion of young unemployed people constituted two-thirds of the total number of unemployed people with lower rates for young men (29 per cent in 1997) than young women (37.7 per cent). The proportion of young people who have been looking for a job for more than 12 months is exceptionally high in this country (approximately two-thirds of the young unemployed). Finally, Spain shows the highest rate of youth unemployment. In addition to a continuous rise in the 1970s, unemployment figures rose in the late 1970s and early 1980s to a peak value of nearly 40 per cent. Especially among the 16–19 year olds, the rate sometimes exceeded 50 per cent.

To provide an in-depth view of the situation and experience of young unemployed people, 300 interviews were conducted (50 interviews in each country). The comparability of the sample—taking into account different schooling, qualification, and welfare support systems within the six countries participating in the project—was ensured through the adoption of common selection criteria. Those interviewed had to be between 20 and 24 years of age[2] and officially registered as unemployed for at least 12 months. The distributions by gender and qualification level reflected the country patterns (Table 3.1). It was decided not to include immigrants in the study as this would have heightened the diversity of the sample. In addition, language barriers might have made it too difficult to conduct the interviews. Due to strong regional disparities in unemployment rates of young people within most countries, the research teams were asked to select the interviewees from more than one area. With the exception of Sweden, each national study contained samples from two areas reflecting differences in low versus high unemployment rates, urban versus semi-urban contexts, and in the case of Italy and Germany regions (Southern and Northern Italy; Eastern and Western Germany).

The study populations largely coincide with the statistics concerning qualification level of unemployed youths in the respective country: in the Belgian, the German, and the Swedish studies, it is primarily young people with lower qualification levels that have difficulties in accessing the labour market. In the Greek, the Italian, and the Spanish studies this is also the case for those with a higher educational background.[3] It should be stressed, however, that the samples should not be regarded as a representative of the overall population of long-term unemployed young people (Table 3.2).

---

[2] This selection criterion could not be achieved from all countries. In four national studies (Greece, Italy, Sweden, and Belgium) people aged 25 have also been included.

[3] In the Swedish study 49 instead of 50 are included in the analysis: one individual dropped out at a fairly late stage of the analysis when closer inspection showed that a central selection criterion was not filled.

Table 3.1 *Gender in respective national study population distributed by region*

	Region A		Region B		Total	
	Male	Female	Male	Female	Male	Female
S	Interviews conducted only in one region				20	29
B	11	14	9	16	20	30
GER	14	12	9	15	23	27
GR	10	22	7	11	17	33
I	7	13	14	16	21	29
SP	13	21	6	10	19	31
All					120	179

Table 3.2 *Qualification level in respective national study population distributed by region*

	Region A		Region B		Total	
	Higher	Lower	Higher	Lower	Higher	Lower
S	Interviews conducted only in one region				38	11
B	11	14	10	15	21	29
GER	10	16	15	9	25	25
GR	26	6	17	1	43	7
I	15	5	25	5	40	10
SP	24	10	10	6	33	17
All					200	99

The method chosen for carrying out the qualitative interviews with long-term unemployed youth was the 'problem-focused interview' which was developed at the University of Bremen in the 1980s and which contains both standardized and narrative elements (Witzel, 1987, 1995). The interview schedule contained seven thematic fields based upon Kronauers' (1998) six dimensions of social exclusion, together with a section on psychosocial strains which included questions about feelings of victimization, shame, financial hardship, and also experiences in the submerged economy. For the Southern European countries additional questions were included on the submerged economy to assess the situation in greater depth.

Youth Unemployment and Social Exclusion

It is clear from the analyses that the main factors creating a high risk of social exclusion among young people were unemployment and its economic effects. This supports the assumption in earlier social–psychological literature that work is one of the main mechanisms for overall societal integration. The inability to enter the labour market in the first place must be recognized as a central factor in determining the further development of young people. It might be justified to say that, in the long run, having work versus not having work sets the agenda for integration into, or exclusion from, society.

One of the main reasons for exclusion from the labour market is the absence of qualifications, or the possession of generally low (or not-matching) job qualifications. Without vocational training that meets the (future) requirements of the labour market, lasting inclusion into work seems to be extremely difficult. It is therefore understandable that job qualification schemes are usually regarded as the most effective measures against unemployment and social exclusion. However, the relatively exclusive focus of policy interventions on this type of institutional answer underestimates the importance of other institutions and their potential effects in reducing the vulnerability of adolescents. In particular, the research highlighted the significance of earlier school experience in preparing young people for their future job situation and in reducing risks of social exclusion. Here there is clear evidence of the cumulative nature of disadvantage. Absent or low qualification levels are often found among young people who have grown up in a situation of relative poverty, in deprived areas that lead to multiple socialization deficiencies.

Despite these general tendencies in the data, there were also marked divergences between individuals in their risk of social exclusion. The individual cases were assigned to three groups according to whether the person faced a high risk of social exclusion, an increased risk of social exclusion, or only a low risk of social exclusion. Three dimensions—labour market exclusion, economic exclusion, and social isolation—were found to be *central dimensions* for the risk of exclusion in all countries. The group of long-term unemployed young people at *high risk of social exclusion* is made up of cases which show at least three aspects of social exclusion, of which at least two had to be central dimensions. The group of long-term unemployed young people at *increased risk of social exclusion* consists of those for whom two central but no other criteria apply or of those with not more than one of the central dimensions and any number of non-central aspects.

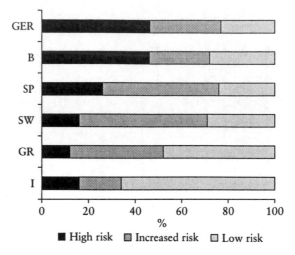

Figure 3.3 *Types of social exclusion in six countries of the EU (each country N = 50, in %).*[4]

The group of long-term unemployed young people showing *a low risk of social exclusion* is made up of cases that show exclusion tendencies in no more than one area, and that area not being one of the central dimensions. Such operationalization provides a balance between the requirement of a common basis for comparison, and the need to take account of national specificities in risk factors.

There were marked country differences in the prevalence of these different risk categories. As can be seen in Figure 3.3, in Belgium and Germany, cases at high risk of social exclusion were most common. In contrast, most of the young people in Sweden and Spain were part of the middle type with an increased risk of social exclusion. In Greece and Italy, people at a low risk of social exclusion make up the biggest group.

Type 1: 'High Risk of Social Exclusion'

In most of the national studies, a high risk of social exclusion arises if young people experience at the same time a high risk of labour market exclusion, economic exclusion, and social isolation (Figure 3.4). They had longer durations of unemployment in all countries compared to other groups. The single most important factor that increases the risk of social exclusion is low qualification. Providing access only to poor and precarious jobs, low qualifications are an obstacle to building a professional career and make it difficult to escape from

[4] The rank order of national studies is given according to the weighted types (high risk = 3, increased risk = 2, low risk = 1).

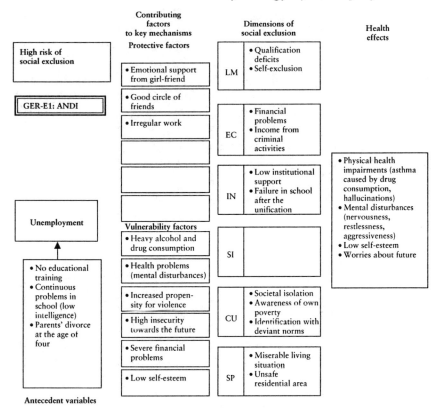

Figure 3.4 *Case chart type 'High risk of social exclusion'.*

Note: LM = Labour market exclusion; EC = Economic exclusion; IN = Institutional exclusion; SI = Exclusion through social isolation; CU = Cultural exclusion; SP = Spatial exclusion.

unemployment. Furthermore, they came from lower social classes or from families with major social and financial problems. Due to financial and other problems in their family of origin, these young unemployed are at a disadvantage from childhood onwards. Their qualification level and their self-esteem are low, they are not sufficiently supported by their social environment and governmental institutions, and they tend to be passive or in some countries even tend toward problematic behaviour such as drug dependency and deviant behaviour. The young people in this group also exhibit a high degree of passivity towards the labour market. They see few or no chances of finding regular work; often they are no longer actively seeking work or only in a limited way. Besides diminished job search activity, their efforts to improve their qualifications are also significantly lower.

A low level of institutional support is a vulnerability factor for all study populations except Sweden, where some members of this group received a relatively high amount of institutional as well as social support. In Belgium, Germany, and Sweden, people in this group were also likely to experience cultural exclusion, while in Greece and Italy the risk of spatial exclusion was common. Finally, it was observed in all countries that personality-related factors such as low self-esteem and poor mental health increase the risk of social exclusion.

Andi is an example of a person in the high-risk group. Twenty years old, he comes from East Germany and has been without work since he left school at the age of 14. He lives alone in a one-room flat and has a girlfriend who is expecting his child. Problems with his family and socialization deficits led to failure in school and, in turn, impeded his integration into the labour market. Other circumstances make him vulnerable to the various dimensions of functional exclusion that can lead to social exclusion. Alcohol and drug consumption and the increased propensity for violence, for example, make his social exclusion all the more likely. The only countervailing forces are a circle of friends and the emotional support of his girlfriend. He experiences illnesses that are both a cause and effect of his exclusion. He has asthma and hallucinations, which mainly result from drug consumption. He also shows signs of nervousness, restlessness, and aggressiveness. Furthermore, he has low self-esteem and expresses high insecurity towards his personal future.

Type 2: 'Increased Risk of Social Exclusion'

The group of young people at increased risk of social exclusion seems to be relatively heterogeneous. In all countries it involves the risk of labour market exclusion. But the other relevant exclusion dimensions for this type vary in each country: they may be institutional exclusion, spatial exclusion (Greece), or economic exclusion (Sweden, Spain). The qualification levels reveal a general lack of educational resources. The risk of social exclusion for this group is mainly counteracted by a high degree of family support (Greece, Italy, Sweden, Spain) or of support from the social environment (Belgium, Germany). Furthermore, general activity is at a high level, which is also likely to be a protective factor.

Strong social connections (friends and family) counteract the risk of social exclusion. The dimension that makes the difference between 'high' and 'increased' risk of social exclusion is social isolation. The strong link to the family described in the Italian, Greek, and Spanish studies, however, is not unambiguously positive. Although the existence of good social networks (especially family, but also friends) reduces the immediate threat of economic exclusion, a feeling of economic dependence on the family undermines people's capacities for autonomous choice.

Olga is an example of the type at increased risk of social exclusion. She lives in West Germany, is 23 years old, lives without a partner, and has been unemployed for 2 years. Problems before being unemployed are deficits in education and a three time failure in vocational training. Her situation at the time of unemployment is marked by a balance of protective and vulnerability factors. By living with her parents, her financial as well as her spatial situation is secured. Furthermore, she can count on help from her circle of friends. Factors which are an obstacle to integration into the labour market are demotivation due to several failures in vocational training schemes and a lack of willingness to be mobile geographically. She feels that she does not receive sufficient institutional support. Furthermore, security through the family means at the same time dependence on the family. The psychological consequences she experiences as a result of unemployment are feelings of shame, irritability, and boredom (Figure 3.5).

Type 3: 'Low Risk of Social Exclusion'

Long-term unemployed youth in this group are at most affected by one dimension of social exclusion and this is not one of the central dimensions. The risk of social exclusion is reduced by a range of protective factors: high qualification, active behaviour at the labour market, secure financial situation, social support, institutional support, high self-esteem, and high level of socio-cultural activities. Compared with the other two groups, the young people at *low risk* of social exclusion in all studies are younger, are more highly qualified, and have been unemployed for a shorter period of time. They are more actively seeking a job, are in a relatively secure financial situation, and are supported by their social environment. The risk of labour market exclusion is low because unemployment is regarded as a temporary situation, and also as a time for personal development and planning. People at low risk of social exclusion neither feel socially isolated nor economically excluded. In Southern Europe they receive sufficient financial support from their families and in Northern Europe from state institutions. They are also satisfied with the support they receive from governmental institutions.

Moreover, the interviewees are not only actively looking for a job but are also more committed to socio-cultural activities than those in the other risk groups. Most of them are continuously occupied with activities of personal interest. They participate actively in associations

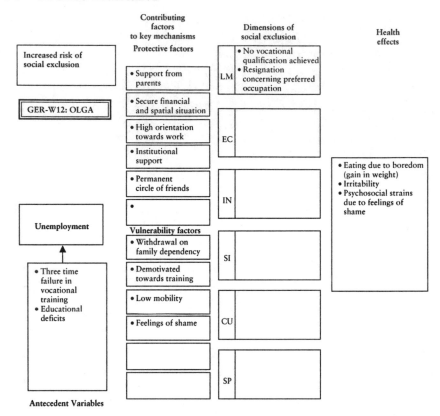

Figure 3.5 *Case chart type 'Increased risk of social exclusion'.*

Note: LM = Labour market exclusion; EC = Economic exclusion; IN = Institutional exclusion; SI = Exclusion through social isolation; CU = Cultural exclusion; SP = Spatial exclusion.

and organized groups. Different kinds of support (financial, social, and institutional) are of major importance for this group. For some interviewees social support enables them to subordinate the search for a job to the maintenance of their current lifestyle, which is characterized by temporary jobs and personal interests like music (Italy). For others, unemployment is closer to a free choice (Belgium). Youth at low risk of exclusion usually have protective personality features. All have a high level of self-esteem and good communication skills. They are able to make decisions, to plan out and implement positive changes in their lives, and to cope with new requirements. Some of the young people at low risk of social exclusion depend to a lesser extent on institutional support due to their ability to help themselves (Sweden).

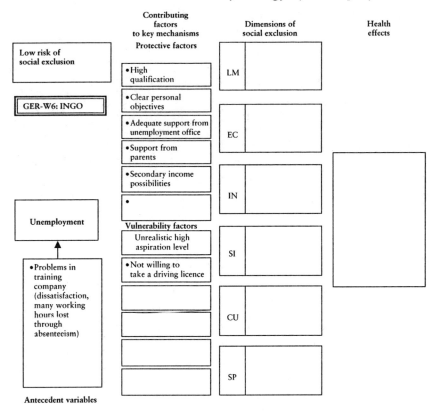

Figure 3.6 *Case chart type 'Low risk of social exclusion'.*

Note: LM = Labour market exclusion; EC = Economic exclusion; IN = Institutional exclusion; SI = Exclusion through social isolation; CU = Cultural exclusion; SP = Spatial exclusion.

Ingo is an example of this type (see case chart in Figure 3.6). He is 22 years old and has been without work for a year. He comes from West Germany. He has completed a vocational training and lives with his parents. He has not been taken on after his apprenticeship possibly due to losing too many working hours through absenteeism. His situation at the time of unemployment is marked by a number of protective factors. Due to his educational and vocational training he is relatively highly qualified. He has clear objectives concerning his career and receives adequate support from the unemployment office. He is emotionally and financially supported by his family and has good secondary income possibilities. However, his unrealistically high aspiration level, as well as his unwillingness to obtain a driving licence, are barriers to quick integration into the labour market.

Nevertheless, none of the six dimensions of social exclusion emerge clearly and there is no evidence of health problems.

Youth Unemployment, Social Exclusion, and Health

Despite the limited number of studies and the quality of empirical evidence (mainly cross-sectional data), the analysis of previous research evidence from the different countries revealed rather homogenous results on the link between youth unemployment and ill health (Kieselbach, 2000*b*). In general, it was reported that, compared to their employed peers, young unemployed people had a distinctly higher risk of health-related problems. This is especially true for mental health and psychosocial problems leading to an increase in depression and a poorer quality of life, but also for objective health indicators for instance with respect to the higher risk of suicidal behaviour among unemployed youth. This is also reflected in the health behaviour of young unemployed people, especially with regard to alcohol and cigarette consumption.

Our research showed that, in addition to the effect of such individual differences, the health of the long-term unemployed youth and the health-related effects resulting from unemployment varied considerably between the different countries. In particular, the cultural and social differences between Northern and Southern European countries had significant implications for health. To a considerable degree, this reflected the implications of such factors for the likelihood that people were in particular categories with respect to social exclusion risks. However, cultural differences also led to some differentiation in the health implications of unemployment within specific social exclusion risk categories.

High Risk of Social Exclusion

For those at high risk of social exclusion, all studies, except the Greek, reported a number of *psycho-social strains* directly resulting from unemployment. These effects were mainly passivity, the feeling of lack of opportunities, as well as apathy, and a sense of resignation. Furthermore, in nearly all countries, low self-esteem or low self-confidence was observed among youth at high risk of exclusion. However, in the Northern European countries, a greater number of psycho-social stress factors were reported compared to the Southern European countries. In Belgium, Germany, and Sweden, financial stress was considered to be the crucial stress factor. Fear of the future, missing a perspective for life, and feelings of dependency were also common. This indicates that, among people at high risk of social exclusion, the diversity of psycho-social strains is greater in the Northern European countries than in Greece, Italy, and Spain. In Greece, in general, the health problems of long-term unemployed young people were a pre-existing condition rather than a result of unemployment. In Spain, psycho-social strain in connection with social problems within the family and circle of friends was particularly salient: if support did not exist or was insufficient, young people were particularly likely to feel lonely, bored, afraid of the future, and depressed.

In most of the countries, there is a homogeneous picture with respect to the *health related behaviour* (tobacco and alcohol consumption, abuse of drugs and medicine, as well as lack of physical activities) of long-term unemployed youth. But Greece and Italy are exceptions, in that no negative effects on health due to unemployment were observed.

Increased Risk of Social Exclusion

In all six countries, the health of those at increased risk of exclusion was considerably better than of youth at high risk of exclusion. Nevertheless, there was substantial variation within the category with respect to the prevalence of strain. Whether or not young people were supported by their parents had a major influence on their health. Young Italians in this situation hardly show any ill-health effects. The only strains reported are a lack of control of their situation, as well as a lack of structure in their everyday life. In the Greek study, the health of unemployed youth within this group was largely independent of their employment status. In the Northern European studies, financial difficulties (Germany, Sweden) or financial insecurity (Belgium) were more important psycho-social stressors than in the Southern countries.

In all countries, *protective factors* can be found for youth at increased risk of exclusion, but the specific form they took differed between countries. In Greece, the relative absence of financial difficulties had an important buffer effect. The situation in Italy and Spain is similar: social support especially from friends, but also as a result of integration into the family, reduced vulnerability. In Northern Europe, there were additional protective factors to those of social integration and economic protection. In Germany and Sweden, a higher level of qualification was important. In Belgium, Sweden, and Germany, the level of personal initiative young people could exercise played an important protective role.

In summary, in Southern Europe, economic protection (by parents or irregular work), as well as social integration were the crucial factors mediating the risks of strain, whereas in Northern Europe, higher levels of qualification and opportunities for personal initiative were also of considerable importance.

Low Risk of Social Exclusion

In all countries, youth in the group with a low risk of social exclusion were in considerably better health than those in groups at higher levels of risk. All countries reported cases that were relatively free from strain. The young people were described as being active, having high self-esteem, and good communication skills. No case of risky health-related behaviour is reported. In the three Northern European countries, social support and financial protection were equally important protective factors. In Belgium and Germany, a high level of qualification also reduced risks of strain. Sweden was distinctive in that some young people with a low-risk of social exclusion used their unemployment as a time for orientation. Similarly, in Belgium, unemployment was a deliberate choice for some. In both countries, people in these situations assessed the strain resulting from unemployment as rather low. In the Southern European countries, it was above all economic security and the availability of social support that reduced vulnerability to strain.

Societal Variations in Vulnerability and Protective Factors

Although the studies in all of the countries show high congruence with respect to the importance of school education, duration of unemployment, and to some degree of social origin in determining exclusion risks (and hence vulnerability to mental ill-health), there are marked differences with respect to other factors. In particular there were substantial differences in types of vulnerability and protective factor between the Northern and Southern European countries. In Greece, Italy, and Spain, two factors played a much more crucial role in the prevention of social exclusion: the family and the submerged economy.

The Role of the Family

Both in the Northern and Southern European countries work plays a central role in the developmental process of young people. The denial of access to the labour market implies above all financial limitations. In Belgium, Germany, Spain, and Sweden, there is usually access to some type of benefit system. In contrast, in Southern European countries young people who have never entered the labour market are in most cases totally excluded from any type of state support. This means that the family has to take on the responsibility of economically supporting the children.

Dependence on the family, which partly takes the form of living with the parents, has an important protective role in that it increases the level of social support. Problems of social isolation were much rarer in the Southern countries and this was reflected in higher levels of psychological well-being. However, forcing young people to be dependent on the parental family also prolongs the juvenile phase of the life cycle. Although family support is an important buffer, this protection may also hinder the development of young people to independent adulthood. This risk is much more important in Southern European countries, given that young people are rarely eligible for transfer payments.

At the same time, the crucial role of the family means that the welfare of the young unemployed is more heavily conditioned by their milieu of origin. In the Southern European country studies, poverty and other social problems in the family of origin play a decisive role in accentuating financial dependency and lack of social support among young unemployed people. While in all studies, a *low* level of social support contributes to an increased risk of social exclusion, in the Italian, Greek, and Spanish studies the emphasis lies on lack of support by the family, whereas in the Belgian, German, and Swedish studies, it is the lack of, or decrease in, local social contacts that is of central importance.

The Submerged Economy and Social Exclusion

The research carried out in the six countries revealed that the submerged economy plays only a limited role in the lives of long-term unemployed young people in the *Northern European* countries.[5] In some cases, resorting to irregular employment is seen as justified as

[5] The discussion in this section is based on Borghi and Kieselbach (2002, 2003).

the only answer to severe economic difficulty, and sometimes as a preventative measure to ensure that the situation does not precipitate criminal activity. The submerged economy is also a means to give people a certain financial independence and allows them to maintain their standard of living at an acceptable level.

The situation in the three *Southern European* countries is, however, very different. National estimates have pointed to a substantial informal sector in the economies of these countries. Our field research confirms that work in the informal sector is also a much more important part of the experiences of the unemployed in the Southern European countries. Thirty-six cases (24 per cent) of involvement in the submerged economy were discovered among the 150 interviewees from Central and Northern Europe, many of which were only sporadic and of little importance; in Southern Europe, on the other hand, 121 cases of long-term unemployed (81 per cent) with experience of irregular work (thirty-eight in Spain, forty-one in Greece, and forty-two in Italy) were discovered (out of a total of 150 people interviewed in the three countries), albeit of different kinds and with differing results.

The form of involvement of the unemployed in such work, however, could take very different forms. Broadly speaking, it is possible to distinguish between the following patterns:

(1) *permanent irregular employment*: this category includes those jobs that take up a significant part of the individual's time during the course of the day and the week; these are real, permanent jobs of a full-time nature lacking any kind of social security and welfare protection or trade union rights;

(2) *irregular seasonal employment*: this category of job is characterized by an intense period of employment (often with longer than normal working hours) for a limited period of time;

(3) *casual irregular employment*: this category includes all those jobs of a strictly casual nature; often unconnected jobs which last for a very short period and are in no way associated with the education or training of the unemployed.

It is clear that the greater presence of irregular employment in the Southern European countries reflects the need to soften the financial burden of unemployment on those affected. In those countries where the unemployed receive very little or no financial support at all, there is clearly a much greater incentive for involvement in the submerged economy (Leonard, 1998). Nevertheless, the economic dimension is not the only one with which to measure the consequences of irregular employment.

The studies conducted in Greece, Italy, and Spain highlight the ambivalent role played by the involvement of young unemployed people in the submerged economy with respect to the risk of social exclusion. Income earned through irregular work, despite being low, often discontinuous and rarely sufficient enough for a person to be financially independent, does nonetheless constitute a temporary solution, often a kind of 'waiting wage', whilst seeking a regular employment contract. It partially satisfies the individual's financial requirements. Moreover, in some local contexts, these 'shadow' jobs may constitute the only available alternative to unemployment, given the unsatisfactory nature of employment measures and the paucity of chances to create regular employment, even short-term, low-paid work, and work suitable for first-time workers. However, while softening the phenomenon of economic exclusion, irregular employment reveals a more problematic side, especially where it constitutes relatively full-time employment. The studies conducted in the three Southern countries, show that it often threatens to subtract valuable resources (time, motivation, etc.) from the search for regular work. In the case of those jobs that do not reflect a person's professional training, education, or job aspirations, it can often lead the individual into a professional 'blind alley'.

The studies also highlight the ambivalent nature of irregular employment with regard to the risk of *socio-cultural exclusion*. On the one hand, there is the opportunity to develop new social contacts through work, regardless of its irregular nature, and thus to develop a relational network which enables the individual to escape his or her restrictive family circle and to broaden social experiences which otherwise would be almost impossible to develop within the family. Such working experiences contribute, albeit in a limited way, to a process whereby life skills are further developed. On the other hand, the experiences reported during the interviews show that irregular employment can also be associated with exploitation, the denial of basic rights, and the creation of humiliating, arbitrary relations, which can accentuate socio-cultural exclusion. Even in less extreme situations, the fact that such activity often takes place within the family sphere, or within a social milieu similar to the individual's, and consists of simple, uninteresting tasks, considerably restricts its potential with respect to the development and widening of life-skills.

With respect to the risk of *social isolation*, if the expansion of the submerged economy does not lead to criticism of the individuals directly involved (and this does not seem to emerge strongly even in Northern European countries, such as Germany, where such a phenomenon is much less frequent), then it allows for a partial degree of social inclusion, a reduced form of citizenship for these unemployed young people, the individual and social price of which ought to be seen not so much in relation to the present as to the future.

We can identify, then, two contrasting scenarios of the impact of irregular employment on the social exclusion of long-term unemployed young people. In the first, irregular employment contributes towards increasing the complexity of an unemployed young person's social relations and broadening (or keeping) the options available to that person. By softening the economic hardship created by unemployment, irregular work enables an individual to persist in his search for regular employment whilst not binding him in an exclusive manner: it may even render this search more effective through the social contacts created by irregular employment. In some cases, irregular employment may increase an individual's professional and social skills through the widening of his range of experiences. In the second scenario, irregular work contributes towards reducing this complexity—that is, the range of accessible alternatives—in an almost irreversible manner. It makes socio-cultural deficiencies (as well as economic difficulties) increasingly chronic, through a combination of poor quality work, restricted social contacts, and limited provision of cognitive and social resources due to the family and social setting of the work.

While in the first case, it is clear that the submerged economy can be seen as a form of protection from the risk of social exclusion, in the second it leads towards marginalization and to increased exposure to the risk of permanent exclusion. In general, this second case emerges in situations where irregular work—taken up as the only available possibility for a young unemployed person in a deprived area—is characterized by jobs of extremely poor quality not only in economic terms, but also with respect to the social and cognitive opportunities they offer. In such a situation, irregular work reinforces (instead of limiting) the disadvantages of the milieu of origin. Hence, depending on the quality of the jobs taken, such involvement can act either as a buffer or as a trap for unemployed young people.

Conclusions

Unemployment is a central risk factor for young people, which in the long-term threatens the overall integration of young people into society. This chapter has discussed the potential contribution of unemployment research based on the concept of social exclusion compared to previous perspectives focusing on individual outcomes, analyzing stigmatization effects or the role of activities as moderators of the unemployment experience. The question arises of whether the concept of social exclusion enables us to conceptualize the individual and social impact of unemployment in a way that significantly extends the present knowledge (Kieselbach and Beelmann, 2003). The dominant approaches of effect-related unemployment research (Wirkungsforschung) try to systematize the unemployment and health relationship and identify a number of moderators (Warr, 1987; Kieselbach, 1991). They deploy a conceptual and methodological approach in which effects tend to remain purely additive. The social exclusion approach, focusing on the key mechanisms increasing or counteracting the process of marginalization, adds a more structured as well as a more dynamic perspective to social–psychological unemployment research. It offers a more complex and systematic explanation of the effects of unemployment, by moving away from a set of isolated variables and bridging the individual and the social effects of unemployment in a way that is indispensable for a *social* psychology of unemployment.

Social exclusion processes can be considered as complex moderators of the health effects of unemployment. The detection of key mechanisms that increase vulnerability to social exclusion will help to identify crucial turning points of the individual biography; susceptible phases where social support will be needed to help people in coping adequately with their life situation. This knowledge is a necessary prerequisite for developing intervention schemes intended to limit the detrimental effects of joblessness.

Our research confirmed many of the specific factors contributing to exclusion risks identified in previous research. The most important vulnerability factors that contribute to an increase of the risk of social exclusion for young unemployed people in the long-term are in all countries low qualification, passivity in the labour market, a precarious financial situation, low or missing social support, and insufficient or non-existent institutional support. The most important protective factor for unemployed youth is social support. However, the research also revealed a factor that has been rarely emphasized in earlier psychological studies: the importance of social origin. Social origin can be a protective factor for the youth as well as a decisive vulnerability factor: poverty and other social problems in the family can increase the risk of social exclusion for the youth. This can be interpreted in the sense that the effects of social origin are reinforced by the experience of long-term unemployment.

Most crucially our research showed that it is the specific combination of these vulnerability and protective factors that determines the risk of poor mental health. Moreover, these combinations have been found to vary in a structured way between societies as a result of different institutional frameworks and different cultural traditions, with major implications for the individual experience of unemployment. This is most evident in the striking contrasts between Northern and Southern European countries. The lack of state welfare provision in the southern countries leads to a much more central role for the family in supporting unemployed people. While integration into social networks is of great importance for youth from Northern Europe, in Southern Europe the family is more important. Especially due to the high level of family support, the number of youth at high risk of social exclusion in general is lower in Southern Europe compared to Northern Europe. Increasing individualization processes in Southern European countries, however, may weaken the buffer effect of family support in the future. Given the very low level of institutional support in these societies, this would create a major need for social policy reform.

Another central result of our study is the crucial role of the submerged economy in the southern countries for the psycho-social well-being of young people without formal employment. The higher involvement of young people in the Southern European countries in irregular work acts at the same time as a psycho-social buffer, moderating the risk of social exclusion, and as a barrier to re-entering the primary labour thus entrapping those involved. This points to the need to develop bridges out of irregular work into the labour market that may reduce the stigmatizing impact of the submerged economy.

Overall, the normalization of youth unemployment, the prolongation of the youth period (despite its negative consequences for the maturation needs of young people), and the wide acceptance of the submerged economy strongly influence individual experience of unemployment. In the Southern European countries, these factors moderate tendencies of blaming oneself, considerably lower the risk of social exclusion, and concomitantly reduce ill-health effects associated with long-term unemployment and social exclusion.

The necessity to develop more inclusive policies in the European Union, as outlined in many programmatic documents of the European Commission and most specifically in the Employment Guidelines (CEC, 2001), is dependent on the thorough analysis of the key mechanisms linking adverse life events to the degree of social integration into society. The evidence is now incontrovertible that the absence of employment is a central factor determining poverty, social exclusion, and social integration.

CHAPTER 4

Gender Differences in Employment Commitment among Unemployed Youth

TORILD HAMMER AND HELEN RUSSELL

This chapter focuses on gender differences in employment commitment among unemployed youth. The level of employment commitment among the unemployed is important for a number of reasons: first, as a potential influence on chances of re-employment; second, as a negative outcome of unemployment; and third as a moderator of the psychological impact of unemployment. Gender differences in employment commitment may therefore be a significant factor in differentiating the experiences and destinations of unemployed men and women. Exploring commitment levels among unemployed young people is of particular interest, as this is a group which has both experienced persistently high levels of unemployment and has been sometimes singled out as having a relatively weak attachment to the labour market.

Employment Commitment and Unemployment

There are two strands to the literature on employment commitment and unemployment. The first is concerned with the role of employment commitment in moderating the impact of unemployment on psychological distress, while the second addresses the issue of the inter-relationships between unemployment and employment commitment. This second research theme addresses questions such as whether unemployment reduces employment commitment and whether employment commitment influences employment prospects.

Employment Commitment as a Mediator of the Effects of Unemployment

A number of authors have suggested that an individual's level of employment commitment will influence the extent to which unemployment is psychologically distressing. Those who define themselves in terms of their employment and value their work role very highly will experience greater distress if this role is taken from them. This argument has been used to underpin an expectation of gender differences in unemployment experience. Ashton (1984) and Hakim (1996) have argued that because women's role as mothers and homemakers often takes precedence over their role as workers, unemployment poses 'no serious threat' to women's identity and therefore women will experience less psychological distress from unemployment than men. A similar line of reasoning has been applied to unemployed youth—here the contention is that, because young people have not yet developed a strong attachment to the work role, unemployment will have less impact on their mental well-being. An expectation of gender differences in employment commitment is also to be found in arguments emphasizing the differential financial consequences of unemployment. Financial explanations of unemployment experience also adopt a traditional view of gender roles, assuming that men, as primary breadwinners, will confront greater financial hardship than unemployed women. This greater financial pressure in turn is thought to lead to gender differences in employment commitment as a result of men being more financially motivated to find re-employment.

However, there is little support for any general claim about unemployed women being less committed to employment than men. Research in the United Kingdom found that there was no difference in the employment commitment of adult unemployed men and women (Russell, 1996). Gallie and Alm (2000) extended these findings to the European Union and found that unemployed women had higher employment commitment than unemployed men in all countries, excluding Belgium, West Germany, Ireland, and Portugal. Similarly, at least in the case of young unemployed people, the empirical support for the assumptions underlying the financial argument for lower employment commitment among women has been shown to be weak. Analysing the financial situation of unemployed youth in six countries, Hammer and Julkunen (2003) found that young unemployed women reported higher levels of deprivation and lower disposable income in all countries.

There is, however, evidence that in much more restricted groups and contexts, unemployed women record lower levels of employment deprivation and lower work involvement than unemployed men (Malmberg-Heimonen and Julkunen, 2000; Russell and Barbieri, 2000). Russell and Barbieri found that only women with highly demanding care commitments, that is, children under age six or who held traditional gender role attitudes had significantly lower levels of employment deprivation than unemployed men. Malmberg-Heimonen and Julkunen (2000) found that unemployed young women with children had lower work involvement than young men with children in Norway, Denmark, and Scotland (but not in Sweden, Iceland, or Finland) and had less negative attitudes to unemployment (in Iceland, Norway, and Denmark). Significant differences were also found in relation to job search behaviour, however these need to be interpreted with caution since job search activity is influenced by resources (including income and time) as much as by commitment to employment (Russell, 1996).

The Effects of Unemployment on Employment Commitment

The second set of literature has centred upon the question of whether the experience of unemployment affects employment commitment. There are sharply opposing views on this issue. First, in theories of the underclass and the culture of dependency/poverty it is often argued that prolonged unemployment erodes commitment to paid work, especially amongst the young (Murray, 1990). Several studies have suggested that young unemployed people may form their own social networks within groups of unemployed (Carle, 1987). These groups may develop their own culture, a subculture that rejects the norms and values of society, and lead to a devaluation of work. Similar conclusions are reached by those who argue that the unemployed may re-evaluate the importance of employment in their lives as a method of coping with job loss (Jackson et al., 1983).

Other writers, however, have suggested a very different relationship between unemployment and employment commitment. Jahoda (1982) has argued that a spell of unemployment will highlight the importance and centrality of employment in a person's life, and therefore lead to an increase in employment commitment. This position has also received some empirical support. Gallie and Alm (2000) found that the unemployed were just as committed to work as those in jobs; indeed, the unemployed displayed higher levels of non-financial employment commitment than those currently in work in all countries. There are also studies that have found that employment commitment is still very high among young people (Jackson et al., 1983). In fact, Banks and Ullah (1988) found a higher level of employment commitment among unemployed youth than among those in employment. While the balance of research evidence supports the hypothesis that unemployment is associated with increased employment commitment, the evidence is less consistent for young people and this group requires further investigation.

Despite their conflicting conclusions, both of these arguments tend to assume that there is an invariant effect of unemployment on employment commitment. However, it is possible that the impact of unemployment may depend upon structural and institutional factors prevailing within particular societies. For instance, it has been argued (Marsh and Alvaro, 1990) that the level of unemployment in a country will influence employment commitment among both men and women. In areas with high unemployment, there may be a general decline in work ethic, since there will be less stigma attached to unemployment when it is a highly generalized condition and there may be a greater tendency to demote the value of employment where the chances of obtaining work are very poor. There may also be an effect of high levels of unemployment in accentuating gender differences, through strengthening traditional gender role expectations. Where jobs are scarce, there may be strong normative pressures to give employment priority to men.

The overall level of unemployment and employment may also lead to different selection effects. In periods or areas of high employment the people who remain unemployed are likely to be those with the least favourable characteristics, including low employment commitment. In contrast, in a situation of high unemployment individual characteristics will play a secondary role to structural conditions. This would mean a weaker distinction between employed, unemployed, and inactive groups in terms of personal characteristics such as employment commitment.

It may also be the case that employment commitment varies according to the support for female labour market participation in countries with different welfare regimes. The organization of the welfare state is important because of what it reflects about the nature of gender relations within the society, and of the norms and expectations about gender roles which we would expect to influence women's employment commitment. The specific elements of the welfare state such as eligibility rules, level of benefits, and access to services are also likely to have a very direct impact on the lives of the unemployed women and men. For example, they may affect the level of financial hardship experienced (see Chapter 5), and as a result lead to gender differences in experiences and behaviour (Gallie and Paugam, 2000; Russell and Barbieri, 2000). We might also expect that, in countries with strong support for employed mothers, having children will not effect women's employment commitment in the same way as in countries without such support.

Hypotheses

The literature emphasizing universal gender differences in role priorities leads to two general hypotheses:

1. Unemployed young women will show lower employment commitment than unemployed young men and there will be no significant differences in the strength of this effect between countries.
2. Unemployed young women with young children will show particularly low levels of employment commitment and again the pattern should be same across countries.

However, the cross-national differences recorded in some previous studies suggest that, contrary to the universalistic hypotheses of gender differences, it may not be the case that unemployed women will share a single orientation to employment and the family across countries. We examine then four additional comparative hypotheses:

3. Higher unemployment rates will lower the level of employment commitment because, when non-employment becomes the norm amongst young people, there is less social pressure to find a job. This effect should be particularly strong among women due to the reinforcement of traditional gender role norms.
4. Alternatively, higher unemployment rates will have a *positive* impact on levels of employment commitment because people are reminded of the value of employment.
5. The selection hypothesis suggests that in countries with a high unemployment rate there will be less distinction between the employment commitment of unemployed, inactive, and employed young people, as employment outcomes will be more constrained.
6. In countries where there is a stronger tradition of female breadwinning and greater support for working mothers there will be no gender gap in employment commitment among the unemployed, while in more traditional societies employment commitment will be lower among young women with family responsibilities.

Design of the Study

The Countries

The nature of these hypotheses makes it essential to examine gender differences in employment commitment among unemployed youth in a comparative framework. Five countries have been selected for the analysis: Germany, Spain, Norway, Sweden, and Finland. These countries were chosen to provide contrasts in terms of both the level of unemployment and of the gender models implicit in their welfare regimes. Two of the countries (Germany and Spain) represent the traditional male breadwinner welfare model. Of these Germany had relatively low unemployment, while Spain had exceptionally high unemployment. The other countries are examples of the dual breadwinner welfare model. Two of these (Norway and Sweden) had relatively low unemployment conditions and the third (Finland) had relatively high unemployment.

Table 4.1 shows the youth unemployment rate among men and women in the countries included in our study as well as the female participation rate in the labour markets.

The table shows that there are substantial gender differences in the level of unemployment in Spain, where women have a much higher risk of unemployment than young men, while unemployment is more evenly distributed across the sexes in the other countries in our study. The female participation rate is much lower in Spain and Germany compared with the Nordic countries. The proportion of women who work part-time also varies across countries, with a very low proportion in Finland and Spain.

Table 4.1 *Labour market statistics for study countries*

	Youth unemployment rate			Female activity rate	Part-time (% of employed women)
	Male	Female	Total		
Finland	25.5	25.0	25.3	72.0	16.9
Norway	10.2	11.1	10.6	76.5	43.2
Sweden	21.6	20.3	21.0	76.4	36.2
Spain	19.5	33.1	25.5	51.8	17.1
Germany	8.1	7.2	7.7	63.2	37.9
EU15	14.3	17.1	15.6	59.8	33.6

Note: Figures refer to 2000.

Source: OECD employment outlook 2001, ELFS 2000.

With respect to welfare regime models, previous policy analyses suggest that these countries differ in the extent to which their welfare states support traditional male-breadwinner household forms and treat women primarily as mothers or workers (Lewis, 1992; Daly, 1996; Gornick et al., 1997). Within these comparative classifications the Scandinavian countries are identified as encouraging *male and female breadwinning*, through generous leave schemes, individualized tax and benefit systems, and the provision of public services, in particular state-subsidized childcare. However, Lewis has argued that Sweden and Denmark seem to give a better support for working mothers than Norway, while Leira (1992) has noted that Norway was much later than the other Scandinavian countries to develop public childcare and more generous parental leave schemes.

Germany is defined as having a strong male breadwinner regime because access to welfare is strongly linked to labour market participation. This means that the risks covered by the welfare state are mainly male risks and women's entitlements within the system are primarily as dependents of men (Daly, 1996). Furthermore, care is largely privatized in the family, and there is relatively little support for working mothers. The tax and benefit system and social service provision provide greatest support to families that conform to the male breadwinner/female carer model (Dingledey, 2001). In Spain large gaps in welfare provision are assumed to be covered by the family and the lack of public involvement in the provision of care means that this responsibility continues to fall on women. The benefits that are available are strongly linked to labour market status rather than need.

Data

The study draws on a new comparative data set of unemployed youth in Europe funded by the European commission 'Youth unemployment and social exclusion in Europe' (YUSE). In all countries, representative samples were drawn from national unemployment registers, with eligible respondents defined as young people between the ages of 18 and 24 who had been unemployed for a period of at least 3 months during the last 6 months. They were interviewed one year later. The total sample in all countries therefore consists of young unemployed people with a variety of work histories who, at the time of the interviews, were located in a wide range of positions inside and outside of the labour market. This survey design makes it possible to compare young people with unemployment experience, some of whom have managed to acquire positions in the full-time labour market, others who have re-entered full-time education, and others who have remained unemployed, withdrawn from the labour market, or become marginalized in some other way.

In Scandinavia, the surveys were carried out in 1996/97. The surveys were initially based on postal questionnaires with additional strategies employed to minimize bias due to skewed response rates. Those who failed to respond to the initial questionnaire after having been sent a reminder were interviewed by telephone. National register data from the unemployment register has been coupled to the surveys enabling us to analyse attrition as well as the reliability and validity of the survey data (Carle, 2000). In Spain and Germany, the data collection was in 1999/2000. In Spain postal questionnaires were used (as in the Scandinavian countries), while in Germany, the data was collected through telephone interviews.

To sum up, the study draws on comparative surveys among representative samples of unemployed 18–24 year olds who had been at least 3 months continuously unemployed and were interviewed 12 months later. The response rates and completed sample sizes in the five study countries were: Finland 73 per cent $n = 1736$; Norway 56 per cent $n = 1106$; Sweden 63 per cent $n = 2534$; Germany 65 per cent $n = 1918$; and Spain 52 per cent $n = 2523$ (see Hammer, 2003 for further information on data and research design).

Results

The Effects of the Level and Persistence of Unemployment

When considering an individual's employment commitment it is important to take account of current labour market status. While all the young people in the study share a recent experience of unemployment, they occupied a number of different employment statuses at the time of interview up to one year later. Table 4.2 summarizes the employment outcomes for respondents in each country. Three main outcome categories are identified: employment (including occasional/ irregular employment), continued unemployment, and activities outside the labour market including education, training, full-time home-duties, and military service.

The proportion of young people who were still unemployed was highest in Finland (42 per cent) and lowest in Germany, which is

Table 4.2 *Employment status at time of interview*

	Unemployed	Employed	Out of LM	Total
Finland				
Male	47.6	21.5	31.0	100.0
Female	34.9	19.8	45.3	100.0
All	42.1	20.8	37.1	100.0
Norway				
Male	29.4	35.5	35.1	100.0
Female	27.3	26.2	46.5	100.0
All	28.5	31.5	40.0	100.0
Sweden				
Male	33.6	32.2	34.3	100.0
Female	28.6	28.7	42.6	100.0
All	31.1	30.5	38.4	100.0
Spain				
Male	23.3	52.1	24.6	100.0
Female	30.7	41.4	28.0	100.0
All	27.9	45.5	26.7	100.0
Germany				
Male	26.7	26.3	47.0	100.0
Female	22.8	30.6	46.5	100.0
All	25.0	28.2	46.8	100.0

consistent with the divergent levels of youth unemployment experienced in these two countries. The proportion of young people who had found jobs was greatest in Spain, where 46 per cent of unemployed respondents were in jobs when interviewed 12 months later. Given the high rates of youth unemployment in Spain compared to Germany, Norway, and Sweden this result might not be anticipated. However, it is important to bear in mind the very high level of temporary work in Spain that increases flows into, as well as out of, employment. It is notable that in Spain only 18 per cent of the unemployed had found a permanent position, the rest were in temporary jobs. The results post-date the Spanish labour market reforms to increase temporary employment opportunities. The lowest rate of entry into employment was in Finland, where only 22 per cent of respondents were in jobs at the time of the interview.

The proportion of young people outside the labour market ranged from a low of 27 per cent in Spain to a high of 47 per cent in Germany. The destinations of those outside the labour market are quite varied: with the exception of Germany, education was the most common destination for this group, in Germany training was the biggest subcategory. Working in the home accounted for around 4 per cent of respondents except in Norway where 9 per cent of the previously unemployed were in this category when interviewed.

The figures in Table 4.2 also show that there were significant gender differences in the destinations of the unemployed. In Finland, Sweden, Germany, and to a lesser extent in Norway, young women were less likely to be still unemployed than young men when interviewed. In Spain the situation was reversed, so that a higher proportion of women than men remained unemployed. This reflects the wide divergence between male and female youth unemployment rates recorded in the national statistics for Spain (see Table 4.1). The wide gender gap in unemployment in Finland is due to a much higher level of withdrawal from the labour market among Finnish women compared to Finnish men. All three Nordic countries have significantly higher rates of economic inactivity among young women than among young men. In Sweden and Finland this is due to higher rates of re-entry into education and higher rates of home duties among women, but in Norway it is almost entirely due to differences in working at home. However, controlling for age and gender differences in work experience, women had a higher probability of entering education than men in all countries (Hammer, 2003). The destinations of unemployed men and women were most similar in Germany, although even in Germany there are gender differences in the activities of those outside the labour market.

Do these differential outcomes across countries and gender relate to respondents' employment commitment? As seen above, previous research suggests that the adult unemployed tend to express somewhat higher levels of employment commitment than the employed. In this analysis we can examine whether this holds true for young people with recent unemployment experience. In general we would expect those who are economically inactive to have a lower commitment to employment than the active. However, this assumes that withdrawal from the labour market is a matter of choice. Some of the unemployed may be *pushed* out of the labour market because of a lack of employment options rather than choosing to leave. This would lead us to expect that where employment opportunities are most constrained the economically inactive may retain relatively high levels of employment commitment (hypothesis 5).

The measure of employment commitment used in this study was developed by Warr et al. (1979).[1] The scale is devised from respondents' agreement/disagreement with six statements:

- It is very important to me to have a job.
- If I won a lot of money I would want to work.
- I hate being unemployed.
- I feel restless if I do not have a job.
- Work is one of the most important things in my life.
- I would prefer to work even if unemployment benefits were generous.

The response categories for each item are: strongly agree, agree, neither agree nor disagree, disagree, and strongly disagree. The scale has a Cronbach's alpha of 0.83, and scores range between one and five, with higher scores indicating greater employment commitment.

The mean employment commitment scores for those in different employment statuses are presented in Figure 4.1. Overall, those in employment had higher employment commitment scores than either the unemployed or the economically inactive. The difference between the employment commitment scores of the employed and unemployed was statistically significant in Finland and Norway but not in the other three countries. This result differs from the findings of previous research, outlined earlier, which found lower employment commitment among the employed compared to the unemployed. However, since all respondents in our sample were previously unemployed, we are comparing the re-employed to those remaining unemployed. These results suggest that higher employment commitment may facilitate exits from unemployment to work but we lack the longitudinal information to test this formally. Another explanation is suggested by Gallie et al.'s (1998) research in Britain which found that amongst the *employed*, those who had experienced unemployment in the last 5 years were more committed to employment than other workers. Therefore, it is possible that the recent unemployment experience shared by all our respondents reduces the impact of current employment status.

In Norway, Sweden, Spain, and Germany those remaining unemployed were somewhat more committed to employment than the

---

[1] We use the term employment commitment rather than work commitment throughout the chapter as it is conceptually clearer than 'work commitment' which could also include unpaid domestic/caring work or voluntary work. Warr et al. (1979) call their scale a 'work' commitment scale, however several items in the scale refer to a 'job' which is likely to frame respondents to answer in terms of paid employment.

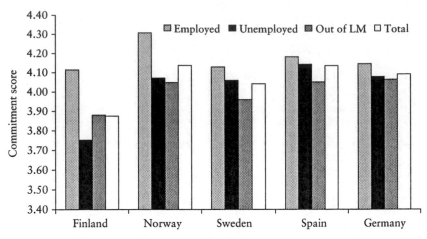

Figure 4.1 *Employment commitment score by labour market status.*

economically inactive; however, in Finland the inactive had higher scores than the unemployed. Given that the Finnish respondents had by far the lowest levels of re-employment, this result is consistent with the hypothesis that withdrawal in these circumstances is not entirely voluntary and therefore does not reflect a lack of employment commitment. But the low scores of both the non-employed and unemployed relative to the employed in Finland runs contrary to the general selection hypothesis above.

Overall, the comparison between countries does not support the hypothesis that the national level of unemployment influenced employment commitment, at least among young people with recent unemployment experience. Employment commitment was highest in Norway and Spain, countries that had very different youth unemployment levels. However, it is possible that the low levels of employment commitment in Finland, especially among the unemployed and non-active, may be related to the poor exit rates there.

Does the evidence support the view that there are substantial gender differentials in employment commitment, with women showing lower levels of commitment than men? The results presented in Table 4.3 show that, despite higher economic inactivity, young women recorded higher levels of employment commitment than young men in four of the five countries, with Norway being the only exception. The biggest gender gap in employment commitment was observed in Sweden and Germany. When we look at gender differences within labour market groups the pattern remains the same; where there are statistically significant gender differences they

Table 4.3 *Employment commitment scores by current employment status and sex*

	Employed	Unemployed	Inactive	All
Finland				
Male	4.10	3.71	3.85	3.83
Female	4.14	3.83	3.91	3.92
Norway				
Male	4.28	**4.21**	4.10	4.20
Female	4.35	**3.87**	3.99	4.06
Sweden				
Male	4.05	3.97	3.80	3.94
Female	**4.22**	4.17	**4.09**	**4.15**
Spain				
Male	4.11	4.14	3.98	4.08
Female	**4.24**	4.15	4.10	4.17
Germany				
Male	4.07	4.03	3.94	4.00
Female	**4.23**	4.16	**4.23**	**4.21**
All[a]				
Male	4.11	3.95	3.92	3.99
Female	**4.24**	**4.07**	**4.08**	**4.13**

Note: Bold indicates significant gender difference at 0.05 level.
[a] The total figure does not weight for differences in sample or population sizes across countries.

are in the direction of women having higher commitment scores than men. Indeed, it is notable that in three of the countries the scores for the female unemployed were higher than those for men who were in jobs. The only case where men were significantly more committed is among the unemployed in Norway. Therefore, the evidence does not support the view that unemployed young women are less committed to employment than men in general. Nor is there evidence that the pattern of gender differences across countries reflect gendered welfare regimes that encourage female employment to a greater or lesser extent (hypothesis 6 above). In Spain and Germany, where institutions support more traditional gender roles, young women had higher employment commitment than young men in nearly all categories.

There is little evidence that high unemployment reinforces traditional gender roles at least in the form of any general reduced employment commitment among women, since it is only in Norway

where youth unemployment is relatively low, that there is any sign
that young women have lower commitment than young men. In the
next section of the paper we examine whether there is evidence of
reduced employment commitment among a more restricted category
of young women, that is, those with family responsibilities.

The Effects of Family Situation

Earlier research suggested that gender differences in employment
commitment and work involvement are confined to unemployed
women with particular family characteristics. Figure 4.2 shows that
the living arrangements of respondents differed very widely across
the study countries. The proportion of young people living with parents varied from 71 per cent in Spain and 51 per cent in Germany to
a third or fewer in the three Scandinavian countries. The proportion
living with a partner (either married or cohabiting) ranged from a
low of 14 per cent in Spain to 43 per cent in Sweden. These broad
country differences remain very much the same among those in
different current employment situations (not shown).

Strong cross-national differences are also observed in the proportion of respondents who had children. Only 7 per cent of Spanish
youth had a child compared to 28 per cent in Norway (Table 4.4).
These figures reflect broad demographic differences across countries
as shown in the national fertility statistics. The national figures suggest that the Finns should have a higher fertility rate than Sweden
and Germany. However, in the Finnish sample most young registered

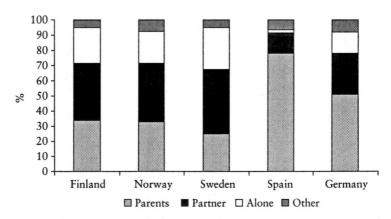

Figure 4.2 *Living arrangements of respondents by country. (Eurostat
New Cronos Database)*

Table 4.4 *Proportion of respondents with children*

	Finland	Norway	Sweden	Spain	Germany
No children	89.9	71.9	84.9	93.1	84.7
Children	10.1	28.1	15.1	6.9	15.3

unemployed are first-time job-seekers and they are therefore younger than in the other countries.

In the following analyses we investigate whether employment commitment among young men and women is influenced by their family situation (living with partner, and having children). We also examine whether the impact of the family situation varies across countries with different welfare models. Is it the case that the impact of family is less important for women's employment commitment in welfare regimes supporting mothers' employment?

For this analysis we focus on those who were still unemployed at the time of the interview. The data presented in Figure 4.3 show that, when we take all countries together, single unemployed women have a higher employment commitment score than single unemployed men but married/cohabiting unemployed men have a higher score than married/cohabiting women. This pattern is evident in Finland and Spain, while in Germany and Sweden there is no gender gap in

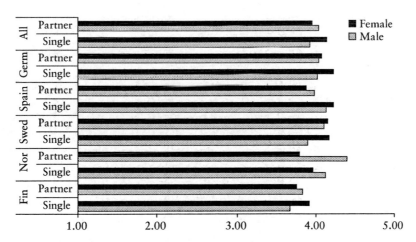

Figure 4.3 *Employment commitment score among currently unemployed by partnership status and gender.*

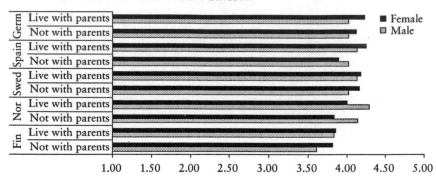

Figure 4.4 *Employment commitment scores among currently unemployed by living with parents.*

commitment scores among respondents living with a partner. In Norway, young men have higher commitment scores than women within both the single and married/cohabiting groups.

It is also possible to compare the employment commitment scores of those living or not living with parents.[2] If having an alternative source of financial support within the household reduces commitment to employment among the unemployed, we would expect both males and females living with parents to have a lower commitment score. However, the results show that unemployed young people who live with their parents have higher commitment scores than those in other living arrangements (this difference is significant in Finland, Norway, and Spain). Gender differences among those living with their parents are limited to Spain and Germany, where results show that women are more committed than men in this position (see Figure 4.4).[3] The fact that living with a partner has a different impact on women's employment commitment than living with parents suggests that it is not alternative financial support per se that is decisive (this issue is investigated further below).

In Figure 4.5 we compare the commitment levels of the unemployed with and without children. Overall, unemployed women without children have higher scores than men without children, however among those with children, men score higher. This finding holds true for all the countries except Norway where childless unemployed men have higher scores than childless women.

[2] Note that those living with a partner are a subset of those 'not living with parents'.
[3] The gap is not statistically significant in Norway because the numbers living with parents is so small.

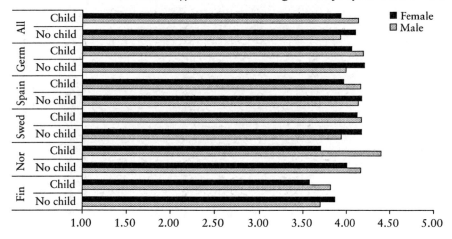

Figure 4.5 *Mean employment commitment scores among currently unemployed by parental status and gender.*

Do these gender-specific effects of family responsibilities remain significant when we control for other relevant characteristics? This is assessed through regression analysis. As can be seen in Table 4.5, the length of time one remains unemployed since entering the labour market still has a small negative impact on employment commitment even when other factors are taken into account. It is possible that employment commitment tends to decrease with the duration of unemployment as a result of a 'discouraged worker effect'. Alternatively, there may be a selection effect, with those with low employment commitment being disproportionately selected into the long-term unemployment group. In the absence of longitudinal data it is not possible to separate these effects. It should be noted, however, that the analysis presented in Table 4.5 explains very little of the variance in employment commitment.

Education is not linked to employment commitment in a systematic way. Those with secondary education had somewhat lower employment commitment than those with elementary school education; but those with third level education did not differ from the least educated.

The interaction effects confirm that the impact of the two family variables vary by gender: both have a positive effect on young men's employment commitment scores but have a negative effect on women's employment commitment. Moreover, the negative impact of cohabitation/marriage and children on the employment commitment

Table 4.5 OLS regression of employment commitment among
currently unemployed

	Model 1			Model 2		
	B	SE	Sig.	B	SE	Sig.
(Constant)	4.08	0.08	0.000	3.95	0.09	0.000
Female	0.33	0.07	0.000	0.30	0.07	0.000
Age	0.01	0.01	n.s.	0.01	0.01	n.s.
Education (ref = elementary)						
Vocational Ed.	−0.04	0.05	n.s.	−0.04	0.05	n.s.
Secondary	−0.13	0.05	0.004	−0.12	0.05	0.006
Third Level	−0.03	0.08	n.s.	−0.02	0.08	n.s.
Other education	−0.21	0.07	0.003	−0.20	0.07	0.005
Any work experience	0.00	0.04	n.s.	0.00	0.01	n.s.
Months unemployed	−0.003	0.00	0.003	−0.003	0.00	0.002
Live with partner	0.11	0.06	0.041	0.11	0.06	0.047
Child(ren)	0.13	0.06	0.074	0.11	0.07	n.s.
Deprivation Scale				*0.23*	*0.05*	*0.000*
Country (ref = Sweden)						
Finland	−0.22	0.06	0.000	−0.24	0.06	0.000
Norway	0.24	0.08	0.001	0.22	0.08	0.004
Spain	0.16	0.09	0.092	0.17	0.07	0.078
Germany	0.02	0.07	n.s.	0.05	0.07	n.s.
Interaction effects						
Female × Norway	−0.47	0.12	0.000	−0.44	0.12	0.000
Female × Finland	−0.11	0.09	n.s.	−0.05	0.09	n.s.
Female × Germany	−0.02	0.10	n.s.	−0.01	0.10	n.s.
Female × Spain	−0.19	0.11	n.s.	−0.17	0.10	n.s.
Female × Partner	−0.23	0.08	0.004	−0.23	0.08	0.003
Female × child	−0.29	0.10	0.003	−0.28	0.10	0.005

Note: Adjusted R square = 0.06; N = 2542; n.s. = not significant.

of young unemployed women was not found to vary significantly
across the five countries (i.e. the three-way interactions were insigni-
ficant). The impact of family responsibilities on the employment
commitment of women who have found work again was different:
having children has no effect upon employment commitment,
although women who live with a partner again have lower employment commitment (see model for employed in Table 4.6).

It might be argued that living with a partner reduces commitment
to employment among unemployed women because they are provided

Table 4.6 *Regression on employment commitment among currently unemployed (n = 2498) and employed (n = 2460)*

	Unemployed		Employed	
	B	**SE**	**B**	**SE**
Constant	2.68	0.09	3.15	0.08
Female = 1	0.12**	0.04	0.15***	0.03
Children = 1	0.12*	0.07	−0.05	0.05
Work experience	0.001	0.001	0.002**	0.001
Months unemployed	−0.002**	0.001	0.001	0.001
Coping problems	0.35***	0.02	0.29***	0.02
Live with partner	0.18**	0.06	0.22***	0.05
Equal men and women[a]	−0.07***	0.02	−0.04*	0.02
Finland	−0.09*	0.04	0.09*	0.04
Norway	0.04	0.06	0.15***	0.05
Spain	−0.09	0.06	−0.05	0.04
Germany	−0.02	0.05	−0.04	0.04
Job search	0.60***	0.06	0.15**	0.05
Live with parents	0.20***	0.04	0.06	0.04
Interaction Effects				
Female × partner	−0.14*	0.07	−0.22***	0.06
Female × child	−0.23**	0.09	n.s.	n.s.
Adjusted R square	0.19		0.12	

Ref = Sweden

[a] Whether the respondents disagree that there should be equal rights for men and women.

*** $p < 0.001$; **$p < 0.01$; *$p < 0.05$

with financial support, which makes the option of remaining out of employment less unattractive. The employment commitment scale used here attempts to tap into non-financial employment commitment, for example, in items such as 'if I won a lot of money I would want to work' and 'I would prefer to work even if unemployment benefits were generous'. Nevertheless, financial deprivation may influence responses to other elements of the employment commitment scale such as, 'It is very important to me to have a job'.

In model 2 of Table 4.5, we include a scale of financial deprivation, based upon eleven questions about the experience of material and social deprivation. It is clear that women with children or a partner had lower employment commitment even controlling for financial deprivation. Increased financial deprivation had a positive impact on employment commitment as anticipated; however, it did not reduce the impact of living with a partner for either sex. Therefore, partnership status is not acting as a proxy for financial support.

It is also possible that the 'family responsibility' effect is mediated through its effects on coping abilities: possibly where women have children or/and a partner they cope better with unemployment and this may reduce their employment commitment. To test such a hypothesis we add to the model a variable on coping with unemployment. Coping with unemployment is constructed as an index based on seven different questions about coping with their latest period of unemployment.

- I have more time for family and friends.
- I do not accomplish anything.
- I have problems planning for the future.
- I am financially dependent on others.
- I can use my time as I please.
- I have more time for my hobbies.

The response categories for each item are strongly agree, agree, neither, disagree, and strongly disagree. The negative items have been recoded in order to make an index. The scale has a Cronbach's alpha of 0.84 and scores range from one to five, with higher scores indicating coping problems. Since job search is also an important coping strategy, we include this information as an additional factor (Kaul and Kvande, 1991). Job search is measured by the number of different methods to find work.

Coping with unemployment has indeed an effect upon employment commitment both in the unemployed group ($\beta = 0.35$) and among the employed ($\beta = 0.29$). Those who have fewer problems with managing the situation of unemployment have lower employment commitment. It could be argued that the causality is the other way round and that those with lower commitment to employment are better able to cope with unemployment and find positive dimensions to their experience. However, the effect of coping was equally strong in the employed group where information refers to previous experience. This suggests that how people cope with unemployment also has an independent effect upon employment commitment. More importantly, the gender interaction effect of having children or a partner upon employment commitment remains significant, so this effect is not attributable to its implications for making it easier for people to cope with unemployment. Taking account of coping ability, however, revealed sharper country differences. There was a three-way significant interaction effect (not shown in the table), indicating that young women with a partner in Norway in both the employed and the unemployed group displayed lower employment commitment than such women in other countries and the same interaction effect was nearly significant in Spain ($p = 0.059$).

To sum up, we did not find gender differences in employment commitment between countries with different welfare models and gender cultures. In four out of the five countries young unemployed women had higher levels of employment commitment than unemployed men. Norway was the exception to this: gender differences were greater in Norway than in the other countries, and more young women in Norway stayed at home with children. This is perhaps surprising given that Norway, together with Sweden, has been characterized as dual breadwinner country. However, as mentioned above, the classification of Norway in this respect has been a matter of some controversy in the literature. Lewis, for instance, selects Sweden as typifying a weak male breadwinner regime, but argues that the Norwegian system has continued to treat women primarily as wives and mothers (p.162). Ellingsæter (1998) has compared parents' perceived norms about equal partnership in economic provision in the three Scandinavian countries. She also concludes that, while the idea of the traditional breadwinner model is rather weak in Denmark and Sweden, in Norway the male breadwinner norm still persists at least at the ideological level.

Both in the employed and unemployed group, young women with a partner had lower employment commitment. Having children also reduced commitment for young unemployed women, but did not have any significant effect in the re-employed group. The effect of family responsibilities on young women's employment commitment is then particularly clear for young unemployed women and appears to be independent of either financial need or of the general ability to cope with unemployment. These results are consistent with the hypothesis that, where unemployed women have access to an alternative role within the home, this reduces their commitment to employment. The fact that this effect is observed amongst young women in Scandinavian countries, where there is strong institutional/policy support for female breadwinning, suggests that unemployment at this career stage may have the effect of reinforcing traditional gender roles (Wallace, 1987; Hammer, 1996).

It is possible, however, that there is an effect of welfare regime on labour market decisions that is independent of employment commitment per se. To examine this, we carried out a multi-nomial logit analysis among women (see Table 4.7). This makes it possible to analyse the influence of family status on being in employment, unemployment, or pursuing education compared with staying at home (the reference group). It is also possible to evaluate the impact of, having children or a partner in countries with different welfare regimes controlling for employment commitment.

As would be expected in terms of welfare regime effects, children have a particularly negative impact on the chances of being either employed or unemployed compared to being involved in household duties in Spain and Germany. Young mothers who have experienced unemployment in Spain and Germany tend to withdraw from the labour market, reflecting the fact that these countries provide very little support for employed motherhood. In the other countries children have no influence on employment and have a positive effect on the likelihood of being unemployed.

Table 4.7 *Multi-nominal regression of employment status among women (n = 3914)*

	Employment		Unemployment		Education	
	B	SE	B	SE	B	SE
Employment duration	0.01**	0.003	−0.01	0.003	−0.01*	0.004
Unemployment duration	−0.02***	0.004	0.01**	0.004	−0.02***	0.005
Emp commitment	0.74***	0.22	0.03	0.18	0.67*	0.26
Age, year of birth	−0.12**	0.05	−0.12**	0.05	−0.05	0.50
Compulsory education	0.16	0.34	−0.19	0.31	−0.10	0.35
Vocational	0.21	0.32	−0.31	0.30	−0.18	0.33
Secondary general	0.20	0.32	−0.32	0.29	0.27	0.33
Tertiary	0.24	0.37	−0.65*	0.34	0.29	0.40
Partner = 1	−0.29	0.16	−0.49**	0.15	−0.76***	0.17
Children = 1	−0.40	0.55	1.84***	0.50	−2.02	1.26
Finland	−0.59*	0.24	−0.36	0.23	−0.26	0.24
Norway (NO)	−1.9	1.01	−0.10	0.81	−2.80*	1.19
Spain	1.01*	0.41	0.89*	0.35	−0.94	1.06
Germany	0.23	0.29	−0.12	0.26	−1.63*	0.64
Interation effects						
Children* Spain	−1.51***	0.47	−2.71***	0.42	−1.16	1.09
Children* Germany	−1.84***	0.36	−2.29***	0.33	−0.62	0.67
Emp commit.* NO	−0.46*	0.24	0.05	0.20	−0.58*	0.28
Intercept	2.12	0.59	3.60	0.56	3.13	0.63

Chi-square = 1,542.87, df = 85, $p < 0.001$, Pseudo R-Square, Cox and Snell = 0.33.
***$p < 0.001$; **$p < 0.01$; *$p < 0.05$.

Conclusions

This chapter focused on gender and cross-national differences in employment commitment among the unemployed. In relation to gender differences the most notable finding was that, in all countries except Norway, employment commitment was higher among young unemployed women than among young unemployed men. We did not find that employment commitment among women was affected by the level of female labour market participation in a country or by different welfare regimes with different breadwinner models. Nor were commitment levels of men or women systematically related to the national level of unemployment—the highest levels of employment commitment were noted in Norway, which had below average youth unemployment rates and in Spain, which had the highest youth unemployment. However, the low levels of commitment observed in Finland where the chances of existing unemployment were poorest suggest that poor employment prospects may have a discouraging affect. National comparisons of gender differences in commitment did not support the hypothesis that high levels of unemployment affect gender roles in a general way.

However, our investigation of the relationship between gender, family status, and employment commitment found that having children or a partner affects employment commitment negatively among unemployed females in all countries, while the reverse is the case among men. Unemployed females with partners reported lower employment commitment than others it seems, not for financial reasons, but perhaps because of role anticipation. If future plans include raising a family and a woman's current employment prospects are poor, this may lead to lower levels of employment commitment.

Although welfare regimes were not related to employment commitment, it is however notable that, once employment commitment has been taken into account, young women with children in Germany and Spain, which are countries with traditional male breadwinner models, were more likely to withdraw from the labour market. In other words, welfare regimes do not influence gender differences in employment commitment, but do influence actual labour market behaviour. Spain and Germany have little support for working mothers, and so if unemployed women have children they tend to withdraw from the labour market.

It is important to stress that we have analysed gender differences in employment commitment among unemployed youth. People in this group have low levels of education, have mainly experience from low-skill jobs and have experienced several spells of unemployment. We would expect more traditional gender roles among these young women compared with women with better qualifications. The results may imply increasing differences between women within dual bread-winner societies, not only in Norway but also in Sweden and Finland, leading to a broad similarity between countries in the situation of this particularly vulnerable group.

Acknowledgement

The authors wish to thank Duncan Gallie for his insightful and helpful comments.

CHAPTER 5

What Difference does a Job Make?
The Income Consequences of
Joblessness in Europe

HERWIG IMMERVOLL AND
CATHAL O'DONOGHUE

Introduction

The level and structure of European taxes and transfer payments
have been the subject of much attention and discussion in recent
years. There has been considerable pressure to reduce budget deficits
in order to meet national or European targets. On the revenue side,
room for manoeuvre was limited due to tax burdens which are
already considered too high in many European countries. As a result,
the reduction of public expenditures associated with existing social
protection systems is argued to be the most likely route towards
achieving 'sound' public finances (Buti et al., 2000). Furthermore,
certain state transfers have frequently been criticized as giving rise
to adverse incentive effects and have—next to labour market 'rigidities' and over-regulation—been named as one of the main causes of
slack economic growth and unemployment (Bean, 1994; IMF, 1999;
European Commission, 2000a).

  In particular, there is a concern that by intervening in the labour
market, tax-benefit systems create incentives that negatively affect
the behaviour of both employees and firms. On the demand side,
high tax burdens increase the cost of labour while on the supply side,
high marginal tax rates reduce the reward for additional work
efforts. In addition, generous out-of-work benefit payments are seen
as leading people to reduce their efforts to remain in work or to seek

gainful employment (Björklund et al., 1991; Snower, 1997). Of course, the absolute benefit level also determines the public expenditure necessary to finance benefit payments. Because the burden of financing is to a large extent borne by employers and employees, generous benefits raise the cost of labour which may in itself lead to decreasing employment.[1] Moreover, generous benefits tend to improve the relative bargaining position of employees and may therefore lead to higher wages (Layard et al., 1991).

There is no consensus as to the quantitative significance of these effects[2] and, in any case, any negative implications of state interventions in the market have to be weighted against their success in achieving economic and social policy goals for which they were originally designed (Atkinson, 2000). For example, in Southern Europe, there have been concerns that the state does not provide protection against contingencies such as long-term unemployment.

While excessively high replacement rates may give rise to adverse *work incentives*, very low degrees of *income maintenance* will have negative consequences from both an economic and a social policy perspective. In measuring and discussing the coverage and generosity of benefits, it is therefore essential to take both dimensions into account.

Whether or not one thinks that the role of the state in this area should be reduced, it is essential to carefully measure the extent of these interventions in order to be able to study their effects. In particular, since existing measures of replacement rates are subject to a number of shortcomings (discussed in the section titled 'Measuring Replacement Rate'), it is very difficult to draw any conclusions about their effects. As a first step it is therefore important to improve measurement methods. In this chapter, instead of addressing the question of whether net transfer payments should be more or less generous, we establish their impact on household incomes. More specifically, we are concerned with measuring the levels of incomes that are available to those out of work relative to their in-work incomes. From a social policy point of view, the *absolute* level of out-of-work income is important since it determines the minimum living standard that people are able to secure during periods of unemployment. On the other hand, the level of income out-of-work measured *relative* to in-work income (the replacement rate) is a measure of the relative drop in living standards that people experience when losing

---

[1] Carey and Tchilinguirian (2000) provide recent estimates of taxes on labour in OECD countries.

[2] Buti et al. (2000).

their job. This latter measure is also relevant for looking at work incentives. Is there enough potential financial gain from employment to make it worthwhile for unemployed people to look for jobs? And, looking at the same issue from a different and rather more pointed perspective, is the hardship caused by being out of work 'sufficient' to make work and the efforts needed to secure employment the more attractive alternative?

There are, of course, other dimensions to the situation of being unemployed, that will be equally or more relevant for decisions of whether or not to seek or stay in employment. Among them are non-financial rewards (both of being in-work and out-of-work), the negative stigma of being unemployed (whether with or without benefits), people's perception as to the availability of benefits, and the likelihood of finding a suitable job, as well as other aspects of benefit systems such as eligibility conditions or duration of entitlement (for the latter, see Atkinson and Micklewright, 1991). There is a danger that because benefit levels are relatively straightforward to measure (and because they are often the only dimension of benefit systems featuring in economic models) they would receive too much attention by both researchers and policy-makers while other determinants of work incentives are ignored.

However, even with replacement rates, there has been considerable disagreement about what is the most appropriate measurement method. In addition, the identification of unemployment as a Europe-wide problem has led to increasing demands for measures that are comparable (ideally) or reconcilable (at least) across countries (European Commission, 2000*b*: ch. 5). Consistent measurement of replacement rates across countries is a prerequisite for addressing related policy questions at the European level.

In this chapter, we use an integrated European tax-benefit model, EUROMOD to study replacement rates across Europe. In the following section we review existing approaches and explain how ours differs from them. The microsimulation model used in this chapter provides a large degree of flexibility and transparency and therefore allows the sensitivity of estimates with respect to different assumptions to be assessed. Some of these assumptions and their implications are discussed in the section titled 'Conceptual Issues'. As an illustration of the approach, we compute distributions of replacement rates for four different countries: Denmark, France, Spain, and the United Kingdom. This specific choice of countries is intended to allow us to throw some light on how different types of welfare state system affect people's income situations in and out of work.

The model and simulation details are discussed in the section titled 'Simulations'. In the next section, we briefly describe the national tax benefit systems. Simulation results are presented in the section titled 'Distribution of Replacement Rates'. In the section titled 'What Drives Replacement Rates?', we take a closer look at what particular income components determine the distribution of replacement rates. The final section emphasizes some caveats and discusses how they could be addressed in future research.

Measuring Replacement Rate

Social and fiscal policy instruments that affect people's incomes are subject to a well-known trade-off. An instrument that performs well from an income maintenance perspective may have unintended behavioural consequences. For example, if the operation of the tax-benefit instrument depends on characteristics that people can influence, then this link will have a potential impact on people's behaviour. In many cases, changing people's behaviour is an intended consequence of the policy and is, thus, desirable. Examples include taxes and fines on activities which negatively affect others, the tax-deductibility of charitable donations or unemployment benefits enabling job-seekers to undertake a more thorough search process.[3] Frequently, however, the incentives that such instruments give rise to are unintended. For instance, high marginal tax rates caused by either the tax system or the withdrawal of benefits reduce the net gain from any additional income and will, thus, make efforts to increase incomes less attractive. Similarly, benefits or taxes that depend on a certain status of the recipient/taxpayer (such as being unemployed) have an impact on the desirability of entering or leaving this status.

Replacement rates are a measure of the degree to which individuals' (and their households') standard of living while employed is maintained during periods of unemployment. The higher a household's replacement rate, the more protected they are from the impact of losing work income. At the same time, however, high replacement rates may reduce peoples' efforts to secure employment. This chapter does not try to answer the question as to where the dividing

---

[3] On the latter, see Acemoglu and Shimer (1999), who discuss under which conditions unemployment insurance systems increase economic efficiency.

line between achieving the objectives of income maintenance and maintaining work incentives might be. Instead we merely report the distribution of replacement rates.

It is a fact, however, that there are concerns that out-of-work bene-fits may lead to insufficient efforts to escape unemployment or avoid slipping into it. The opportunities that unemployed people face may be such that accepting jobs offered to them would not result in any or little financial gain. They are thus locked into unemployment—a situation often referred to as the unemployment trap—with prospects of finding a job deteriorating as time passes. Similarly, those currently employed may, under certain conditions and for a certain period of time, not lose much by becoming unemployed. In this context, the replacement rate can be relevant even if, as is often the case, benefits are not paid if termination of an employment relationship is judged to be 'voluntary': Employers may use the availability of unemploy-ment insurance to smooth over demand cycles by laying off people when demand is weak and re-employing them when business is stronger.[4]

Individual replacement rates depend strongly on the individual situation. Obviously, the current or prospective wage level plays a decisive role. For a given level of benefit, lower wages will generally correspond to higher replacement rates. There will generally also be other incomes, received either by the same person or by other persons in the household, which have an influence on total household income and, thus, the (household based) replacement rate. In addition, expenses which have to be incurred in one labour market situation but not in the other, may have an important effect on disposable income (e.g. union fees, costs of commuting to work, costs of pro-viding care for dependants during working hours, job search costs, etc.). However, in terms of policy makers' control, all these income components are less readily accessible than taxes and benefits. Partly for this reason and because policy-makers have more control over tax and transfer policy than over household decisions, the influence of tax-benefit systems has received most of the attention.

Early studies have analysed the level of (gross) unemployment benefits as a fraction of employment income in isolation from the rest

---

[4] There has been some evidence that such temporary layoffs are important phe-nomena especially in the United States but also in some European countries. See Fitzroy and Hart (1985), Jensen and Westergard-Nielsen (1989), and Felli and Ichino (1988).

of the tax-benefit system (OECD, 1994*a*). It has since been recognized that the omission of taxes and benefits other than unemployment benefit produces over-simplified results that can be seriously misleading. People are concerned about their total net incomes and the measurement concept needs to reflect this. Progressive income taxes on earnings combined with a favourable or tax-free status of benefit payments mean that replacement rates before taxes are markedly lower than the so-called net replacement rates which are measured net of tax and contribution payments (OECD, 1997). Equally important is the fact that the more extreme values of replacement rates found for some people are frequently caused by very complex (and sometimes unintended) interdependencies between parts of the tax-benefit system which have been introduced at different times, with different objectives, or are administered by different authorities. Unless all relevant parts of the tax-benefit system are taken into account, these 'anomalies', which can have very serious implications for work incentives, will not show up in the resulting replacement rate calculations.

In Immervoll and O'Donoghue (2001*b*), we have considered the implications of a number of different methods of calculating replacement rates, including:

- Replacement rates of stylized households
- 'Data driven' replacement rates and
- Simulation based replacement rates.

We have argued that simulation based methods using tax-benefit models offer a number of advantages when computing replacement rates. Because tax-benefit models are computer programs that represent the rules governing a country's tax and benefit system, by applying these rules to a set of households that is representative of the population it is possible to evaluate the effects of existing tax-benefit systems as well as policy changes in terms of income distribution and government revenue. Using this approach, one can avoid the main problem of stylized calculations that do not take into account the actual structure of the population. In addition, the simulation method allows us to explore replacement rates of the entire workforce rather than being restricted to look at those individuals whose change of employment status can be observed in the data as happens in the data-based replacement rate. We can thus produce distributions of replacement rates for all people whose behaviour they can *potentially* affect. But in terms of policy relevance, the most important feature of this method is that it permits analyses of the effects of policy *reforms* on replacement rates. Because tax-benefit models simulate the rules of a wide range of fiscal and social policy instruments, they allow an integrated approach to be taken in analysing replacement rates. Policy changes in many different areas (whether they are hypothetical or have actually taken place) can be examined. By holding 'everything else' constant, the simulation approach isolates the effects of such policy changes—an important advantage vis-à-vis the 'data-driven' approach where one is restricted to analysing policy changes that have actually taken place.[5]

While the treatment of unemployment as a European problem would clearly indicate an important role for comparable multi-country studies, most previous studies adopting the simulation approach have been limited to individual countries (Atkinson and Micklewright, 1985; Callan et al., 1996; ESO, 1997). National tax-benefit microsimulation models are constructed with a view to satisfy national priorities. The structure, concepts, and definitions used in these models therefore reflect very country-specific requirements that make informative comparisons of results across different models very difficult and frequently impossible. EUROMOD, being an integrated European tax-benefit model, can avoid these problems.

Conceptual Issues

In this section, we will outline the issues that have to be resolved before measuring replacement rates in practice. Notwithstanding the fact that the replacement rate is a relatively simple concept in theory, the number of issues and the number of alternative approaches of dealing with them make actual measurement quite difficult.

Direction of Transition

An individual of working age faces a set of feasible labour market states. Each of them is characterized by, among other things, a certain level of income (either actual or perceived: discussed later) that

---

[5] Moreover, a 'data driven' analysis of policy changes is only possible after some delay since one has to wait for the changes to feed through to the data and then for the data to be collected and processed. Even then, one cannot easily isolate the effect of the policy change since, along with the tax-benefit rules of interest, many other effects will potentially have influenced replacement rates as well.

plays a part in determining the relative attractiveness of this state. Many studies of replacement rates have focused exclusively on the unemployed and have computed their current income as a fraction of the prospective income they would earn if entering employment (e.g. Central Planning Bureau, 1995; European Commission, 1998b; Salomäki and Munzi, 1999). In this chapter we extend our analysis to the following labour market states: employed or self-employed (A); unemployed (B); out of work other than unemployed (C). The transitions we consider are:

- from B to A (we will call this replacement rate RR_{ba})
- from C to A (RR_{ca})
- from A to B (RR_{ab})

RR_{ba} and RR_{ca} thus represent what we call out-of-work replacement rates. RR_{ba} is the out-of-work replacement rate applying to those who are currently receiving unemployment benefits or who classify themselves as 'unemployed' in the response to the questionnaire underlying our data (see the 'Simulations' section for further details). RR_{ca} denotes the level of current (net) income relative to the prospective (net) employment income of someone currently out-of-work but not 'unemployed' according to the above definition. It is, in other words, the out-of-work replacement rate faced by working age individuals who receive neither income from work nor unemployment benefits (e.g. 'inactive' people; those engaged in unpaid care or domestic work; recipients of pensions, disability benefits, social minimum benefits, etc).[6] It is an advantage that we can investigate the 'inactive' group separately, however one must be cautious in drawing conclusions for this group as a whole as it is very heterogeneous. RR_{ab} measures the *initial* unemployment benefit that people currently in work would receive if they became unemployed relative to current in-work income. In computing RR_{ab} we have to make assumptions about eligibility to unemployment insurance benefit. Lacking information about contribution records in the data, one would need to make assumptions whether people satisfy the contribution conditions for entitlement to contribution based benefits. It is important to note that the correctness of any common assumption will vary substantially across countries. For people declaring

---

[6] It may, for policy purposes, be interesting to look at the different groups of benefit recipients separately. Since the data contain information on who receives which benefit, it is possible to analyse the distribution of replacement rates for each of these groups in isolation.

themselves as being unemployed during at least one month of the year, a recent study based on the ECHP finds coverage rates in Denmark, France, Spain, and the United Kingdom of roughly 95, 85, 40, and 65 per cent, respectively (Alphametrics, 2002). While, for purposes of understanding the generosity of unemployment benefits, it is interesting to know what RR_{ab} would be *if* everybody would satisfy relevant contribution conditions, substantial differences in coverage rates would make such numbers difficult to interpret in isolation.[7] We therefore also provide replacement rate estimates for the opposite transition from out-of-work to in-work (RR_{ba}, RR_{ca}). Since the data provide information on any benefits that people who are out-of-work currently receive, we do not have to make any assumptions about contribution records for these transitions.

Unit of Analysis

Although the transition from one labour market state to another is a process at the individual level, the subsequent change in income potentially affects the well-being of other household members as well. Both from income maintenance and work incentive points of view, it is therefore not appropriate to only evaluate the alternative income situations of the person whose labour market status changes. Our choice of the household as the unit of analysis is mainly a result of three considerations.[8] First, and as asserted above, the level of

---

[7] Similarly, an important question to be addressed in future analyses is what RR_{ab} would be for people who do *not* qualify for unemployment insurance at all and would therefore only receive means-tested social minimum benefits. By allowing analysts to specify assumptions on missing contribution information, EUROMOD permits a range of different scenarios to be explored.

[8] Even though we compute household based replacement rates, we *separately* consider *each household member* who is of working age. If there is more than one person of working age, we thus compute more than one replacement rate for this household. Depending on the member of household's current labour market status, we compute a household based RR_{ab}, RR_{ba}, or RR_{ca} in turn for each person by computing the before- and after-transition household income. For example, for a two-parent single-earner household with one child of working age who is currently looking for work, we would compute one RR_{ab} (for the earner), one RR_{ca} (for the inactive spouse), and one RR_{ba} (for the unemployed child). In doing so, the incomes of all members of household can enter the calculation of taxes and benefits (relevant in cases where benefits or taxes depend on couple, family, or household income). At the same time, it is assumed that all income components other than the simulated taxes and benefits remain unaffected for members of household whose labour market status does not change (i.e. the income of the child and spouse is held constant when evaluating RR_{ab} for the earner, etc.).

resources available in the household as a whole will affect each household member's standard of living. Second, the employment status and incomes of individual household members can have important consequences for the amount of taxes paid or benefits received by other household members (e.g. because of a joint income tax system or the assessment of total household income for computing means tested benefits). While we would ideally want to take into account how such joint taxes and benefits are actually shared within the household, we do not have the required information to identify such sharing arrangements. An analysis at the household level avoids having to specify arbitrary sharing mechanisms.[9] Third, the empirical part of this chapter compares replacement rates across different countries. The generosity and coverage of unemployment insurance benefits varies across countries and, where benefits are more limited, the household assumes an important insurance function, substituting or complementing social insurance schemes. The extent to which households are, in fact, able to provide income security for those experiencing spells of unemployment can only be uncovered by computing replacement rates at the household level.[10]

Purpose of Replacement Rates

As discussed briefly, there are two main reasons why we are interested in replacement rates. One is to measure the performance of tax-benefit systems in providing substitute income for those out of work. The second is the concern about possible disincentive effects of high replacement rates. The choice of the appropriate concept of replacement rate depends on how these questions are to be addressed. The dimensions that are relevant in this context are:

(1) which incomes to include in the numerator and the denominator of the replacement rate;

[9] As we understand it, Salomäki (2001) computes individual-level replacement rates by assuming that any benefits accrue (only) to the person reporting them in the underlying micro-data (normally the 'head of household'). Clearly, the results obtained this way are rather sensitive to who reports benefits where entitlement is established for the family or the household as a whole (e.g. family benefits, minimum income schemes, or housing benefits).

[10] For policy purposes, it is clearly relevant to know whether a certain level of income maintenance is due to out-of-work benefits or to incomes provided by other household members. This point of how to decompose replacement rates is taken up in the sections titled 'Distribution of Replacement Rates' and 'What Drives Replacement Rates?'.

(2) which direction of labour market transition to compute the replacement rate for; and

(3) for whom to compute the replacement rates.

In measuring the degree of *income maintenance*, we have two main alternatives regarding dimension (1). If we see out-of-work benefits as an insurance system then one could be interested in measuring the extent to which in-work incomes are insured. In this case, the numerator would be (net) out-of-work benefit income and the denominator would be (net) income from work. Only incomes of the person whose labour market status changes would be taken into account while all other household members' incomes would be disregarded. Or one could be interested in the living standard out-of-work as opposed to in-work. In this case, both numerator and denominator would also include all other incomes including, for example, investment income, benefits which are independent of work status, and the incomes of all other members of household. We adopt the latter type of calculation since we regard the question of relative living standards the more interesting one. As regards dimension, (2) we are, in addressing questions of income maintenance, only interested in the transition from in-work to unemployment (RR_{ab}). A more interesting question is for whom to compute RR_{ab}. To give an accurate picture of the level of income maintenance across the entire population, one has to compute RR_{ab} for those currently in-work *and* those currently out-of-work who have had a job previously. Limiting the analysis to those in-work may potentially introduce a sample selection bias since people who have *actually* experienced job loss, and the income, and lifestyle associated therewith are not taken into account.

Because *work incentives* are relevant for all types of labour market transitions, the replacement rates to be computed under this heading are more varied. Since we are interested in all three directions of labour market transitions discussed above, we compute RR_{ab}, RR_{ba}, and RR_{ca}. In our calculations, we use the same formula as for the 'income maintenance' replacement rates, that is, with total household disposable income in both numerator and denominator. However, since transitions into work (RR_{ba}, RR_{ca}) are computed only for those who are currently out of work, we now have to estimate income from work. Basically, there are three approaches we can choose from. We can use (*a*) an arbitrary earnings level (such as the minimum wage, if it exists in the country under consideration); (*b*) actual previous in-work income; or (*c*) estimate potential in-work earnings based on relevant characteristics, such as education level. If we were to use previous in-work income, we could only compute RR_{ba} and RR_{ca} for those who have previously been in work rather than for all people for whom the decision whether or not to enter work is relevant. There is also a theoretical argument for using a general earnings equation. In terms of economic models explaining job search behaviour, it is the *distribution* of job offers (characterized by the associated wage level) which is crucial in determining the probability of someone accepting a job.[11] This distribution might be better represented by a statistically estimated earnings equation than by an arbitrary earnings level or by actual previous in-work income which, in terms of the distribution of offers, may be an outlier. Lastly, in the microdata underlying our simulations we do not, in fact, observe previous work income for all unemployed individuals. For these reasons, we are using a standard earnings equation to estimate in-work income for those currently out of work, utilizing the Heckman procedure to account for sample selection bias (see Heckman, 1979).[12] This method adjusts earnings to account for the selection bias associated with the fact that we only observe earnings for those who are shown to work in the data (and not the past or potential earnings of those currently without a job).

For RR_{ab}, we do not face these problems since in-work replacement rates are only computed for those in-work. The counterfactual out-of-work income is then computed by setting in-work incomes to zero, altering all work related variables to indicate that this person is now unemployed and then applying the tax-benefit model to find all relevant taxes and benefits for the entire household.

In Table 5.1 we summarize the discussion of the properties of different replacement rates. The table shows alternative choices for each of the dimensions considered above. The approach adopted in our simulations is indicated using **bold** typeface.

Other Assumptions

An issue related to the previous point is the time period relevant for determining the replacement rate. In measuring replacement rates,

---

[11] Atkinson and Micklewright (1991) provide summaries and critiques of these and other popular economic models underlying theories of labour market transitions.

[12] We thus assume that the selection bias is the same for all 'out-of-work' groups whereas it may be more conceptually appropriate to treat different 'out-of-work' groups such as involuntary unemployed differently from, for example, those on early retirement or home-workers. However, for cross-country studies like the present one, the use of a single participation equation seems preferable to us on transparency grounds.

we are concerned with the income of one situation relative to another. Income, however, is a flow-concept. As a result, one needs to be clear about the time period over which it is measured. Since both in-work and out-of-work incomes can change over time, the replacement rates will potentially be different depending on the time period we chose for measuring them. We have chosen the year as the relevant period. More precisely, it is the 12 months following the transition (which is assumed to take place on the first day of the fiscal year). The employment status is assumed to remain unchanged during the entire year. However, the simulations do take into account that benefits may only be available during part of the year (e.g. the fact that the maximum period for receiving UK insurance based Job Seekers Allowance is 6 months). The simulation of annual out-of-work income also takes into account any waiting periods that apply before a benefit can be received.

While limiting the analysis of replacement rates to the year following the transition may be regarded as a simplification, there are other aspects of our approach that may in fact be 'too precise'. The tax and benefit rules modelled in a tax-benefit microsimulation model are very detailed—often exceeding any information which may be easily available to non-expert individuals (e.g. from information brochures). In fact, individuals may not even be aware that some of the simulated instruments exist. Since most benefits or tax reductions are not available automatically but have to be applied for, this leads to the issue of non-take-up of benefit, where individuals do not claim benefits to which they are entitled. The bias introduced by any take-up issues is not a priori clear since benefits and tax reductions may be available only while in-work, only while out-of-work, or independent of income and employment status. In addition the quality of information about taxes and benefits that people have access to may be different in different labour market situations. The importance of these issues will also depend on whether labour market transitions are planned individually or in association with the employer or a union (e.g. in the case of temporary lay-offs). There is, however, clear evidence that the issue of take-up is an important one.[13] While EUROMOD permits the effects of different take-up assumptions to be explored we assume 100 per cent take-up (and no tax-evasion) in the simulations reported here.

---

[13] See, for instance, Atkinson (1989) and Department of Social Security (2000) for the United Kingdom, and Riphahn (2001) for Germany.

Simulations

The model used is EUROMOD, an integrated European tax-benefit model. EUROMOD provides us with a Europe-wide perspective on social and fiscal policies that are implemented at European or national level. It is also designed to examine, within a consistent comparative framework, the impact of national policies on national populations or the differential impact of coordinated European policy on individual Member States. Within the context of the present chapter, the most relevant feature of EUROMOD is that it can provide conceptually consistent and, thus, comparable output for different countries.[14]

Simulations are run for four countries: Denmark, France, Spain, and the United Kingdom. The micro-data sets underlying the simulations are derived from wave 3 (Spain), and wave 2 (Denmark) of the ECHP (User Database), the 'Family Budget' (BdF) survey 1994–5 (France), and the UK 1995–6 Family Expenditure Survey. As mentioned above, we consider the replacement rates of working-age individuals (in-work, unemployed, or 'inactive'). Those currently in-work are defined for the purposes of this study as those who had income from employment or were self-employed during the year, while the 'unemployed' are classified as either declaring themselves as unemployed and seeking work or receiving unemployment benefits in the data. Working-age individuals who are neither working nor unemployed are considered 'inactive'.[15]

The simulations are based on the systems of tax and benefit rules current in June 1998 and all monetary variables in the micro-data are updated to this year using the most appropriate uprating index available for each type of variable. The standard instruments simulated in EUROMOD and relevant for this exercise are income taxes, social insurance contributions, child benefits and other family benefits, and income-tested benefits. For the present study we also simulate unemployment benefits for the transition into unemployment (RR_{ab}). For those currently unemployed or inactive, we simulate a transition into full-time employment (RR_{ba}, RR_{ca}). Prospective earnings are imputed using Heckman type earnings functions estimated separately for men and women and accounting for selection bias through the use of a participation equation. All coefficients are

---

[14] See Immervoll et al. (1999) and Sutherland (2001) for more details on the model.
[15] For information regarding sample sizes, coverage, non-response, etc., see Immervoll and O'Donoghue (2001*b*) and Sutherland (1999).

significant at the 95 per cent level and take the expected signs (see Immervoll and O'Donoghue, 2001*a* for results and details). For all types of transition we exclude people younger than 18 or in pursuit of education and those aged 60+. For comparability reasons we have opted to exclude civil servants in the results reported here.[16]

In simulating unemployment benefits and computing the relevant replacement rates, a number of noteworthy assumptions are made:

- Past unemployment insurance contributions of individuals currently in work are 'sufficient' to be eligible for the relevant benefit(s)
- We disregard provisions made for unemployment compensation in collective agreements
- We disregard any special legal provisions for seasonal unemployment
- We assume that all transitions into unemployment are *involuntary*
- We disregard any back-to-work measures (e.g. retention of benefits on employment)
- We assume that in the case of transitions from work to unemployment, individuals have been made unemployed at the start of the current tax year and we measure replacement rates over this year as a whole
- In computing incomes we do not include *in-kind* benefits such as the provision of social/subsidized housing or childcare. Also not taken into account are work-related expenses (union fees, commuting, childcare costs, etc.), expenses incurred only by the unemployed (job search costs) and any discounts or rebates that may be available to benefit recipients (e.g. public transport, medical expenses, school-related expenses).

Replacement rates are then calculated by simulating, for each individual in turn, the household disposable income for their original state (in-work, 'inactive', or unemployed). After changing their relevant status and income variables in the microdata to the counterfactual state, the tax-benefit model is again used to recalculate household disposable income. When simulating the transition from work to unemployment, we utilize in-work income as previous income. Lacking

[16] In two of the countries examined (Denmark and the United Kingdom), civil servants are covered by unemployment benefits as there is a possibility of unemployment, while in France and Spain, civil servants are not covered by unemployment benefits since, by virtue of their employment contracts, they are protected from unemployment.

contribution records in the data we compute unemployment benefits based on the assumption that people satisfy the conditions for receipt of the unemployment benefits. For this reason, and although we assume more limited contribution histories for young employees,[17] the replacement rate results for the transition into unemployment (RR_{ab}) will nevertheless have to be interpreted as *upper bound* estimates. The definition of replacement rates used is the ratio of household disposable income out-of-work over household disposable income in-work, where disposable income is defined as gross incomes from market activities, plus social benefits, minus income taxes, and own social insurance contributions.

National Tax-Benefit Systems

We have selected four countries that represent different welfare state regimes: Denmark, a 'universal' or 'social-democratic' welfare state; France a 'continental' welfare state; Spain, which, like France relies strongly on social insurance principles but with a stronger focus on the family as a provider of financial security; and the United Kingdom as an example of an 'anglo-liberal' welfare state with a combination of universal and market-based welfare principles. Table 5.2 shows the importance (as per cent of aggregate disposable income in the household sector) of different components of the tax-benefit systems in each of the countries. Focusing on benefits and public pensions, France shows the highest relative expenditures, followed by Denmark, Spain, and the United Kingdom. This reflects the relative lack of development of state benefits in Spain and the importance of private provisions (particularly in the case of pensions) in the United Kingdom. In terms of revenue sources, Denmark places relatively little emphasis on employer contributions, with income taxes the highest percentage of all countries. In France employee and employer contributions are the most important. In Spain, social insurance contributions are also important, with income taxes having a higher share of total revenues than in France.

While unemployment insurance benefits in the United Kingdom are a flat amount, they are earnings related in Denmark, France, and Spain. In all cases potential coverage is limited to insured employees. In France and Spain, the self-employed are excluded. However, in

[17] We assume that people in employment have started their uninterrupted contribution payments at the age of 18.

France only about 9 per cent of workers we examine are self-employed, compared with nearly 20 per cent in Spain, indicating that social insurance coverage will be lower in Spain. In France, individuals who are not eligible for unemployment related benefits may be eligible for social assistance, while in Spain, there is no comparable instrument. Once individuals exhaust entitlement to unemployment benefits, workers in France are eligible for unemployment assistance. Certain older workers and those with children in Spain may be eligible for unemployment assistance, but entitlement is generally quite limited. In the United Kingdom, unemployment benefits are payable only for at most 6 months, after which individuals may be eligible for social assistance. Social assistance can also top up family incomes to the social minimum while in receipt of unemployment benefits or low earnings. This is not the case in Denmark, where, in addition to income conditions, social assistance is conditional upon 'social events' (such as unemployment, sickness, divorce, etc.) and can therefore not generally be received by low-wage earners. Another important determinant of income while out-of-work (or in low-paid jobs) are housing benefits available in Denmark, France, and the United Kingdom.

Turning to income taxation, Denmark and the United Kingdom employ largely an individual income tax. Nevertheless, large tax-free allowances, which can be transferred between spouses, make household composition an important determinant of tax liabilities in Denmark. The link between other household members' incomes on own income taxes is even more direct in France and Spain, where income is taxed on a joint basis.

Distribution of Replacement Rates

Table 5.3 presents results for the four countries, broken into 20 per cent bands of replacement rates, and shows the proportion of the relevant target group facing replacement rates within each band.[18] The top section shows the distribution for those currently in work (RR_{ab}). We notice that France has a higher incidence of 'high' in-work replacement rates than the other countries. Seventy-nine per cent of workers face in-work replacement rates of 80 per cent or more, implying that more than 20 per cent of French labour income earners

---

[18] All results have been derived using weighted data.

would, in the event of becoming unemployed, be confronted with a rather substantial decrease in *household* income by more than 20 per cent—even under the strong assumptions that unemployment is involuntary and each employee's insurance contributions have been built up without interruption. Denmark has the next highest incidence of 'high' replacement rates with 61 per cent of workers with rates of 80 per cent or more and 89 per cent with 60 per cent or more. Next comes Spain with 58 per cent (80 per cent) with replacement rates of 80 per cent (60 per cent) or more. For the United Kingdom, where unemployment benefits are not earnings related, we see a much less concentrated distribution and markedly lower replacement rates with only 25 per cent (55 per cent) of workers having replacement rates of 80 per cent (60 per cent) or higher. As a result of the relatively low flat rate unemployment benefit, we also see very few people in the United Kingdom being financially as well or better off without a job than in work. For the transition from work to unemployment, the largest number of people with '100+' replacement rates is found in Denmark and is mainly a result of floors built into the unemployment benefit system: earners of very low in-work incomes may, in the event of becoming unemployed, receive benefits exceeding their previous earnings.

Turning to the second part of Table 5.3 and to those who are currently unemployed, we find a very different distribution of replacement rates (RR_{ba}). It is much more similar across countries than the distribution of RR_{ab} discussed above. About 53 per cent (80 per cent) of French unemployed face out-of-work replacement rates of 80 per cent (60 per cent) or higher compared with 52 per cent (79 per cent) of Danish, 46 per cent (72 per cent) of Spanish, and 22 per cent (58 per cent) of British unemployed.

Clearly, compared to those in work, fewer unemployed in Denmark and France have 'high' replacement rates (≥ 80 per cent) while in Spain and the United Kingdom, the differences are less pronounced. This is essentially due to the fact that the unemployment benefits (UB) *observed* for those making the transition into employment (RR_{ba}) will generally be lower than the *simulated* unemployment benefits for those becoming unemployed (RR_{ab}). First, RR_{ab} are the replacement rate in the first year of (involuntary) unemployment under the assumption of uninterrupted contribution histories while RR_{ba} are computed for all people reported to be experiencing a spell of unemployment and are based on the UB amounts that unemployed people actually receive. As the duration of entitlement to UB is normally limited, those who have been unemployed for longer may cease to be eligible for these benefits.[19] Second, UB may fall in value over time as in the case of France or the United Kingdom.[20] Consequently, even for those long-term unemployed who are still in receipt of UB, benefit levels (and, hence, RR_{ba}) may be lower. In short, because the duration of unemployment will often be longer for our unemployed sample (RR_{ba}) than for those who we 'make' unemployed in our simulations (RR_{ab}), institutional factors such as duration dependent eligibility and benefit amounts will result in lower replacement rates for the sample of unemployed compared with the sample of working individuals.

On the other hand, the earnings we predict for those moving into work (RR_{ba}) will be an important factor. Due to differences in education level, experience, etc., the earnings potential of actually unemployed people going into work will often be low compared to the earnings of those currently in work. These factors influencing potential earnings will be picked up by our earnings model: it will, on average, predict lower earnings for those currently unemployed. Compared to RR_{ab}, the in-work incomes (the denominator) used for computing RR_{ba} will therefore tend to be lower causing replacement rates to be higher. The two effects therefore run in opposite directions, with the 'earnings' effect being relatively stronger in the United Kingdom (median $RR_{ab} <$ median RR_{ba}) and the 'institutional factors' dominating in Denmark, France, and Spain (median $RR_{ab} >$ median RR_{ba}).

The third type of replacement rates we examine concerns those who are currently 'inactive' (RR_{ca}, bottom part of Table 5.3). Again, we compare net household incomes in the current (out-of-work) situation with net household incomes that would result if the 'inactive' individual would move into work. Here, Spain shows the highest proportion of currently 'inactive' people (41 and 71 per cent, respectively) with replacement rates of 80 per cent (60 per cent) or more compared to France with 38 per cent (74 per cent), Denmark with 38 per cent (80 per cent), and the United Kingdom with 25 per cent (66 per cent).

---

[19] They may then become eligible for lower valued unemployment or social assistance benefits (France, United Kingdom) or nothing as in the case of many unemployed in Spain. In Denmark, where membership in the unemployment insurance scheme is voluntary, those who are observed to be unemployed in the data and are not members of the insurance scheme will not be receiving any unemployment benefits at all (in cases where family income is 'low', they would receive social assistance instead).

[20] In the United Kingdom, benefits become means-tested after 6 months and may thus also fall in value.

The median values as well as the incidence of 'high' replacement rates (≥ 80 per cent) are generally lower than for the unemployed group. This is not true, however, for the United Kingdom. Upon first inspection, this may seem peculiar as 'inactive' people are not eligible for (unemployment) benefits. However, in many cases 'inactive' people are in receipt of disability benefits or early retirement pensions which can be more generous than unemployment benefits (which are generally clearly lower in the United Kingdom than in the other countries). Also they are likely to have lower potential earnings than the unemployed, whose in-work experience is typically higher than for the 'inactive' group.[21] In general, and as mentioned before, one must be cautious in drawing conclusions based on replacement rates computed for the 'inactive' group as a whole as it is very heterogeneous.

What Drives Replacement Rates?

In this section we consider the factors that influence replacement rates, by separately analysing (*a*) the results for different demographic groups; and (*b*) the influence of different income sources within the household.

Replacement Rates for Different Demographic Groups

Table 5.4 describes the distribution of replacement rates decomposed by gender. We see that for those currently in work, women's replacement rates (RR_{ab}) are higher than men's in all four countries. In absolute percentage terms we find that Denmark and Spain exhibit the largest differentials of 'high' replacement rates (80 per cent or more) with a difference of 31 and 34 percentage points, respectively. In relative terms, the United Kingdom has the highest differential: the percentage of working women with 'high' replacement rates is 2.6 times the percentage of males. There are a number of reasons for these differentials. First, it is important to note that they are *not* due to more generous benefits for women. Rather, women are likely to have lower earnings, both in terms of their hourly wage rates and because

---

[21] In our earnings model, we use potential experience as an explanatory variable since we do not observe actual experience in our data (see Immervoll and O'Donoghue 2001*b*). Notwithstanding the argument that 'inactive' people will, in reality, often have lower (re-)entry wages than the unemployed, our simulations will therefore not generally be able to pick up this effect.

of shorter working hours. In addition, and as we shall see below, household composition plays an important role, with working women having a high probability of living with partners who have higher earnings. If the husband is the main earner then income will, in relative terms, not fall by very much if his wife loses her job. The (household based) replacement rate she is facing will therefore be relatively high.

For the unemployed (RR_{ba}), the absolute difference between men and women is again greatest in Denmark and Spain with 16 and 13 percentage points differences respectively in the 'high' replacement rate category. For inactive women (RR_{ca}), the differential is generally lower than for the unemployed. Indeed, in France and Spain the differential is going in the opposite direction, with more men having higher replacement rates. The explanation for this is related to our broad definition of 'inactivity': while men may be more likely to be inactive and receiving disability benefits, inactive women will more often be (unpaid) homeworkers.

Table 5.5 decomposes the distribution of replacement rates by age group. Here we note that the replacement rate for the under 25s in work are in general much higher than for older age groups. The reasons are similar to those for observing higher replacement rates for women. First, younger people will have lower predicted in-work income than older people and thus have higher replacement rates as unemployment benefits typically provide minimum payments ('floors') that younger people are more likely to benefit from. This effect is particularly strong in the United Kingdom (where benefits are flat rate) and in Denmark. Second, they are more likely to live at home with other earners. Again, if young people living with their parents are made unemployed then the effect on overall household income is likely to be small.

The age group differences for unemployed people are smaller than for the in-work group. One of the reasons is that average out-of-work benefits will, relative to their potential earnings, often be lower for younger unemployed people than for older individuals because young people may not have built up sufficient contributions to be entitled to unemployment benefits.[22] In the case of both Spain and France, they will, due to age restrictions, then not be eligible for

---

[22] Note that this is particularly relevant for the out-of-work groups (RR_{ba}, RR_{ca}) for whom we take unemployment benefits as reported in the data (i.e. benefits are, for these groups, not subject to any assumptions about contribution histories).

unemployment assistance or social assistance benefits either. For the inactive group, we find that age differentials generally lie in-between those for the in-work and unemployed groups. These results reflect the variation in the two main determinants of replacement rates for young people; benefit rules and household structures. The variation in these dimensions tends to be more pronounced between in-work and out-of-work groups than it is for older individuals.

To see more directly to what extent household composition, and particularly the presence of other potential earners in the household, have an effect on the levels of replacement rates, we now decompose the distribution of replacement rates by the number of adults (Table 5.6). For in-work individuals, the number of adults in the household exerts the biggest influence on the extent of 'high' replacement rates (80 per cent or more) of all three classifications explored here (gender, age, number of adults).[23] Spain exhibits the largest absolute differential. While 59 per cent of workers in households with two or more adults face 'high' replacement rates of 80 per cent or higher, this is true for only 9 per cent of single-adult households. France is second with 83 versus 51 per cent. In Denmark the figures are 65 and 40 per cent followed by the United Kingdom with 27 and 11 per cent. In relative terms, the percentage of households with two or more adults facing 'high' replacement rates is about 6.4 and 2.5 times the percentage for single-adult households in Spain and the United Kingdom respectively compared with 1.6 for Denmark and France. For unemployed and inactive people, the direction of the differential is the same although it is generally smaller.

Decomposing Replacement Rates by Income Source

So far we have considered the distribution of replacement rates by demographic influences. As the definition of a replacement rate is a

---

[23] The presence of children has often been seen as a reason for high replacement rates as out-of-work benefits often include extra amounts paid for dependent children, while in-work incomes do not. Consequently, out-of-work incomes should be relatively higher than in-work incomes for those who have children. The extent to which this is true depends, of course, on the size of any child-related benefit payments. Policies such as the UK Working Families Tax Credit and other family related *in-work* benefits aiming to increase the financial incentives of employment will reduce this differential. In Immervoll and O'Donoghue (2001*b*), we present replacement rate results separately for households with and without children. Although it is the case in our results that more families with children have higher replacement rates, the differential is greater for other characteristics such as gender, age, or the number of adults.

function of household incomes, it is the impact of these demographic characteristics on incomes that drive the replacement rates. Both market incomes and tax-benefit systems depend upon demographic characteristics. As outlined above, gender and age differentials can influence wage rates, while household composition will influence the scope for multiple earners in a household. While there are rarely direct gender influences on the operation of tax-benefit systems, gender inequalities in work patterns will result in differential entitlement to benefits and progressive taxation may result in different average tax rates. Different age groups will have similar impacts, but in addition there may be some age-related instruments such as reduced eligibility for young people and perhaps increased eligibility for people nearing the retirement age. In this section we consider the relative importance of different income sources on the distribution of replacement rates (drawing upon a more detailed analysis in Immervoll and O'Donoghue, 2001*b*).

To address this question, we now turn to a decomposition of replacement rates in terms of the incomes that drive them, focusing in particular on the group who are identified as being unemployed in our underlying microdata (RR_{ba}).[24] Figure 5.1 presents decomposition results. The replacement rate calculation consists of four parts; incomes out-of-work *less* taxes and contributions out-of-work divided by incomes in work *less* taxes and contributions in-work. In this figure, in-work (left) and out-of-work (right) components are shown in separate bars. The bars are then split up into the main subcomponents; income taxes, own social insurance contributions, own earnings, spouse's earnings, other earnings (i.e. earnings of other household members apart from the spouse), benefits, and other market incomes (such as earned interest on savings or other investment income). In comparing the out-of-work bar with the in-work bar own earnings, taxes and contributions will fall while benefits should rise. Other market incomes and other household member's incomes are not affected by the transition and should therefore remain unchanged.

Incomes are in national currency per month (1998 levels) and at the household level (left hand scale). Breaking replacement rates up into bands as in Tables 5.3–5.6, the graphs show, for each replacement rate band, the composition of household incomes for the in-work (left hand bar) and out-of-work (right hand bar) situation averaged across all people in the relevant band (the vertical dotted lines separate the

---

[24] In Immervoll and O'Donoghue (2001*a*) we report on income decompositions for the 'in-work' and 'inactive' groups as well.

different replacement rate bands while the bold line shows the distribution of replacement rates from Table 5.3 by replacement rate band).[25] Average gross incomes are represented by the height above the axis and average taxes/contributions are shown as negative income components. Average disposable incomes can thus be derived by subtracting the bar below the axis from the bar above. The relationship between the resulting in-work and out-of-work bar disposable incomes is the replacement rate: the higher out-of-work incomes, the lower out-of-work taxes/contributions, the lower in-work incomes, and the higher in-work taxes/contributions, the higher the overall replacement rate. In addition and if applicable, work-conditional benefits, such as the UK Family Credit (in 1998, later replaced by the Working Families Tax Credit), contribute to lower replacement rates by providing earnings subsidies (shown as benefits in the graphs) that are withdrawn during periods of joblessness.

Based on the results, an important finding relates to the role of spouses' and other household members' earnings relative to benefits. With the possible exception of France, we see that for those with high replacement rates, spouses' and others' earnings are, on average, more important components of (out-of-work) income than benefits. Thus, other people's earnings would on average do more to preserve a household's living standard than benefits. This fact is consistent with our finding above that the presence of more than one adult in a household is an important determinant of high replacement rates. We see that other household members' earnings are as or even more important than the incomes of spouses. They represent typically the earnings of parents of young people living at home, hence resulting in the high potential replacement rates for young people. Spain, where young people tend to stay in the family home longer than in the other countries, provides a vivid example in this respect.

Conclusions

In this chapter, we have measured the distributions of replacement rates in four European countries and considered the forces, both

---

[25] It is important to note that, due to few observations, the decomposition results are, in a statistical sense, not significant for some replacement rate bands (such as the 0–20 per cent band in all countries).

economic and demographic, that drive these measures. Going beyond simple calculated replacement rates for 'typical' or 'average' households, we have produced detailed distributions of net replacement rates in four EU Member States representing different welfare state regimes showing how many people in each country face different levels of replacement rates. Using actually existing households as the basis for such calculations is particularly important when considering employment related issues due to accelerating trends towards 'atypical' households and 'non-standard' types of employment and their consequences for people's labour market choices and constraints. Using the EUROMOD tax-benefit model, we are also able to isolate the influence of demographic and policy influences that determine relative income levels in- and out-of-work.

We could draw three main conclusions from the above analysis. They all relate to the need for analysing in detail all income sources relevant for people's material well-being as well as their incidence within the household.

First it is, on a conceptual level, important to take into account the household context when comparing measures of well-being both in- and out-of-work across countries. It is only by considering all household members' incomes that the different degrees to which welfare state regimes rely on the household as an insurance mechanism can be captured. For instance, according to the 'welfare state regime' classification, Spain and other Southern European countries rely strongly on the family as a mechanism of income maintenance. Yet, while we do find an important role of other household members in providing a degree of income maintenance, our results show that almost half of all Spanish employees would see total *household* income drop by more than 20 per cent in the event of becoming unemployed—even if we assume that all of them had contributed to unemployment insurance during their entire adult life.

Second, and related to the first point, replacement rate *levels* alone cannot be used to draw firm policy conclusions. Instead, one needs to analyse the driving factors behind observed levels. In particular, we found marked differences between the distributions of replacement rates faced by those currently in work versus those who are currently unemployed or 'inactive'. By showing which income components are driving replacement rates, it is possible to clarify if this discrepancy is mainly due to different earning prospects of those currently out-of-work or whether they are due to differences in eligibility to, and coverage of, out-of-work benefits. Similarly, there is an important differential between household-level replacement rates faced by women and young people when compared to men and older persons. Yet, in our results, the fact that the former two groups tend to face higher replacement rates is not due to having access to more generous unemployment benefits. Instead, their labour market opportunities seem to be such that their earnings potential may, for a range of different reasons, be inferior to that of other household members. The same line of argument applies more generally to people moving in and out of low-quality jobs. Indeed, targets to increase employment rates, which feature prominently on the European policy agenda, may increase the number of low-paid, low-security jobs. Should replacement rates go up as a result of such developments then attempting activation through a reduction of out-of-work benefit levels would likely be the wrong 'lever to pull'. A detailed analysis of the factors underlying replacement rates is an important way to prevent the adoption of misguided policies.

As a final observation, the case for looking at replacement levels in conjunction with the wider household context can also be made by considering the income levels of those people for whom our results indicate high replacement rates. Unsurprisingly, the highest replacement rates are frequently (but clearly not always) found for groups with the lowest household incomes while in-work. Given that a primary purpose of safety nets is the provision of a reasonable standard of living during transitional periods of unemployment and given the concern about social inclusion as one of the main European policy aims, this points towards the need for a comprehensive analysis of the income situation in the different labour market states. High replacement rates in isolation tell us nothing about people's financial well-being since 100 per cent of too little is still too little. Clearly, if standards of living are a concern then looking at replacement rate levels alone is not sufficient if employment does not guarantee adequate income levels.

Table 5.1 *Replacement rates: choices of income concepts.*

	Income maintenance		Incentive effects	
	Out-of-work	In-work	Out-of-work	In-work
Incomes in-and out of work	b_{UE}	y_w		RR_{ab}: $y_w + b_{oth} + y_{oth}$ $+ Y_W + B_{oth} + Y_{oth}$
	$b_{UE} + b_{oth} + y_{oth} +$ $Y_W + B_{oth} + Y_{oth}$	$y_w + b_{oth} + y_{oth} +$ $Y_W + B_{oth} + Y_{oth}$	$b_{UE} + b_{oth} + y_{oth} +$ $Y_W + B_{oth} + Y_{oth}$	RR_{ba}: $e_w + b_{oth} + y_{oth}$ $+ Y_W + B_{oth} + Y_{oth}$
				RR_{ca}: $e_w + b_{oth} + y_{oth}$ $+ Y_W + B_{oth} + Y_{oth}$

Notes: UE means unemployed. The notation for the income components is as follows. B_{UE}= Own Unemployment benefit; B_{oth}: benefits other than B_{UE} (e.g., child benefits); Y_w: Actual income from work as recorded in the data; E_w: Income from work as predicted by the earnings equation; Y_{oth}: Primary income other than Y_w (e.g., investment income). All income components are net of taxes and contributions payable on them. Income components shown in lower case are incomes of the person for whom the replacement rate is calculated while UPPER CASE income components are those of all other household members. All income components are net of taxes and other deductions.

Table 5.2 *Characteristics of tax-benefit systems (1998)*

	Denmark	France	Spain	UK
Instrument as percentage of disposable income[a]				
Employer SICs	3.2	28.1	13.1	6.3
Income tax	51.9	11.0	15.1	20.0
Employee SICs	13.5	18.6	5.3	5.5
Benefits and public pensions	31.0	33.4	28.5	21.3

[a] Disposable income is defined as market incomes minus income taxes and (own) social insurance contributions plus all public pensions and cash benefit payments.

Source: EUROMOD.

Table 5.3 *Distribution of household replacement rates (1998)*

Replacement rates [%]	DK	FR	SP	UK
In-work (RR_{ab})				
Median RR	85.0	87.0	84.0	62.0
Sample size	2,238	9,856	4,905	6,101
0–20	0.5	0.8	6.3	3.2
20–40	1.9	1.8	5.3	11.9
40–60	8.3	2.5	8.1	30.1
60–80	28.2	15.8	22.8	29.6
80–100	46.7	74.2	52.6	22.9
100+	14.3	4.9	4.9	2.4
	100.0	100.0	100.0	100.0
Unemployed (RR_{ba})				
Median RR	81.0	81.0	77.0	64.0
Sample size	627	2,054	1,778	582
0–20	2.9	0.5	3.0	1.5
20–40	5.7	5.4	9.0	11.8
40–60	12.6	14.4	15.9	28.3
60–80	27.0	26.6	25.5	36.6
80–100	34.0	34.5	31.1	20.5
100+	17.7	18.5	15.4	1.3
	100.0	100.0	100.0	100.0
Out of work but not unemployed (RR_{ca})				
Median RR	76.0	74.0	74.0	68.0
Sample size	337	3,692	3,461	2,555
0–20	1.5	0.7	3.9	1.4
20–40	3.9	6.0	7.9	8.0
40–60	15.0	18.4	17.3	24.1
60–80	42.0	37.4	30.1	41.1
80–100	37.5	31.4	36.2	23.8
100+	0.0	6.1	4.7	1.5
	100.0	100.0	100.0	100.0

Note: Target sample sizes refer to the number of persons aged 18–59. The in-work/unemployed/inactive groups are not mutually exclusive as it is possible to have different states in a particular year.

Source: EUROMOD.

Table 5.4 Distribution of household replacement rates decomposed by gender (1998)

	DK		FR		SP		UK	
	Women	Men	Women	Men	Women	Men	Women	Men
In-work (RR_{ab})								
Sample Size	887	1,351	4,207	5,649	1,644	3,261	2,900	3,201
Replacement Rate [%]								
0–20	0.0	0.8	0.2	1.3	1.7	8.7	1.1	4.9
20–40	0.2	3.0	0.7	2.5	1.7	7.1	4.8	17.9
40–60	3.0	11.7	1.1	3.6	3.5	10.5	19.8	38.7
60–80	17.0	35.3	9.6	20.4	13.1	27.7	36.2	24.0
80–100	59.9	38.4	83.1	67.7	70.6	43.4	34.7	13.0
100+	20.0	10.8	5.3	4.6	9.3	2.7	3.4	1.6
	100.0	100.0	100.0	100.0	100.0	100.0	100.0	100.0
Unemployed (RR_{ba})								
Sample Size	338	289	1,058	996	813	960	236	346
Replacement Rate [%]								
0–20	1.0	5.1	0.4	0.6	0.6	5.2	0.0	2.3
20–40	2.5	9.3	4.2	6.8	7.4	10.5	3.1	16.7
40–60	7.4	18.4	13.9	15.0	12.9	18.7	22.0	31.9

Table 5.4 (*continued*)

	DK		FR		SP		UK	
	Women	Men	Women	Men	Women	Men	Women	Men
60–80	29.6	24.1	26.8	26.4	26.0	25.1	50.5	28.8
80–100	34.6	33.3	36.0	32.9	36.5	26.1	23.6	18.8
100+	24.9	9.8	18.6	18.4	16.6	14.4	0.8	1.6
	100.0	100.0	100.0	100.0	100.0	100.0	100.0	100.0
Out of work but not unemployed (RR_{ca})								
Sample Size	195	142	2,358	1,334	2,566	895	1,647	908
Replacement Rate [%]								
0–20	1.2	2.0	0.5	1.1	2.5	7.5	0.7	2.5
20–40	2.8	5.3	5.7	6.6	7.6	8.7	3.4	15.0
40–60	12.4	18.6	17.7	19.8	18.3	14.2	22.2	27.1
60–80	42.7	41.1	39.3	34.1	32.0	25.0	48.0	30.7
80–100	40.9	33.0	32.6	29.3	36.3	36.0	24.3	23.1
100+	0.0	0.0	4.3	9.1	3.2	8.6	1.5	1.6
	100.0	100.0	100.0	100.0	100.0	100.0	100.0	100.0

Note: Target sample sizes refer to the number of persons aged 18–59. The in-work/unemployed/inactive groups are not mutually exclusive as it is possible to have different states in a particular year.

Source: EUROMOD.

Table 5.5 *Distribution of household replacement rates decomposed by age (1998)*

	DK		FR		SP		UK	
	<25	≥25	<25	≥25	<25	≥25	<25	≥25
In-work (RR_{ab})								
Sample size	475	1,763	1,275	8,581	894	4,011	825	5,276
Replacement rate [%]								
0–20	0.0	0.6	0.0	0.9	1.0	7.4	0.6	3.6
20–40	2.3	1.8	0.5	1.9	0.7	6.2	4.1	13.3
40–60	5.8	9.0	0.5	2.8	0.6	9.6	15.3	32.7
60–80	11.9	32.9	6.3	17.2	6.2	26.1	36.1	28.4
80–100	39.7	48.8	85.5	72.5	81.2	46.8	41.9	19.5
100+	40.3	6.9	7.3	4.5	10.3	3.8	1.9	2.5
	100.0	100.0	100.0	100.0	100.0	100.0	100.0	100.0
Unemployed (RR_{ba})								
Sample size	131	496	532	1,522	521	1,257	144	438
Replacement rate [%]								
0–20	1.3	3.4	0.0	0.7	2.4	3.2	0.0	2.0
20–40	4.8	6.0	1.7	6.7	3.5	11.1	4.0	14.6
40–60	11.5	13.0	10.0	15.9	11.0	17.8	23.0	30.3
60–80	23.3	28.0	23.6	27.7	27.0	25.0	37.4	36.3

Table 5.5 (continued)

	DK		FR		SP		UK	
	<25	≥25	<25	≥25	<25	≥25	<25	≥25
80–100	43.4	31.5	45.1	30.9	44.7	25.9	34.5	15.5
100+	15.8	18.2	19.7	18.1	11.5	16.9	1.1	1.4
	100.0	100.0	100.0	100.0	100.0	100.0	100.0	100.0
Out of work but not unemployed (RR_{ca})								
Sample size	75	262	489	3,203	726	2,735	362	2,193
Replacement rate [%]								
0–20	0.5	1.8	0.8	0.7	3.5	3.9	0.2	1.6
20–40	0.4	4.8	2.1	6.6	2.1	9.3	5.6	8.5
40–60	11.4	16.1	11.3	19.6	8.4	19.4	16.9	25.4
60–80	31.2	45.0	30.0	38.5	26.2	31.1	40.2	41.3
80–100	56.5	32.2	49.8	28.6	58.5	30.9	36.7	21.5
100+	0.0	0.0	6.1	6.1	1.2	5.5	0.5	1.7
	100.0	100.0	100.0	100.0	100.0	100.0	100.0	100.0

Note: Target sample sizes refer to the number of persons aged 18–59. The in-work/unemployed/inactive groups are not mutually exclusive as it is possible to have different states in a particular year.

Source: EUROMOD.

Table 5.6 *Distribution of household replacement rates decomposed by number of adults (1998)*

	DK		FR		SP		UK	
	1	2+	1	2+	1	2+	1	2+
In-work (RR_{ab})								
Sample size	415	1,823	1,094	8,762	162	4,743	639	5,462
Replacement rate [%]								
0–20	1.5	0.3	1.2	0.8	19.6	6.0	11.2	2.0
20–40	5.1	1.3	2.4	1.7	10.2	5.2	33.0	8.8
40–60	20.6	5.8	2.0	2.6	14.4	8.0	32.7	29.7
60–80	32.9	27.3	43.9	11.6	46.7	22.2	12.3	32.1
80–100	25.0	51.1	45.3	78.6	7.4	53.6	9.4	24.9
100+	14.9	14.2	5.3	4.8	1.7	5.0	1.5	2.5
	100.0	100.0	100.0	100.0	100.0	100.0	100.0	100.0
Unemployed (RR_{ba})								
Sample size	167	460	282	1,772	28	1,750	113	469
Replacement rate [%]								
0–20	10.0	0.5	2.3	0.2	21.9	2.8	4.2	0.6
20–40	8.1	4.9	17.0	3.3	19.5	8.9	28.1	6.5
40–60	15.0	11.8	20.8	13.3	14.9	16.0	38.5	25.0

Table 5.6 (continued)

	DK		FR		SP		UK	
	1	2+	1	2+	1	2+	1	2+
60–80	22.4	28.6	21.3	27.6	18.5	25.6	16.9	43.0
80–100	23.8	37.5	18.4	37.5	1.8	31.3	9.3	24.2
100+	20.8	16.7	20.2	18.2	23.4	15.4	3.0	0.8
	100.0	100.0	100.0	100.0	100.0	100.0	100.0	100.0
Out of work but not unemployed (RR$_{ca}$)								
Sample size	81	256	225	3,467	50	3,411	459	2,096
Replacement rate [%]								
0–20	7.1	0.0	2.8	0.5	24.7	3.6	2.5	1.1
20–40	4.7	3.6	17.5	5.1	21.4	7.7	17.5	5.7
40–60	22.2	13.0	21.7	18.2	8.7	17.4	31.9	22.2
60–80	50.8	39.6	20.8	38.6	9.5	30.4	35.3	42.6
80–100	15.2	43.8	19.3	32.4	1.0	36.7	11.3	26.9
100+	0.0	0.0	17.9	5.1	34.7	4.2	1.6	1.5
	100.0	100.0	100.0	100.0	100.0	100.0	100.0	100.0

Note: Target sample sizes refer to the number of persons aged 18–59. The in-work/unemployed/inactive groups are not mutually exclusive as it is possible to have different states in a particular year.

Source: EUROMOD.

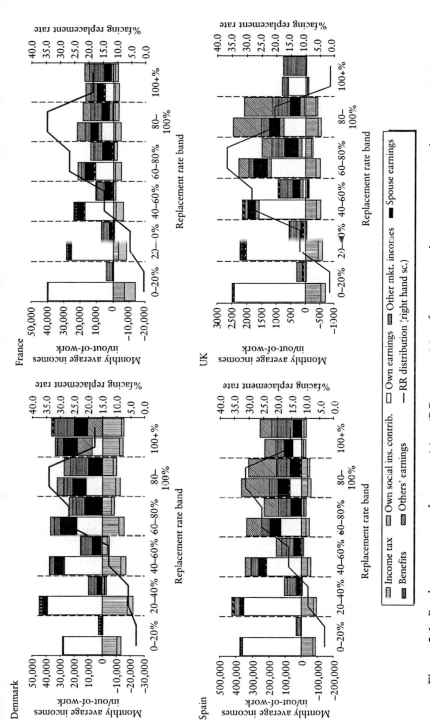

Figure 5.1 *Replacement rate decomposition (RR_{ba}: transition from unemployment into employment, 1998).*

Notes: Incomes are monthly, at the household level and in 1998 national currencies. The left bar consists of in-work and the right bar out-of-work income. Net incomes in each state are found by subtracting taxes and contributions from the positive income components.

Source: EUROMOD.

CHAPTER 6

Skills and Unemployment

STEVEN MCINTOSH

Introduction

The fact that labour market conditions have turned against low-skilled individuals in European countries over the last 20 years or so, and seem set to continue to do so, cannot be denied. The demand for skilled workers has risen, while the demand for the low-skilled has fallen. Without a corresponding fall in the supply of workers with elementary skill levels, simple economic analysis of supply and demand would suggest that the wages of this group should fall relative to their more skilled counterparts. Alternatively, if their relative wages were artificially maintained at existing levels via some institutional mechanism, then their employment rate would be expected to fall. Either way, reduced income and possibly poverty, economic marginalization, and social exclusion could result. This chapter outlines existing evidence, and presents some new evidence, as to how correct this prediction is. Specifically, the chapter wishes to investigate the source of the problem in the falling demand for low-skilled workers, the consequences in terms of the economic position and employment opportunities of the low-skilled, and how this position varies across countries, which may provide potential insights into how to deal with the problem.

The new evidence presented here is based upon some of the results to come out of an European Union Targeted Socio-Economic Research (TSER) project, entitled *NEWSKILLS*, which analysed the position of the low-skilled in six European countries.[1] The countries

---

[1] This chapter describes the results of the project that refer specifically to the relationship between skills and unemployment, although the *NEWSKILLS* project considered a much wider range of issues to do with the supply of and demand for individuals with low skills.

were chosen to represent a range of experiences for the low-skilled. Thus, in addition to the three largest economies of France, Germany, and the United Kingdom, a Scandinavian country (Sweden), a Central European country (Netherlands), and a Southern European country (Portugal) were studied. This allowed us to consider a good range of countries along a number of dimensions, for example with respect to protection against unemployment and other labour market institutions, which can affect labour market outcomes following changes in the relative demand and supply of skilled labour, and also with respect to the labour supply response of skilled workers.

The chapter begins by outlining the facts regarding the level of unemployment amongst the low-skilled, including some discussion of exactly how to define low skills, based on our research into the issues involved in such a definition. We then move on to discuss the factors behind the fall in demand for low-skilled labour, before completing the review with a discussion of remaining employment opportunities for such workers.

Unemployment and Low Skill

The introduction above suggested that the low-skilled face high levels of unemployment. However, assessment of the evidence for this raises important issues for the way in which 'low-skill' should be defined and measured. Since we are principally interested in the ability to obtain work, information about skills as required and used in the workplace would be the most useful. Unfortunately, such data are hard to come by. There are some international surveys that seek to directly assess low-skill in the sense of basic literacy and numeracy competencies. The International Adult Literacy Survey (IALS) appears to be an obvious candidate. However, only a single cross-section of the IALS exists for any one country, and so these data can tell us nothing about changes over time. The International Association for the Evaluation of Educational Achievement (IEA) has produced a series of studies since 1960, such as the well-known TIMSS study of mathematics and science. The greatest drawback of such studies for the measurement of labour market competence is that they test at the early age of 14 before individuals have acquired labour market experience. If we require information on skill levels over time and across countries, then we need to search for alternatives.

One possibility is to define workers' skills by the jobs that they do. Hence, Table 6.1 draws on Labour Force Survey data to describe the unemployed by the broad occupation category of the previous job undertaken, for various European countries. The list of occupational groups is broadly hierarchical, with the more skilled occupations at the top of the table. The results show that those workers who worked previously in elementary occupations form the largest group of the unemployed (22.1 per cent) in the European Union as a whole, followed by craft and related trades workers (19.0 per cent), and service and sales workers (17.9 per cent). The same three occupations frequently emerge as the most represented amongst the unemployed in the individual countries of the European Union, although the ordering varies across countries. There are some differences by gender, reflecting the different nature of jobs typically undertaken by men and women. Thus amongst males, the occupational group most represented amongst the unemployed in the European Union as a whole is craft and related workers (30.1 per cent), whilst amongst females it is service and sales workers (26.7 per cent). For both men and women, however, those who previously worked in elementary occupations figure highly amongst the unemployed. In terms then of a definition based on previous occupation before becoming unemployed, it would appear that the pool of unemployed workers consists predominately of low-skilled workers.

There are, however, numerous problems associated with using such figures to investigate the relationship between skills and unemployment. For example, although it was stated that the ordering of occupational groups in Table 6.1 represents a broad hierarchy of skills, it is not necessarily clear, for example, that clerks or sales workers are more or less skilled than craft workers. In addition, the occupations listed are very broad, and there will be a range of more specific occupations, and hence a range of skills, within each of these broad categories.

Another key problem is the identification of individuals' skills with the jobs that they perform. The literature[2] on overeducation takes as its starting point that individuals are not always appropriately matched to the jobs that they do, so that the 'overeducated' have a higher level of skills than those used in their jobs, while the 'undereducated' do not have the necessary skills for their work. In either case, classifying an individual's skills by the job that they did would misrepresent these skills.

---

[2] See for example Hartog (1997) or Groot and Maassen van den Brink (2000) for an overview.

Another problem with the statistics as presented is that the proportion of the unemployed who previously worked in unskilled occupations will depend upon the proportions actually working in these occupations. In countries with a high percentage of workers in low-skilled occupations, such individuals are naturally going to be heavily represented amongst the unemployed. Thus, a conclusion of an acute problem of low-skill unemployment could be drawn, when in reality the number of low-skilled in unemployment is merely representative of the number of low-skilled in the economy. One solution could be to derive an unemployment *rate* for each occupation, with the number of unemployed who previously worked in a particular occupation expressed as a proportion of the total number working in that occupation in the previous period. However, the use of two different stocks in the numerator and denominator of this proportion (this year's unemployed compared to last year's work-force in the occupation) would be a little confusing, and would depart from the usual method of calculating unemployment rates.

A final problem with this method of investigating low-skilled unemployment is that individuals who have never worked are necessarily excluded from the numbers, since they do not have a previous occupation. The low-skilled are probably more likely to have never worked than those with a higher level of skills, and so will be under-represented in the table of unemployment by previous occupation.

An alternative method with which to define low skills is to use education level. Table 6.2 displays unemployment rates, labour force participation rates, and employment/population ratios by education level in the year 2000 for a number of European countries, as well as for the United States, for comparison purposes. In every country tabulated, individuals with less than upper secondary level education have a higher unemployment rate than their more educated peers. On average across the whole European Union, 10.6 per cent of individuals who completed their education before upper secondary level are unemployed, compared to 7.2 per cent of individuals who reached upper secondary level, and 4.1 per cent of individuals with a tertiary education. The effect is particularly pronounced in the United Kingdom and Ireland, where the 'lower secondary or below' unemployment rate is about twice that for upper secondary education, which is again twice the unemployment rate amongst those with a tertiary education in the United Kingdom. The final row in the table shows that the situation in the United States is similar to that in its English-speaking cousins in Europe.

Looking at unemployment rates only tells half the story, however. For every country in the table, individuals with less than upper secondary education are also less likely than those with more education to participate in the labour force at all.[3] Across the European Union as a whole, 60 per cent of those with less than upper secondary education participate in the labour force, compared to 80 per cent of those with upper secondary education, and 88 per cent of those with a tertiary education. Putting these two facts together—a higher unemployment rate and a lower participation rate—there are far fewer low-skilled individuals in employment relative to those with higher level skills. The employment/population ratios in Table 6.2 reveal that just over half (54 per cent) of individuals who did not progress beyond lower secondary education are in employment, compared to 75 per cent of those with upper secondary education and 84 per cent of those who proceed to tertiary education. There appears to be a distinct break at the end of lower secondary education, whereby individuals who do not progress beyond this point have significantly lower employment opportunities.

There are again some problems, however, with using education level as an indicator of skills. First, skills can be obtained from sources other than formal education, for example many working skills are likely to be gained through workplace training or simply work experience. This will be particularly the case amongst those individuals who leave education early to learn a trade, so that the lower education categories may not be as low-skilled as supposed. An additional problem when making international comparisons of education levels is the comparability of the classifications across countries. Does, for example, reaching an upper secondary level of education imply a similar level of skills in different countries?

A considerable section of the research programme was spent on developing a working measure of low skills. Because of the difficulty in obtaining a time-series of workplace skills variables across countries, it was decided that our measure had to be based upon qualifications achieved and courses followed. Therefore, unfortunately, skills learned through work experience and informal learning-on-the-job will not be covered by our measures. We did try to improve on using only measures of educational achievement,

---

[3] Participation in the labour market is defined as being in employment, self-employment, or unemployed under the ILO definition of unemployment, that is, actively looking for work. The remainder of a given population are classified as 'inactive'.

however, by using the International Standard Classification of Education (ISCED). This classification system assigns the various qualifications that individuals acquire to a particular level[4] in the hierarchy. As far as information sources allowed, we included vocational qualifications obtained in our classification, assigning them to the most appropriate ISCED level. Therefore, the skills of those individuals who leave school early, and thus appear low-skilled on a formal education measure, but who nevertheless go on to acquire a skilled trade through a vocational training course, will have these skills included in our measure. Considerable care was taken over the assignment of the various qualifications to the ISCED levels, to make these as comparable as possible across countries. Table 6.3 details which qualifications were assigned to each level in the European countries studied.

The next decision to be taken was which ISCED levels should be classified as low-skilled. We decided to classify all those at ISCED level 2 or below (no higher than lower secondary education or equivalent) as low-skilled. This choice of cut-off point was based on a number of criteria. First, the data in Table 6.2, discussed above, show clearly that individuals with no more than lower secondary education appear to be a very distinct group in terms of their employment rates, relative to those with more education. Second, those with no or only primary education (ISCED 0/1) are concentrated disproportionately in the older age groups. This is the result of cohort effects produced by the chronology of educational reform in European countries (compulsory secondary education was introduced either immediately before or shortly after the Second World War). Therefore, those likely to have failed to complete secondary education will be primarily those born in the late 1930s and early 1940s. Defining low skills as only the ISCED 0/1 group would therefore focus the analysis on these older cohorts, with perhaps less relevance to current labour market policy. An additional disadvantage of using the ISCED 0/1 group is that it is numerically very small in some of these countries (particularly Germany and Sweden), thus reducing the precision of any statistical results.

---

[4] The ISCED categories are as follows: ISCED 0: education preceding the first level (pre-primary); ISCED 1: education at the first level (primary); ISCED 2: education at the lower secondary level; ISCED 3: education at the upper secondary level; ISCED 5: education at the tertiary level, first stage; ISCED 6: education at the tertiary level, first stage, leading to first degree; ISCED 7: education at the tertiary level, second stage, leading to a postgraduate degree.

In further tests, we used the Third International Mathematics and Science Study (TIMSS) to examine the reliability of using the ISCED 0–2 group as a low-skill measure across countries (Steedman and McIntosh, 2001). We chose thirty maths questions, selected from the full range of TIMSS items, that we thought tested the simplest mathematics normally taught by the age of 11 or 12. We were therefore considering the most basic competencies that are most likely to be required in an employment setting, rather than the whole mathematics curriculum. The results for 12/13 year olds (international grade 7) reveal that students at this age in the six European countries are far from mastering this mathematics material. On only 4 of the 30 questions did more than 90 per cent of European 12/13-year olds achieve the correct answer. Since students aged 13/14 (international grade 8) were also given identical tests in TIMSS, we could measure the annual rate of improvement in test scores, and then extrapolate this forwards to age 16, the point at which lower secondary schooling is completed. The results still reveal a lack of mastery of these basic competencies in mathematics at the age of 16. In France, only half of the thirty basic questions were predicted to be answered correctly by 90 per cent or more of the students, with the other countries performing even worse, achieving mastery of less than half of the questions. We therefore conclude that individuals who do not continue their education beyond the lower secondary level (i.e. those at ISCED level 2 or below) do not, on the whole, possess the necessary mathematical skills to function in the workplace, and that this is a reliable measure of low skills in all of the European countries.

We further checked the validity of using the ISCED 0–2 measure as an indicator of low skills, by ensuring that this group contains most of those defined as low-skilled according to the more objective measure of skills found in IALS. Although the lack of data over time means that the IALS cannot be used as our main measure of skill, it does provide a very good test of validity of the other measures. IALS Level 2 is widely considered to be a low-skill level, below the minimum required of most new employees (OECD/CERI, 1997). Two-thirds (66 per cent) of the ISCED 0–2 group in Europe[5] score at IALS levels 1 or 2. Thus a significant majority of this group is low-skilled according to the IALS measure. In addition, of all those at

---

[5] This figure is the weighted average of the figures across the five European countries in IALS for which reliable data were available; Belgium, Great Britain, Ireland, Sweden, and Switzerland.

IALS levels 1 or 2, 73 per cent (weighted average) are also at ISCED 0–2. We can therefore be confident that ISCED 0–2 captures most (three-quarters) of those at the IALS levels considered to be below the minimum required for new employees.

We are therefore confident that those at ISCED 2 or below form a usable definition of low skills in Europe. As part of the research programme, we then used this definition to investigate the unemployment and inactivity situations of the low-skilled in our European countries (Kirsch, 1999). This involved developing an index to indicate the propensity of the low-skilled to be unemployed or inactive. Specifically, the analysis calculates the number of low-skilled workers who would be expected to be unemployed/inactive, based on the number of low-skilled workers in each country. For example, if there are 1000 low-skilled individuals in a population, and that country's unemployment rate is 10 per cent, then we would expect 100 low-skilled workers to be unemployed, if the experience of unemployment is distributed evenly across all skill levels. If there are in fact 150 low-skilled workers unemployed, then the index number will be $(150/100) \times 100 = 150$, suggesting that the low-skilled are particularly prone to unemployment. If, on the other hand, there are only fifty low-skilled workers who are unemployed, the index will take the value of 50, implying that low-skilled workers have a low propensity to unemployment. The propensity of the low-skilled to be unemployed or inactive in each country, in 1996, is displayed in Table 6.4.

It can be seen that in each country except Portugal, the low-skilled are very much over-represented within the stocks of the unemployed and, particularly, inactive individuals, as all of the 'propensity indexes' are greater than 100. There appears to be some sort of pattern in that the low-skilled have a higher propensity to unemployment and inactivity in the countries where their number is smallest.[6] Indeed there is a perfect negative rank order correlation between the proportion of the workforce that is low-skilled in a country, and the propensity of this group to inactivity. Thus, although countries such as Sweden have done much to reduce the number of low-skilled workers in the population, those who remain low-skilled are particularly likely to be unemployed or inactive. We shall return to this point later.

---

[6] Murray and Steedman (1998), in another *NEWSKILLS* paper, report that the proportions of the working age population at ISCED level 0–2 in 1996 is 28 per cent in Sweden, 41 per cent in the Netherlands, 43 per cent in France, 52 per cent in the United Kingdom, and 77 per cent in Portugal.

Performing similar calculations for all years from 1985–96 (not shown in Table 6.4) reveals an upward trend in the likelihood of unemployment for the low-skilled in France, although in the other countries, the unemployment situation for this group does not seem to have deteriorated to any great extent over this period. However, the propensity towards inactivity does show clear upward trends in every country except Portugal. It therefore appears that some stability in the likelihood of unemployment for the low-skilled has been achieved at the cost of higher inactivity rates. Just looking at unemployment rates is therefore likely to underestimate the problems being faced by the low-skilled in the modern labour market.

Further analysis of the unemployment and inactivity propensities by gender and age reveals that in the United Kingdom, the Netherlands, and France, men at ISCED 0–2 have a higher likelihood of unemployment or inactivity (relative to all men) than women (relative to all women). In the United Kingdom and France, the gap has widened between 1985 and 1996 while in the Netherlands it has narrowed. In Sweden and Portugal the situation is the reverse and women have a greater likelihood of unemployment—in the case of Sweden the gap widened slightly between 1985 and 1996. In the case of Portugal the gap remained small and at much the same level over time. With respect to age, in all countries except Portugal the low-skilled likelihood of unemployment is higher for the young age group (<30 years), compared to the older age group. In France, the United Kingdom, and the Netherlands the differences are considerable while in Sweden the difference is small. Between 1985 and 1996, the likelihood of unemployment increased for the ISCED 0–2 young age group in all countries except Portugal. In the same four countries, inactivity rates are also considerably higher for the <30 age group than for the older group. In France, the Netherlands, and the United Kingdom, the likelihood of inactivity for the <30 age group at the ISCED 0–2 level is substantially higher in 1996 than in 1985. Sweden shows a fall in the likelihood of inactivity for the young age group, as does Portugal. We now turn to an investigation of why the labour market has turned against the low-skilled.

Technological Change, Trade Competition, and the Demand for Low-skilled Workers

The previous section described the relatively weak position of the low-skilled in all OECD countries. A now large body of research has attempted to explain why this is the case, focusing in particular on the decline in their labour market position. As indicated above, a falling demand for low-skilled workers appears to be the main culprit for this decline, given the general increase in educational achievement, and hence falling supply of low-skilled workers, that has been observed in all developed countries. If the supply of low-skilled workers is declining then, with an unchanged demand, we would expect the short-supply to drive up wages for the low-skilled. The fact that this is not the case, and that in some countries (notably the United Kingdom and the United States[7]) wages for the low-skilled are falling in relative terms, suggests that the demand for such workers has also declined.

What has caused the rise in the relative demand for higher-level skills? Two possible explanations have been pushed to the fore in the available literature. One possibility is competition from industrializing economies (Wood, 1994). In the trade sectors of the economy increased competitive pressures have resulted from the great increase in world trade. In particular, competition from developing countries that specialize in typically low-skill, manufactured goods reduce the price of such goods, and hence the demand for and the wages of low-skilled workers in developed countries. In order to retain their competitive advantage, developed countries need to specialize in high-skill, capital-intensive products, and therefore require highly-skilled employees. The alternative possibility is the increasing role of technology in production (Berman et al., 1998). If technological change has been 'skill-biased' in the sense that more skilled workers are required to use the new technology, while low-skilled and semi-skilled jobs are replaced by the technology, then we would expect demand for low-skilled workers to fall.

A number of papers have attempted to distinguish between these two theories and determine which has caused the fall in demand for unskilled workers. This literature has focused mainly on changes in wage inequality as an indicator of the declining labour market position of the low-skilled. The method used is to decompose the change in wage inequality into its within-industry and between-industry

---

[7] See for example Bluestone and Harrison (1988), Katz and Murphy (1992), Levy and Murnane (1992), and Murphy and Welch (1992) for the United States, as well as the special issues of the *Journal of Economic Perspectives* in 1995 and 1997, and Gregg and Machin (1993), Gosling et al. (1994), and Schmitt (1995) for the United Kingdom.

components. The argument is that the within-industry component is associated with skill-biased technological change, as industries upgrade their workforces, while the between-industries component is associated with trade competition, as developed countries move out of the low-skilled industries in which they cannot compete with the developing countries, and into more skilled industries. Even when the industries used in the analyses are very disaggregated, the results always show that the vast majority of upgrading in skilled wages/downgrading in low-skill wages has occurred within industries, suggesting that skill-biased technological change is the key instigator for change (see, for example, Machin, 1996, amongst many other examples).

How do we know, however, that the upgrading in the wages of skilled relative to low-skilled workers is actually caused by skill-biased technological change? A number of papers have examined characteristics of industries, searching for evidence to show that the most technologically advanced industries are the ones where skilled wages are increasing fastest. For example, variables measuring R&D expenditure or innovation counts at the industry level in the United Kingdom are positively related to industries' non-manual wage bill and employment shares, as shown by Machin (1996). At the establishment level, he shows that an increase in computer usage leads to increasing employment of non-manual employees, particularly senior professionals, and declining employment of manual workers, particularly unskilled manual workers. Similar results are obtained in the seven countries considered by Machin and Van Reenen (1998). The pervasiveness of skill-biased technological change is also demonstrated by Berman et al. (1998), who calculate cross-country correlations of the industry-level changes in the proportion of non-production workers in the 1980s. Almost all of the resulting correlations are positive, indicating that the same industries are typically increasing their use of skilled workers the most in each country. These industries are machinery (and computers), electrical engineering, printing and publishing, and transportation, which all tend to be technologically advanced. Other research has focused more directly on computer usage as the source of the skill-biased technological change. For example, Autor et al. (1998) show that computer usage has a positive and statistically significant impact on industry-level changes in the employment shares of educated workers. In a similar vein, Haskel (1999) reports that the increased use of computers can explain over half of the increase in wage inequality in the United Kingdom during the 1980s. Gregory et al. (2001) use a different methodology from all papers considered above, in an attempt to estimate the factors underpinning the rise in the demand for skilled labour and the declining labour market position of low-skilled workers, namely input–output analysis. The results again show technological change playing a key role, reducing low-skilled employment dramatically, while leading to an increase in skilled employment (hence supporting the idea that the technological change has been skill-biased). International trade has had a much more skill-neutral effect, with labour at all skill levels being affected by increased global competition.[8]

The rise in the demand for skills has also been documented in a literature specifically examining required skills in jobs, rather than looking for indirect evidence through rising wage inequality. The 1986 Social Change and Economic Life Initiative (SCELI) survey and 1997 and 2001 Skills Survey in the United Kingdom are useful in this respect (see Green et al., 1998; Ashton et al., 1999; Felstead et al., 2002). These surveys show that skill demands have indeed risen between 1986 and 2001, for example via an increase in the proportion of jobs requiring some qualifications, an increase in required training times and an increase in the time taken to master jobs. Hand in hand with this rise in the demand for skills is an increasing use of computers between 1986 and 2001, and at higher levels of complexity, as documented in Felstead et al. (2002). Direct evidence of the link between computers and the rise in demand for skilled workers is presented by Gallie (1991), who uses SCELI data for the United Kingdom to show that those respondents who use automated or computer equipment are much more likely to need qualifications to get their job. Similarly, Simpson et al. (1987) argue that, although an unskilled worker can in principle operate computer numerically controlled equipment, firms are more likely to demand skilled workers, for their ability to judge quality and identify faults. Finally, Haskel (1996) summarizes a range of case study evidence that suggests that microprocessors increase the demand for skilled labour.

What then, of the alternative theory of the increase in trade with less-developed countries being important for the declining labour market position of the low-skilled in developed countries? The theory is that international trade with developing countries, who can produce

---

[8] The authors show that changing patterns of final consumer demand have also been responsible for the rising demand for skilled workers, a point not made by the wage inequality studies outlined above.

low-skilled goods cheaply because of low labour costs, reduces the world price for such goods, harming the profitability of such industries in developed countries, leading to a reduction in the wages they pay to their low-skilled workers, or complete shutdown and loss of low-skilled employment. It may be that even though such direct Stopler–Samuelson type effects of trade on wages seem to be small, there may still be indirect effects, with merely the threat of trade leading firms in developed countries to invest more in technology to differentiate themselves from firms in the newly developed countries, as pointed out by Haskel (1999). Indeed, when he replaces the computer use, small firms and contracting-out variables in his regression equation with variables measuring the level and change in the relative import price, both have the expected negative effect on wage inequality, with the level effect being statistically significant. Thus, the indirect effects of trade may be important. Similarly, Borjas and Ramey (1995) consider the trade argument and conclude that about half of the fall in employment of low-skilled workers between 1976 and 2000 in specifically trade-impacted industries is due to changes in international trade. They acknowledge, however, that trade-impacted industries form a declining part of the overall economy of developed countries, and so conclude that other factors, such as skill-biased technological change, must be important in explaining the declining position of the low-skilled overall. In a review of the evidence, the OECD *Employment Outlook* (1997a) comes to a similar conclusion, while acknowledging the possible indirect effects of trade mentioned above. It is interesting to note that Green et al. (2003) show that computerization has increased fastest outside of manufacturing, casting doubt on the importance of the overall role of international trade in driving technological development.

One of the papers in the project adds to this literature on the underlying causes of the fall in demand for low-skilled workers (Mellander, 1999). It uses data at the industry level, covering twenty-four industries in the Swedish manufacturing sector over the period 1985–95. Four categories of labour are identified, namely workers with qualifications at ISCED 0/1, ISCED 2, ISCED 3, and ISCED 5/6/7, respectively. This paper makes use of the definition of low skills developed by the research programme outlined in the previous section, and thus considers skill structures in more detail than previous work in this area. It was decided to treat ISCED 0/1 and ISCED 2 workers separately in this study, because of the sharply differing age structure across these two groups. Although the previous section made it clear that all workers at ISCED 2 or below should be treated as low-skilled, rather than focusing on a narrow definition of ISCED 0/1 only, which comprises mainly older workers, the results below suggest that it can be important to treat these two groups of low-skilled workers separately.[9]

Mellander adopts the methodology that has been used in the literature to differentiate between the skill-biased technological change and trade competition arguments outlined above, namely decomposing changes in the employment shares of the four skill groups into their between-industry and within-industry components. As with the evidence reviewed above, the results show that the between-industry changes are totally dominated by within-industry changes, consistent with skill-biased technological change being responsible for the rise in the demand for skilled labour. The contributions of within-industry changes to the total changes in employment shares range between 93 and 99 per cent, depending on the category of labour and the time period studied.

The study goes on to examine in more detail whether the dominant within-industry changes can really be attributed to skill-biased technological change, by including a measure of technological change in estimated labour demand functions for workers at each of the four skill levels. The demand equations control for gender, age, immigrant status, and field of study. The results are revealing.

Skill-biased technological change strongly decreases the demand for ISCED 0/1 workers and does so at an increasing rate over time. Compared to the average effect of technical change on the demand for all inputs, the reduction is 4 per cent in 1986 and 16 per cent in 1995. Technical change saves on ISCED 2 workers as well, but here the effect is much less dramatic: the relative reduction is 2 per cent in 1986 and 5 per cent in 1995. For ISCED 3, the relative skill bias is small and stable, reducing demand by around 1 per cent per year, during the whole period. Only for ISCED 5–7 individuals is the relative skill bias positive. In 1986, technical change increases the relative demand for this category by 5 per cent. This rate then falls very slightly over time to end up at 4 per cent in 1995. Skill-biased technological change therefore seems to be an important factor in the declining labour market position of the low-skilled.

---

[9] For the manufacturing sector as a whole, almost 95 per cent of the ISCED 0/1 workers are at least 40 years old in 1990, while for ISCED 2, more than 70 per cent are below 40.

Pay, Sectoral Change, and the Employment Opportunities of the Low-skilled

So far we have established a rising demand for skilled labour in many countries, harming the labour market position of the low-skilled, the evidence for which has frequently been given as a widening wage structure. Wage inequality has not increased in all countries though. For example, Snower (1996) notes only a modest increase in inequality in Austria, Australia, Belgium, Canada, France, Japan, the Netherlands, Portugal, Spain, and Sweden, while inequality has remained roughly constant in Denmark, Finland, Italy, and Norway, and has fallen in Germany. It has been suggested in the literature, for example by Siebert (1997) that some countries' institutions, such as collective bargaining, minimum wages, or the structure of benefits creating an effective wage floor, have not allowed low-skill wages to be flexible, and have maintained relativities between low-skill and high-skill wages. In such countries the fall in the demand for low-skilled workers has therefore had to manifest itself in the form of increasing unemployment for such groups. Where low-skill wages have been allowed to fall, either relative to skilled wages or indeed in absolute terms, then low-skilled unemployment need not rise, although of course widening wage inequality results. In an oft-quoted remark, Krugman (1994) states that 'the European unemployment problem and the US inequality problem are two sides of the same coin'. Empirical support for such a proposition can be found in Mortensen and Pissarides (1999), who argue that unemployment in the United States would have been similar to levels in Europe in the 1980s and 1990s, if the United States had had similar labour market institutions to those in Europe (they specifically consider unemployment benefit replacement ratios and employment protection tax rates). Similarly, Blau and Kahn (1996) obtain results suggesting that the variation in wage inequality across countries can be explained by labour market institutions, and therefore conclude that European unemployment amongst the low-skilled is caused by their wages being held artificially high, following the fall in demand for their services. If this is correct then one way of increasing employment opportunities for the low-skilled would be to increase pay differentials, if necessary by reducing the wages of low-skilled workers.

Evidence for the responsiveness of the demand for low-skilled labour to low-skilled wages is supplied by the labour demand equations estimated by Mellander (1999), as described above. The results reveal that the two low-skills categories (ISCED 0/1 and ISCED 2) both have 'elastic' long-run demand with respect to their own wages, implying that a 1 per cent rise in the wage leads to a more than 1 per cent fall in demand. In fact, the estimated coefficients suggest that a 1 per cent rise in the wages of ISCED 0/1 workers reduced the demand for such workers by 1.7 per cent in 1986, and by a huge 6 per cent in 1995. For ISCED 2 workers, a similar proportional change in wages reduced demand by only 0.8 per cent in 1986, and 1.5 per cent in 1995. For the ISCED 3 and ISCED 5–7 groups, increases in wages lead to much smaller falls in demand.

These results suggest that, given the changes caused by technological change, low-skilled workers may not be able to justify increases in their wages in terms of productivity, leading to large falls in their employment. Putting it another way, smaller increases in wages would have been necessary to keep more low-skilled workers in employment. However, one positive aspect for policy initiatives is that the estimated wage effects on labour demand are symmetrical, and a 1 per cent fall in the low-skilled wage, achieved for example through a wage subsidy, should lead to a more than 1 per cent increase in employment, particularly for the ISCED 0/1 group for whom the estimated effects are very large. We have to be careful here though, as the ISCED 0/1 and ISCED 2 groups may well compete for low-skilled jobs, and the effect of a fall in the wage of one could be a fall in demand for the other, as employers substitute between the two grades of low-skilled labour. Mellander (1999) therefore also calculates the 'cross-wage elasticities of demand' for these two groups, based on his labour demand equations. The results, for 1995, show that a 1 per cent fall in the wages of ISCED 0/1 workers will reduce the long-run demand for ISCED 2 workers by 1.95 per cent. On the other hand, a 1 per cent fall in ISCED 2 wages would reduce the long-run demand for ISCED 0/1 workers by 2 per cent. What do these elasticities actually mean in terms of numbers in employment? Putting the own-wage and cross-wage effects together, the numbers predict that a 1 per cent fall in the ISCED 0/1 wage will increase demand for such individuals by 7200 workers, and reduce the ISCED 2 demand by 2300 workers. The net effect on low-skill employment is therefore an increase of 4900 workers. When we consider a 1 per cent cut in the wage paid to ISCED 2 workers, this will increase the demand for such individuals by 1800 workers, but there will also be substitution against the very low-skilled, ISCED 0/1, workers, whose numbers would fall by 2400. Overall, therefore, low-skilled employment would *fall* by 600.

Thus, marginal wage reductions for ISCED 0/1 workers will be effective in the sense that the increased demand for these workers is not offset by reductions in the demands for ISCED 2 workers. In contrast, marginal wage reductions for ISCED 2 workers will increase the demand for these workers by less than it decreases the demand for ISCED 0/1 workers.

The results presented so far in this section therefore suggest that allowing the wages of the least skilled to fall should raise the demand for such workers, and hence improve their employment position. Unfortunately, cross-country evidence does not support the view that low-skilled employment is higher where wage flexibility is greater. For example, consider Card et al.'s (1999) comparison of the changing structure of wages and unemployment in the United States, Canada, and France. Their results show that wages have indeed grown faster in age-education cells that have a higher computer usage rate (or equivalently in cells with higher initial wages) over the period 1979–89 in the United States, while if anything the reverse is true for France. Results for Canada lie somewhere between these extremes. This is so far consistent with the wage inequality studies described above, with inequality rising more in the United States than in Europe. However, Card et al. (1999) go on to show that changes in employment rates vary positively with computer usage to the same extent in the United States as in France. Thus, the relative employment rates of low paid US workers who make little use of computers have fallen just as much as their contemporaries in France, despite the wage flexibility that has led to their suffering larger falls in relative wages. A similar comparison of the United States and Germany by Krueger and Pischke (1997) reaches the same conclusion, with their results showing no relationship between the change in employment rates and initial wage levels in Germany, while in the United States, such a positive relationship does exist, suggesting relative employment has fallen for the low-paid (and presumably low-skilled) despite the increase in wage inequality in that country.

A likely explanation for these results is that wages have not fallen far enough in countries with flexible wages, such as the United Kingdom and the United States, to maintain low-skilled employment levels. Despite the eroding of artificial wage floors in these countries, wages have still not been allowed to fall sufficiently, because of more natural floors such as minimum amounts for which any individual is prepared to work (reservation wages). The problem is therefore that wages cannot fall far enough to equate the falling demand for low-skilled workers with the large supply of such workers that remains in the United Kingdom and the United States. An alternative approach to stabilizing, or even reducing, low-skilled unemployment might therefore be to reduce the supply of low-skilled workers, leading to a higher equilibrium wage, rather than forcing down wages to try to equate demand with the large supply. Numerous studies have in fact shown that the success of countries such as Germany in moderating low-skilled unemployment, despite relatively inflexible wages, is due to their efforts to reduce the low-skilled labour supply.

For example, Glyn and Salverda (2000) analyse the determinants of employment rate differences between the least-educated quartile and the most-educated quartile in a range of countries (i.e. the relative employment rate of the low-skilled). The authors find no evidence, however, that this relative employment rate is significantly affected by the level of minimum wages, the unemployment benefits replacement ratio, the severity of employment protection legislation, trade union density, or indeed by the general level of wage dispersion. The only institution effect which they find to be statistically significant is that the relative employment rate of the low-skilled is actually higher in countries that undertake centralized collective bargaining, which runs contrary to the predictions of the employment/inequality trade-off hypothesis. However, the authors do find that the difference between the average literacy test score in the top and bottom quartiles of the education distribution has a positive effect on the employment difference, suggesting that employment of the low-skilled is relatively lower in countries where they perform relatively poorly on literacy tests.

Nickell and Bell (1996) and Freeman and Schettkat (2000) consider how Germany (at the time) had achieved unskilled unemployment rates similar to those observed in the United States, without unskilled wages falling, relative to skilled wages. Assuming that the fall in demand for low-skilled workers, due mainly to skill-biased technological change, has been relevant to all countries, then Germany must have achieved these results by also reducing the supply of the low-skilled to a greater extent than observed in the United States. Both papers point to the high levels of ability achieved by the large group with middle-level qualifications in Germany, as measured by standardized test scores, and argue that the availability of such a large skilled workforce allows Germany to respond in a flexible manner to demand shifts. This argument suggests that schooling and training are important for raising the standards of the workforce, to mitigate the consequences of the shift in demand away from the low-skilled.

Similar ideas are presented in a range of papers considering mismatch between the demand and supply of skills (see, for example, Gregg and Manning, 1997; Jackman et al., 1997; Manacorda and Petrongolo, 1999). These papers assess how much unemployment of the low-skilled is caused by a mismatch between the supply of and the demand for skills (i.e. too many low-skilled workers for the number of low-skilled jobs). As described by Gregg and Manning (1997), it is the response of the supply of skills that is more important in affecting the labour market position of the low-skilled, rather than institutions that prevent a rise in wage inequality. Hence, in those countries in which the supply of skills is raised to match the rise in the demand for skills, there is less mismatch, and so fewer low-skilled workers in unemployment.

A final paper to discuss the supply of skills as well as the demand for skills is Muhlau and Horgan (2001). Rather than express skills in terms of qualifications, however, Muhlau and Horgan use the literacy scores supplied in the International Adult Literacy Survey (IALS). The authors find that the average level of literacy skills is higher in Continental European countries (Belgium, Germany, the Netherlands, Sweden, and Switzerland) than in Anglo-Saxon countries (Canada, Ireland, New Zealand, the United Kingdom, and the United States). The relative wages of the low-skilled are lower in the Anglo-Saxon countries than in the Continental European countries, which is to be expected, given what we know about the relative degrees of wage inequality in these two groups of countries. However, the low-skilled in Continental Europe do not 'pay' for their higher relative wages with higher unemployment rates, as would be predicted by the 'institutions' theory. Indeed, low-skilled workers have *higher* employment rates relative to median-skilled workers in the Continental European countries than in the Anglo-Saxon countries. The authors explain this by showing that, while all countries do not have sufficient low-skill jobs to match the supply of low-skilled workers, the difference is smaller in the Continental European than in the Anglo-Saxon countries. Thus, although the Anglo-Saxon countries have more low-skill jobs than the Continental European countries, this is more than outweighed by the supply of low-skilled workers in the former countries, so that the excess supply of low-skilled workers is higher in Anglo-Saxon countries.

Thus, the literature suggests that the low-skilled as a group have had the best labour market outcomes when their number has been reduced in line with the falling demand for workers of their skill level. In this way, the excess supply of low-skilled workers does not build up to such an extent, and fewer low-skilled workers are forced into unemployment and inactivity, with the possible attendant risks of poverty and social exclusion. Of course, the reduction in supply of low-skilled workers is a gradual process, occurring primarily through the introduction of better-educated younger cohorts into the labour force. The research by Murray and Steedman (1998) estimates that, of the countries in the project, only Germany and Sweden will have reduced the proportion of their respective workforces that are low-skilled to below 10 per cent by 2010. Thus, although the literature reviewed above suggests that the low-skilled will benefit most as a group from a reduction in their number, the question must be asked, what of those who remain low-skilled? The section titled 'Unemployment and Low Skill' discussed the propensity of the low-skilled to be unemployed or inactive in various countries, calculated in the project by Kirsch (1999), and revealed that this propensity is higher in the countries that have reduced their low-skilled number the most, such as in Sweden, and lowest in countries where the low-skilled proportion has remained higher, such as in Portugal. Thus, although raising the supply of skills reduces the number of low-skilled workers out of work, those who remain low skilled seem to face a higher individual risk of unemployment and inactivity. It is therefore of interest to investigate employment possibilities for the low-skilled, to see where the hope for their continued employment lies. Such analysis can be found in the research carried out by Kirsch (1999).

Kirsch begins by noting that we cannot simply look at the numbers of low-skilled workers in employment in various sectors, since the low-skilled are a declining number in the population as a whole. Thus, reduced numbers in employment in particular sectors may simply reflect declining supply, rather than falling demand. Kirsch therefore derives a similar index number to that used to calculate the propensity of the low-skilled to be unemployed or inactive, discussed in the section titled 'Unemployment and Low Skill'. In this case, the propensity of the low-skilled to be employed in a particular sector is given by the number of low-skilled working in that sector divided by the number that would be expected to work there if workers at different skill levels are distributed evenly throughout the economy, multiplied by 100. In this way, Kirsch controls for the size of the low-skilled population.

The sectors are identified as two digit industries according to an international industrial classification (NACE, rev. 1, 1992).[10]

The results reveal a polarization of skill groups across sectors, with some sectors having a high concentration of low-skilled workers, and other sectors a low concentration. In the former category, agriculture, certain manufacturing sectors (clothing and related areas), extractive and processing industries, land-based transport activities, and some services (hotels and catering, retailing, and small repairs) stand out as consistently having the highest propensity to employ low-skilled workers, over time and across countries.

Having identified the sectors where the low-skilled are over-represented, it is also necessary to investigate how these sectors themselves are performing. If a sector where the low-skilled are over-represented is declining, then this offers an explanation for rising low-skilled unemployment, as well as offering reduced hope for the future employment prospects of the low-skilled. For example, it has been argued that the manufacturing sector historically hires many low-skilled workers, and the decline of this sector is one of the main reasons for the reduction in employment, and the growth of unemployment, amongst the low-skilled. However, as noted in the previous paragraph, some service sectors are also large employers of low-skilled workers, and if these sectors are expanding, then they may be able to offer the low-skilled work to replace the lost manufacturing jobs. Of course, another factor we have to consider is declining demand for low-skilled jobs *within* sectors, as discussed in the previous section in the skill-biased technological change debate. Even in sectors where the low-skilled are well-represented, this might be changing over time, with the propensity to hire such workers falling as technological change accelerates.

We can thus identify four possible scenarios of change in the sectors where the low-skilled are over-represented.

1. The sector is expanding, and its propensity to hire low-skilled workers is rising.
2. The sector is expanding, while its propensity to hire low-skilled workers is falling.
3. The sector is contracting, while its propensity to hire low-skilled workers is rising.
4. The sector is contracting, and its propensity to hire low-skilled workers is also falling.

---

[10] In some countries, their own industrial classification was revised during the period of interest (1985–95). A lot of work was undertaken to ensure that these were mapped onto the NACE classification as consistently as possible. At the 2-digit level used, we are reasonably confident about this consistency.

Kirsch (1999) analyses each industry in the NACE classification, in each of five of our countries (France, the Netherlands, Portugal, Sweden, and the United Kingdom). The results reveal that in each country except Portugal, the majority of the traditionally low-skilled industries in the agriculture/industry/construction sector are in situation 4. As we would expect, the prospects for low-skilled employment in this sector are not good, and the decline of these industries, as well as the reduced dependence on low-skilled labour within them, is one of the prime reasons for the rise in low-skilled unemployment. Even in the few expanding agricultural/manufacturing industries that are traditionally low-skill, in each case in France and Sweden their propensity to hire low-skilled labour is falling. The United Kingdom can offer NACE 25 (rubber, plastic products manufacture) as an example of a traditionally low-skilled manufacturing industry that is both expanding and increasingly hiring low-skilled labour (situation 1), while the Netherlands can offer NACE 20 (manufacture of wood, straw, cork, wood products), NACE 28 (fabricated-metal products manufacture, not machines), and NACE 45 (construction). These examples, however, are swamped by the negative industries in situation 4. Only Portugal of our five countries seems to be able to offer hope for low-skilled employment levels in agriculture, industry, and construction.

The situation is not quite so gloomy with respect to the service sector. In all of our countries, we notice a large number of expanding service industries, including those traditionally reliant on low-skilled labour, and some are even increasing their propensity to hire such labour. Examples of traditionally low-skill industries in such a situation (i.e. situation 1) are NACE 51 (wholesale trade), NACE 55 (hotels and restaurants), and NACE 63 (auxiliary transport activities, travel agents) in the United Kingdom; NACE 52 (retail trade and minor repairs), NACE 55 (hotels and restaurants), and NACE 64 (post, telecommunications), in the Netherlands; NACE 90 (sanitation, sewage, refuse disposal), and NACE 95 (Private households with employed persons), in France; and NACE 55 (hotels and restaurants), NACE 64 (post, telecommunications), and NACE 70 (real estate activities) in Sweden. In Portugal, all service sector industries are in this favourable situation 1. These sectors therefore represent the best opportunities for continued low-skilled employment. Their continued expansion is important, if we are not to witness further declines in low-skilled employment, and increases in unemployment amongst low-skilled individuals. It can be seen that the catering industry appears particularly important.

It should be pointed out, however, that the service sector as a whole cannot be relied upon to totally replace the low-skilled jobs lost from agriculture, industry, and construction. In each of our countries, with the exception of Portugal, there are service sector industries in situation 4 (declining industries and falling propensities to employ low-skilled labour) that offset the industries identified above as being beneficial for the low-skilled. As a whole then, it is possible that the level of job opportunities for the low-skilled in the service sector has remained approximately constant over the period 1985–95. Coupled with their observed declining opportunities throughout the manufacturing sector, these two facts together predict an increasingly harsh economy for the low-skilled.

Conclusions

Previous research on the labour market position of the low-skilled has demonstrated a fall in demand for their services, apparently due primarily to skill-biased technological change. Countries that have reduced their supply of low-skilled labour as far as possible in line with this fall in demand have fewer low-skilled workers unemployed or inactive, because there are fewer skill mismatches. The research described in this chapter has added to this literature in a number of ways. First, a great deal of attention was paid to the definition of low skills. The result was a definition based upon the ISCED classification of education, with vocational qualifications added to this skills hierarchy at the appropriate level. Using this definition of low skills allowed us to document the numbers of low-skilled workers in each country studied, and their propensity to be unemployed or inactive. The low-skills definition also allowed a more thorough analysis of labour demand by skill level, with the results again revealing the importance of skill-biased technological change. Finally, we used the low skills definition to undertake an analysis of sectoral employment opportunities for this group of workers. In Portugal, the country with the highest proportion of low-skilled workers amongst those studied, many employment opportunities still remain, with the sectors that traditionally employ low-skilled labour both increasing in size and maintaining their reliance on low-skilled labour. This therefore represents one policy approach to the issue of changing skill demands. If the majority of the labour force remains low-skilled, then employers have little choice but to continue employing low-skilled labour, and thus employment opportunities for this group of workers remain. Of course, employers adapt jobs to suit the available workforce, and so the outcome is an economy based upon low-skill low-wage production of goods and services, competing with the countries of the developing world.

The alternative approach to take in the face of skill-biased technological change and structural change in employment is to upgrade the workforce in line with the rising demand for skilled labour. This is the approach taken by the remaining countries covered by the project, although the distance travelled along this route varies across countries, Germany and Sweden having reduced the supply of low-skilled workers the most. A point may be reached where the demand and supply of skills is matched, so that there need be no structural unemployment of low-skilled workers. Until such a point is reached, however, the low-skilled remain vulnerable to unemployment, inactivity, and social exclusion. Indeed, our analyses suggest that although there are fewer low-skilled workers out of work where their number has reduced most, for those individuals who remain low-skilled, the propensity to unemployment and inactivity is actually higher in such countries.

Thus, the policy prescription to prevent high unemployment and inactivity rates, and hence social exclusion amongst those left behind with low-level skills, must be to continue to increase the skills that they hold. Much of the improvement must be amongst the young people emerging from our education systems. The period of basic compulsory education should not be primarily concerned with selection for higher levels of education. Schools need to focus more on ensuring a minimum level for all and on maintaining high levels of self-esteem during the period of compulsory education, to give young people the capabilities and the desire to continue their learning along more vocationally orientated routes, if the academic route is not appropriate. Of course, suitable, high-quality post-compulsory vocational education and training should be available for those who complete their formal education with a low level of skills. ISCED level 3 has been identified by our research as the minimum now required to be able to function successfully in the modern labour market, and thus this should be the aim of policy, for all young people who leave school without reaching higher education, to attain this level through vocational education and training (of course, allowing for subsequent access to higher education, if desired, once abilities have been taught and self-esteem gained).

This does not, however, address the problem of older workers with a low level of skills, who are already established in the labour market, and face the prospect of future marginalization, if they have not been affected already. This group are harder to reach with education and training, because they are further out of the education system. Many may have developed an aversion to learning as a result of their school experiences and the results of this are seen in the reluctance to 'go back to school' to acquire further education and training in later life. For this group, the formal adult education system fails, because it often replicates the school system and is not appealing to such low-skilled individuals already in employment. We therefore must not just provide training, but also address the low demand for training—supply does not create its own demand. To this end, learning must be provided and supported throughout life; it must not only be available in 'school' settings but outside the conventional settings, for example in the workplace and the home. New information and presentation technologies, for example via the internet, should allow learning to take place in such contexts, providing more attractive and flexible learning opportunities.

A possible exception to the skill-upgrading route is for the very low-skilled (ISCED 0/1), for whom our research suggested that labour market opportunities have declined to an extreme extent. The policy response suggested in this case, given low levels of skills presenting little on which to build, and the generally older age of most workers at this skill level, was wage subsidies to help maintain employment until the (nearby) retirement age.

In summary, therefore, a minimum learning platform should be inclusive and open to all. This is an area where policy needs to be radically rethought, since the traditional approach to education has been characterized in a number of countries by successive exclusion at different stages of education and selectivity based on performance. Making a minimum learning level applicable to all should help reduce the marginalization and exclusion that we observe.

Table 6.1 *The unemployed, by previous occupation (% of all unemployed having previously had a job)*

	BE	DK	D	EL	ES	IT	PO	UK	UE15
Males and females									
Legislators/managers	4.7	4.7	2.9	4.9	2.1	1.0	2.8	7.7	3.4
Professionals	5.5	6.6	5.8	5.5	4.8	3.6	3.3	6.4	5.3
Technicians	7.5	13.9	14.1	6.2	6.4	7.9	7.3	6.0	9.4
Clerks	13.5	15.6	11.5	13.7	9.5	8.3	13.3	14.4	11.3
Services/sales	22.0	17.9	12.7	22.7	19.4	22.3	22.3	19.7	17.9
Agriculture/fishing	1.9	—	3.0	1.9	2.4	2.4	—	1.5	2.5
Crafts/related trades	14.3	11.0	24.7	21.5	13.4	20.2	20.8	15.4	19.0
Plant/machine operatives	6.1	9.7	9.3	10.4	6.6	9.2	10.2	11.3	9.0
Elementary occupations	24.4	18.9	15.7	13.1	35.2	25.0	18.5	17.5	22.1
Armed forces	—	—	—	—	0.2	—	—	—	0.1

Table 6.1 *(continued)*

	BE	DK	D	EL	ES	IT	PO	UK	UE15
Males									
Legislators/managers	6.5	6.1	3.6	7.1	2.7	1.3	5.0	7.8	4.2
Professionals	3.4	6.7	5.8	3.5	3.9	2.4	—	6.6	5.0
Technicians	9.9	11.0	9.2	6.5	5.9	6.6	7.5	5.8	7.4
Clerks	6.5	5.2	5.4	7.0	5.2	4.4	9.3	9.3	6.2
Services/sales	13.2	10.9	5.3	17.7	10.3	16.0	11.0	13.2	10.2
Agriculture/fishing	3.9	—	2.8	2.6	3.6	3.6	—	2.3	3.1
Crafts/related trades	26.3	21.2	38.4	29.8	24.1	30.7	33.5	21.8	30.1
Plant/machine operatives	9.1	12.4	12.8	14.8	8.9	10.8	16.4	15.2	12.3
Elementary occupations	21.2	23.5	16.3	10.7	34.9	24.1	12.3	17.9	21.3
Armed forces	—	—	—	—	—	—	—	—	0.2
Females									
Legislators/managers	3.1	—	2.0	3.0	1.6	—	—	7.4	2.4
Professionals	7.1	6.5	5.8	7.2	5.5	4.9	3.4	6.0	5.7
Technicians	5.6	16.5	20.5	5.9	6.7	9.4	7.2	6.3	11.7
Clerks	19.3	24.8	19.4	19.7	13.1	12.7	16.3	23.4	17.1
Services/sales	29.3	24.3	22.3	27.1	27.2	29.2	30.8	31.5	26.7
Agriculture/fishing	—	—	3.3	—	1.4	1.2	—	—	1.8
Crafts/related trades	4.4	—	6.9	14.1	4.4	8.6	11.3	3.9	6.3
Plant/machine operatives	3.7	7.4	4.7	6.5	4.6	7.4	5.5	4.2	5.2
Elementary occupations	27.1	14.8	15.1	15.2	35.4	26.1	23.2	16.9	23.0
Armed forces	—	—	—	—	—	—	—	—	—

Source: Eurostat (2000).

Table 6.2 *Unemployment, labour force participation rates and employment/population rates by educational attainment (age 25–64), 2000*

	<Upper secondary	Upper secondary	Tertiary
Belgium			
Unemployment rate	9.8	5.3	2.7
Participation rate	56.0	79.3	87.7
Emp/pop ratio	50.5	75.1	85.3
Denmark			
Unemployment rate	6.3	3.9	2.6
Participation rate	66.7	84.2	90.8
Emp/pop ratio	62.5	80.9	88.4
France			
Unemployment rate	13.9	7.9	5.1
Participation rate	66.2	82.2	87.5
Emp/pop ratio	57.0	75.8	83.1

Table 6.2 (*continued*)

	<Upper secondary	Upper secondary	Tertiary
Germany			
Unemployment rate	13.7	7.8	4.0
Participation rate	58.6	76.3	86.9
Emp/pop ratio	50.6	70.4	83.4
Ireland			
Unemployment rate	6.8	2.5	1.9
Participation rate	60.7	75.7	86.9
Emp/pop ratio	56.6	73.8	85.2
Italy			
Unemployment rate	10.0	7.4	5.9
Participation rate	53.2	76.6	86.5
Emp/pop ratio	47.9	71.0	81.4
Netherlands			
Unemployment rate	3.5	2.1	1.8
Participation rate	61.8	81.8	88.1
Emp/pop ratio	59.6	80.1	86.5
Portugal			
Unemployment rate	3.6	3.3	2.8
Participation rate	75.8	86.7	92.9
Emp/pop ratio	73.1	83.8	90.3
Spain			
Unemployment rate	13.7	11.0	9.5
Participation rate	62.4	80.9	87.9
Emp/pop ratio	53.9	72.0	79.5
Sweden			
Unemployment rate	8.0	5.3	3.0
Participation rate	73.9	86.2	89.4
Emp/pop ratio	68.0	81.7	86.7
United Kingdom			
Unemployment rate	8.9	4.5	2.1
Participation rate	58.9	82.8	89.8
Emp/pop ratio	53.7	79.1	87.8
European Union			
Unemployment rate	10.6	6.5	4.3
Participation rate	58.8	79.6	87.9
Emp/pop ratio	53.9	74.5	84.2
United States			
Unemployment rate	7.9	3.6	1.8
Participation rate	62.7	79.5	86.5
Emp/pop ratio	57.8	76.7	85.0

Source: OECD Employment Outlook (2002).

Table 6.3 *Principal education and initial training qualifications grouped by ISCED level—France, Germany, Netherlands, Portugal, Sweden, United Kingdom*

Level	France	Germany	Netherlands	Portugal	Sweden	United Kingdom
ISCED 5/6/7	Higher degree licence BTS/DUT or equivalent	All first and higher degrees All *Meister* and *Techniker*	University, 3 years or more HBO Higher professional education	University (1st degree) Bachelor	Tertiary (post secondary) shorter and longer than 3 years	All first and higher degrees. All teaching, nursing qualifications
ISCED 3	*Baccalauréat*, BT CAP, BEP	*Abitur Fachhochschulreife* All apprenticeship passes or equivalent	VWO Pre-university ed HAVO Senior general secondary ed MBO Secondary vocational education	Intermediate courses Upper secondary Secondary (vocational)	Upper secondary education, academic and vocational programme 2–3 years	HNC/HND 1 or more A-level passes, GNVQ 3 and equivalent, NVQ 3 and equivalent Trade apprenticeship GNVQ 2 or equivalent NVQ2 or equivalent
ISCED 2	*Brevet* (all series)	Leaving certificate of the *Realschule* or equivalent Leaving certificate of the *Hauptschule*	MAVO Junior general secondary ed VBO Pre-vocational education	Lower secondary Preparatory	9-year compulsory school	1 or more O-level/GCSE passes, 1 or more CSE passes All other qualifications
ISCED 0/1	CEP, No qualifications	No qualifications	Primary education only	Primary Less than primary	Elementary school shorter than 9 years	No qualifications

Table 6.4 *The propensity of the low-skilled to be unemployed or inactive, 1996*

	Unemployment	Inactivity
Netherlands	147	163
France	138	160
Sweden	129	171
UK	126	132
Portugal	103	106

Note: The numbers refer to the propensity of the low-skilled to be unemployed or inactive, with 100 representing average propensity. See text for full details.

CHAPTER 7

Economic Redundancy: The Paradoxes of Exemplary Protection

M.-L. MORIN, B. REYNES, F. TEYSSIER, AND C. VICENS

Introduction

Throughout Europe in the second half of the twentieth century, protection against collective redundancy has been one of the linchpins of job stability within companies. Given that it is a crucial point at which the economic interests of the company confront those of employment, it has given rise in most countries to exemplary protective legislation. It was also the subject of one of the first European directives dealing with employment, that of 17 February 1975, now replaced by the directive of 20 July 1998.[1]

Given the numerical importance of job loss from atypical forms of employment, collective redundancy represents only a minority of causes of unemployment.[2] Nevertheless, redundancy regulations still

[1] Directive 75/129/CEE of 17 February 1975, modified by Dir. 92/56/CEE of 24 June 1992 and replaced by Dir.98/59/CEE of 20 July 1998, JOCE N°° L225 of 12 August 1998, p.16.

[2] It is difficult to ascertain the importance of economic redundancy in different countries due to the absence of data, and shortcomings in the national information systems. As a reason for leaving a company, economic redundancy is towards the bottom of the list—in Germany, 10 per cent of the total number of departures, 4 per cent in France for companies in the private sector with more than 10 employees. (Source: *Premières Synthèses*, Les mouvements de main d'oeuvre, 97.05, N°°20.02.) A similar result is obtained if the reason for entering unemployment is analysed, which gives 10 per cent for France as well as Italy. (Source: *Bulletin mensuel de statistiques du travail*, La Documentation Française, DARES, December 1997, N°°.12.)

provide the models of best practice. As much for the companies as for the people concerned, redundancy is the critical point when policies for internal employment and for support on the job market come together. The importance of the quality of redundancy measures has become all the greater due to the increased financial demands of shareholders, the pressures on companies resulting from increased competitiveness on world markets, and the economic and social impact of restructuring. Regulations originally devised some 15 years ago have been modified in all member countries and also within the EU statutory framework where, in the wake of the Vilvorde affair, a new directive has reinforced the community regulative edifice.[3] The economic and social importance of the issue can be judged by the intensity and liveliness of the discussions concerning the adoption of that text,[4] recalling the controversies surrounding the social modernization law in France,[5] and the debates on the reform of worker status taking place in Italy.

The aim of this chapter is to study the role of protection against economic redundancy in preventing unemployment, and especially in reducing the risks of becoming entrapped in long-term unemployment and social exclusion. To provide a picture of the nature and significance of institutional differences, we draw on comparative data from research conducted in France, Italy, Spain, and Germany[6]—where there are the important contrasts between the institutional systems.

Economic redundancy, like any job loss, is a major factor leading to vulnerability in terms of both income and social integration. Insofar as the rupture of contract is the result of company circumstances having nothing to do with the employee, it is understandable that some special protection should be put in place. However, the

---

[3] Directive 2002/14 of 11 March 2002 on a general framework concerning worker information and consultation in the Europêan Community, JOCE of 23 March 2002, L 80, p. 30.

[4] See also the fruitless consultation of social partners on the management of restructuring, by the Commission Liaisons sociales Europe, N⁰⁰.48, p. 1; N⁰⁰.52, p. 4; N⁰⁰.53, p. 1.

[5] Social modernization law N⁰⁰.2002-73 of 17 January 2002, JO of 18 January 2002; Constitutional Council Decision N⁰⁰.2001-455 DC of 12 January 2002, JO of 18 January, p. 1008 onwards.

[6] This article is based on a research report for DG XII: Licenciement Èconomique: un risque d'exclusion sociale? coordinated by LIRHE in association with EAT (Gelsenkirchen, Allemagne), IRES (Bologne, Italie) and Universitat Rovira i Virgili (Tarragona, Espagne), contract N⁰⁰.SOE-2-CT97-3054, March 2000.

consequences of redundancy for the people concerned and the risks of drifting into social exclusion also depend on the characteristics of the person and the state of the labour market. The system of regulation must not only give good general protection at the moment when the decision to make someone redundant is taken. It must also ensure that those who are most vulnerable, either due to family circumstances, age or qualifications, are not the first in line, and above all that those who are affected receive adequate job placement assistance and financial support.

To assess the way the regulations operate, it is necessary to examine the responsibilities of the various players: the employer, the employee representatives, and the public authorities with respect both to the redundancy decision and to support measures. Economic redundancy is an intricate process: throughout the proceedings, collective and individual choices are made as to the numbers of people concerned, the job categories to be targeted, the job placement or support measures to be set up, and the selection of those who will actually be obliged to leave.

A study of examples of collective redundancy, and the conditions under which legal protection or social policy measures are applied, highlights at least two paradoxes that prompt reflection as to the nature and effectiveness of existing regulations. In the first place, despite the very different legislative frameworks, our evidence showed that the actual practices concerning economic redundancy in companies are quite similar from one country to another. Why should this be the case? Obviously there is some convergent evolution of the regulations because of European directives, but one probably needs to go deeper than this to understand the similarities. The entire economic redundancy process needs to be analysed, from the initial collective decision to the actual dismissal of the individual, to determine the real responsibility of the different players and how the interactions are organized.

The second paradox is even more important. Why is it that everywhere, even though there is formally greater protection in certain systems of regulation, it is always the same categories of people who, at the end of the day, are the 'victims' of economic redundancy in the different countries? In a nutshell, these are the least-skilled employees and those with the most years of service, for whom the process of job placement is the most difficult.

What can be learned from these two paradoxes? Is the framework of procedural mechanisms governing the *collective decision* to dismiss sufficient to give *individual protection* to those concerned? What does the latter actually imply? Protection against economic redundancy must also set an example in this respect: at the crossroads between job management in the company and labour market management, it remains the place where new forms of protection can be built to ensure job security and a broader set of options can be created with respect to work life trajectories.

In the first instance we will therefore examine the protective regulations surrounding the collective decision to make people redundant and the rights which these give to those affected, and then look at the 'individualization' of this redundancy which is the crucial moment when risk factors appear. Finally, in the third part of the chapter, after examining the distinctive types of measures (financial and labour market support) given to those who are made economically redundant, the outlines of a new conception of employment protection will be presented, centred on the security of employment trajectories.

Protective Collective Regulations

As we have seen above, economic redundancy provisions have a double role in protection, the first relates to the actual decision-making process, and the second to the rights and other measures taken to guide the employees who have been laid off. The 'ethos' of this protection arises from the responsibilities entrusted to, and the interactions between, the different players both upstream and downstream of the redundancy. These interactions are within the framework of what is fundamentally a collective decision.

All countries have specific, and more strongly protective, legislation for economic redundancy, leading to special treatment for those concerned. But they differ substantially at the level of detailed provisions. So first we will analyse the laws offering protection in the different countries, in order to build up a picture of the different functional models of interactions between the players and identify their responsibilities. This will shed some light on the different ways of supporting economic redundancy and how they have evolved.

The Normative Context and the Responsibilities of the Players

Community law has created a framework common to the different member states, starting from which each national law has defined a protective mechanism as a function of its own institutions, norms, traditions, and practices. There is an unquestionable diversity that can be seen as much in the range and depth of worker protection, as in the nature and degree to which the different players are involved. Nevertheless, the comparative approach also highlights the common ground, particularly regarding the social side of company restructuring under the effect of European integration with the development of truly European industrial groups and convergent management practices. This was taken into account to some extent in 1992 at the time of the modification of the 1975 European Directive.

Comparing the legal and industrial relations systems in the four countries studied, we can theoretically identify three distinct normative models. They can be termed the 'employer liability', the 'dialectic', and the 'administrative intervention' models. These models are based on a functional characterization of the main players in the redundancy procedures, that is to say the respective roles of the employer, the workers' representatives, and the public authorities. In no country do the laws correspond exactly to one specific theoretical model, but they do highlight the fundamental choices made by each country. France can be seen as closer to the 'employer liability' model, Germany and Italy to the 'dialectic' model, and Spain to the 'administrative intervention' model.

The Employer Liability Model
The first form of employee protection is centred on the liability of the employer in the management of the workforce. The very existence and range of this liability is largely dependent on the sphere of application of the regulations covering collective redundancy. The dividing line between collective redundancy and individual redundancy represents a parameter that is common to all the normative orders. It reflects the fact that the decision to lay-off is the result of corporate management strategies, and not merely the management of a particular individual and his job.

Under the influence of European law for collective redundancies, the common feature of the normative mechanisms lies in the employer's obligation to respect specific preventive procedural rules: consultation with worker representatives and notification of the project to the appropriate public authority. In the case of individual redundancy, the guarantees given are usually quite different and arise from *a posteriori* controls by a judge as to the justification for dismissal.

But the nature of the protection linked to collective redundancy can vary according to country. What this means is that, although economic redundancy is characterized by having a motive, which is not in itself related to an inherent quality of the employee concerned, how one qualifies for it is far from uniform. Each country has its own particular definition of 'collective redundancy' based on heterogeneous criteria. This variability ends up institutionalizing national systems with different regulative strength, that exclude or modify protection as a function of thresholds (number of staff in the company and/or number of staff affected) or company circumstances (*in bonis* or in difficulty).

In the first instance the employer's responsibility lies in the decision to initiate the process of economic redundancy. This is a core issue, because it allows an assessment of the balance struck in each country between the employer's freedom of management and the protection given to employees' jobs. The limits and ways of dealing with the economic causes for redundancy differ widely according to country.

French legislation is distinctive because the law, backed up by jurisprudence, favours a precise and strict definition of the economic motives that must underlie a collective redundancy, whereas other countries allow the employer much greater freedom, (for instance citing generic causes) and thus greater flexibility (Mallet and Teyssier, 1992). Legally, this difference in approach is tangible: in France the judge has substantial control over the motives for redundancy whereas in other countries judicial control is mainly procedural and thus weaker.

All the countries studied share the same basic idea that economic redundancy must remain a measure of last resort: it is only possible to break off employment contracts when redundancy is inevitable and after all other possible solutions to keep people in employment have been exhausted. This principle underlies the second of the employer's responsibilities, namely the implementation of measures in order to avoid redundancies, or to allow employees to be placed in alternative jobs. However, the company's liability with respect to the level of involvement in the job placement of redundant staff, and the provision of support measures, vary considerably from one country to another.

French law is based on the principle that the employer is fully and solely liable. In addition to the general and prior obligation to adapt employees to the evolution in jobs and to find new jobs for individuals, there is also an obligation in the case of collective redundancy in companies with at least fifty staff, to set out a *job saving plan*[7] whose main thrust is job placement. And this obligation is not just a

---

[7] This new terminology used to designate the planned redundancy scheme derives from the social modernization law of 17 January 2002.

formal one. The plan, submitted for consultation with the staff representatives is subject to strict administrative and legal control with rigorous sanctions. Whereas French law clearly identifies the employer as the guarantor of the professional reintegration of the employees on the labour market, for other countries the employer's responsibility is less or in some instances only marginally important. In Germany, the social plan, which applies to companies with more than twenty employees, has neither the same content nor the same aims. It is limited to predicting and quantifying the financial settlement needed to compensate for the economic prejudice due to restructuring, taking into consideration the employee's chances on the labour market. Reintegration into the labour market of those affected by redundancy is the State's responsibility. In Italy, job placement of employees is entirely up to the public authorities, no planned redundancy scheme is demanded of the company, and the constraints in terms of training and job placement are minimal. Nonetheless, this removal of employer liability regarding the fate of workers made redundant is attenuated in practice, since there are financial incentives for employers who do undertake job placement. In Spain, even when the employer is legally bound to prepare a package of support measures in companies with a staff of fifty, this obligation is largely ineffective.

Finally, the third aspect of the company's social liability in preventing risk of exclusion lies in the rules governing the selection of employees to be made redundant. Most national laws define the criteria to be respected by the employer when establishing the order of departures. This selection must use objective criteria and take into account social factors in an effort to protect vulnerable workers.

Nevertheless, here again the constraints acting on the employer vary, mainly in their intensity—weak in Spain, stronger elsewhere—and according to the relative importance of the role attributed to collective negotiation. The German example is an extreme case in that staff representatives are implicated in the choice of employees to be laid off through the right to co-determination which subjects the employer's decision to the agreement of the works council.

The Dialectic Model
Consultation between top management and workers' representatives in the context of restructuring is a common denominator of all national systems. This approach is reflected in EU law, which attempts to reconcile employee protection and company adaptation. This is why the principle of social dialogue has become so important, in that it can

help facilitate changes in work organization and at the same time promote the individual and collective well-being of employees.

Consultations with employee representatives generally deal more with the social consequences of a project than with its economic justification or rationality. As a function of the various industrial relations systems, there are significant differences between national laws with respect to the time limits for consultation to take place, the rights of workers' representatives, and the nature and outcome of this consultation.

In France, the setting up of job placement measures and potentially a plan to save jobs, remains a unilateral prerogative for the employer. Consultation with staff representatives, which can take more or less time depending on the size of the collective redundancy, is aimed mainly at ameliorating these measures under the eye of the administration and, above all, of the judge.[8] This is why this country belongs by and large to the first model of 'employer liability'.

On the other hand, German redundancy protection law is mainly based on the social dialogue or dialectic model, with minimal control from outside the company. Within the co-determination procedure, an employer wishing to 'modify the company' must negotiate 'compensation benefits' with the works council. Similarly, the contents of the planned redundancy scheme are the result of negotiation and agreement between the different partners. The heart of the process is seeking agreement, and failing this, the appropriate administration may intervene, leading to an obligatory mediation process with a conciliation committee.

Italy resembles Germany in that it shares the idea that the employees' interests are better served within the framework of social negotiation, even if the organization of this encounter is more complex than in the German case. In effect, the procedure, which consists of a joint examination with the unions of the employer's restructuring project, must finish up by concluding an agreement aimed at protecting jobs through the adoption of substitute measures to avoid redundancy. These consultations are not subject to administrative control, but the assistance offered by the administration is crucial in maintaining the social dialogue needed to reach an agreement.

---

[8] This organization does not seem to be really called into question by the social modernization law of 17 January 2002, even if the latter reinforces the dialogue between labour and management especially via a better apprehension of the alternative propositions from the works committee and a right to opposition, giving access to a mediator.

In Spain, the representatives of the personnel are consulted about the reasons for redundancy and the nature of support measures. But whatever the outcome of these discussions (whether or not it leads to a collective agreement), the administration retains an important role. It is for this reason that Spain comes closest to the next model.

The Administrative Intervention Model
The role played by the administrative authority, and how much it is involved in the various aspects of the redundancy process, has been given different forms depending upon the historical period and the legislation and social practices in particular member countries. Although it has evolved a great deal, the role of the administration as a player in the restructuring process and in economic redundancies can still be analysed using a bipolar model.

At one extreme, this can be a model based on the power of administrative authorization of redundancies, which implies prior control. But this is fast disappearing. The prior authorization system has been abandoned in France. The Spanish continue to apply it, but only for collective redundancies, and in an attenuated form which depends on the outcome of consultations with the workers' representatives. In cases where a collective agreement is reached, the administration ratifies it and authorization is almost always granted. The power of authorization and in-depth control only come into their own if there is no agreement between the social partners.

At the other pole, the dominant and expanding model is that of the administration as a source of influence, relying on different resources, including financial, to exert pressure over the contents of employers' decisions and to promote the search for negotiated solutions.

In Italy, this influence is exercised through the conciliatory or mediatory role given to the administration, to encourage and facilitate dialogue between labour and management. The public authority only intervenes in the consultation process if agreement cannot be reached after the first round of talks. In addition, through its control of financial assistance, it can encourage the employer to conclude an agreement with staff representatives on job placement measures.

In France, the administration, which has the duty to ensure that the provisions relating to the consultation process and support measures are respected, has at its disposal not so much a power of constraint but rather a whole range of ways to intervene, going from issuing warnings, to counselling and negotiation, right up to wielding the important lever of public money.

Despite differences in past practice, the Germans are evolving in the same direction. Previously, the role of the administration was limited: it was merely informed and its mission consisted mainly of dealing with the arrival of redundant employees onto the labour market. However, the trend towards using public money for job placement or retraining measures is likely to allow it to have more influence upstream on the behaviour of labour and management and on the substance of the measures in the redundancy plans. This is a recent and important evolution.[9]

For these three countries, the change in the manner in which the public authorities become involved seems to go hand in hand with the search for more effective answers to the problem of facilitating the retraining of employees who are made redundant for economic reasons. These are concerned to go beyond the present exclusive reliance on financial compensation. In particular, the need for new types of policy has become particularly evident for those in a fragile situation as a result of vulnerabilities that are rooted in the way in which redundancy processes become individualized.

Individualizing Redundancy: The Setting for the Paradox?

In all the countries studied, there is a common finding: in spite of highly protective, collective legal mechanisms, especially concerning rules for selecting the employees, those most at risk are the first victims of economic redundancy. This paradox can be explained by similar company practices in all countries, that have the effect of individualizing the initially collective process of economic redundancy.

Company Outcasts: The Employees at Risk

The statistical evidence bears witness to the weak points in the protection commonly offered by economic redundancy regulations, namely that they allow employees to enter trajectories with significant

[9] The law of 1 January 1998 on the promotion of employment, has created new instruments with the aim of facilitating professional job placement of employees made redundant for economic reasons. These are 'grants for measures within the planned redundancy scheme' that the *Agence pour l'Emploi du Land* holds, under certain conditions at the disposal of companies. The employment authorities do not oblige labour and management to take these measures into the planned redundancy scheme; rather they merely offer them to the partners in the negotiation.

risks of social exclusion after the actual lay-off. Those made economically redundant in the different countries have strikingly similar individual characteristics which aggravate the difficulty of achieving reintegration.

Among these, age is a determining factor. Those made economically redundant are on average older than the average job-seeker. In France in 1993, the proportion of job seekers who were victims of economic redundancy over 55 years of age was two and half times that in the overall population of those looking for work. Moreover, recent trends are worrying, since this older group is increasing markedly, with the over fifties representing 30 per cent of those made economically redundant. This is the result of the conjunction between a workforce renewal policy and an evolution in employment policy, that restricts entry into early retirement everywhere in Europe and therefore increases even more the vulnerability to unemployment of older employees who have been made redundant (Rouyer, 2001).

Similarly, the combination of low qualifications with long periods of service in the same company makes for low employability. Witness, for example, the planned redundancy scheme announced in March 1999 by Levi Strauss (Devillechabrolle et al., 2002). Those made redundant, mainly workers with no qualifications or else a CAP (French vocational training certificate) in sewing, had joined the company for the most part when they were 15–18 years old, and had carried out the same tasks (making fly-buttonholes, or button-buttonholes) for years or even decades with no access to training.

These characteristics also explain the higher proportion of older people who are unemployed among this type of redundant employee, and their particularly unstable trajectory following economic redundancy. French statistics show that the average age of those who have been made economically redundant, and are unemployed as a result, is always higher than the average age of job-seekers signed on at the ANPE (French National Employment Office) for other reasons.[10] The proportion of economically redundant people among the long-term unemployed is high: at the end of January 1998, long-term unemployment concerned 37 per cent of those seeking a job, but almost 50 per cent of those who had been made economically redundant. Looking at very long-term unemployment (more than 3 years), 8 per cent of all job-seekers were affected but more than 13 per cent of those were made economically redundant. Studies carried out in

[10]   420 days in 1993 as against 350 (R. Baktavatsalou, 1996).

Italy provide a similar picture:[11] age (over 40) and sex (female) are the main variables which explain both a longer time interval looking for a job and a greater probability of being eliminated from the mobility list without finding one.

Despite their limitations,[12] analyses of the trajectories followed by employees after economic redundancy, illustrate very well the difficulties that accumulate for those with the most vulnerable individual characteristics. In spite of a high level of job placement,[13] the working life of those employees who do get jobs is characterized by severe precarity. Their employment trajectory is, for the most part, unstable, made up of alternating periods in and out of work, and a succession of short-term or agency contracts. The result is a lower level of income and qualification, less interest in work and a strong feeling of uncertainty for the future.

With this in mind, it is important to examine both the company practices at the root of such situations and the respective responsibility of the different parties involved in the economic redundancy.

The Source of Exclusion: The Individualization of Economic Redundancy

Despite special protective provisions for this type of redundancy, there still remain categories of employees particularly at risk and for whom reintegration is highly problematic. Yet these are precisely the type of people whom the legal mechanisms dealing with economic redundancy were designed to protect.

This situation is the result of a process of individualization of the redundancy process, that takes place during the move from the collective decision to axe jobs to the designation of the people who will go, thereby neutralizing the collective protection measures. This process, which we came across in all of the countries studied, can be explained by common considerations that translate into highly convergent practices. Three main factors combine to produce this.

The first is the conflict between on the one hand, the aim of providing legal protection for those most at risk—those supporting

[11] 'Le marché du travail en Emilie Romagne', région Emilie Romagne, 1997.

[12] Because of non-representative samples of restricted size and heterogeneous survey areas making it difficult to compare the results, especially the quantitative ones.

[13] The idea of job placement is taken here in the wider sense to mean the fact of having a job at the moment of the survey with no consideration as to the nature or length of the contract. This figure is 60 per cent in France and 75 per cent in Italy and Germany.

a family, the least-qualified, those with most years of service—and on the other, the company's interests, where the priority of future development means retaining the best employees who are most often defined as the most-qualified and the youngest. This contradiction is even more flagrant in that the resort to economic redundancies is not only made under the pressure of direct economic constraint, but arises above all from structural adjustment strategies.

The second reason comes from the desire of companies to bypass the rules that apply to collective redundancy because they are cumbersome and increase costs for the employer. And thus there is a very widespread adoption of practices designed to get round the rules by staying below the thresholds set for collective redundancies. These practices take different forms from one country to another: in Germany there is 'individual economic redundancy without restructuring the firm'; in France economic redundancies 'in small packages'.

The third reason arises from a social consensus between employers, employees, and industry representative organizations about the desirability of using mechanisms such as voluntary resignation, encouraged by compensation payments and early retirement provisions, which are the commonest ways of individualizing redundancies in the different countries.

Such negotiated departures, as found widely in Germany for example, constitute a very real by-passing of the application of the criteria for the selection of employees imposed by law. The groups of employees who are best protected against redundancy, using these criteria, are encouraged to spontaneously terminate their work contracts under a mutual agreement with the employer. There are particularly attractive offers of compensation, since these are calculated using the same criteria of age, years of service, and income bracket. Practices such as these obviously make it much more difficult to develop active measures.

The widespread use in all countries of these early retirement mechanisms permitted a gentle absorption of overmanning during company restructuring in the 1980s and 1990s, before it became a human resource management tool. The use of age as a selection criterion for redundancy compounds the effects of a sluggish labour market for the oldest workers, putting them in an invidious situation as far as re-employment is concerned.[14] There is again a general agreement on these mechanisms among all the players concerned: as much from employees and the unions, who look upon them as a recompense for

---

[14] 'Les quinquagénaires entre l'activité et la retraite', *Premières Synthèses*, DARES, October 2001, Noo.41.2. 'Le marché du travail en février 2002', in *Liaisons Sociales*, Noo.31/2002, 23.04.02, cahier joint au Noo.13632.

years of service and a chance to retire from an active working life under good financial conditions, as from the company which favours them because they largely transfer costs to the wider community and are conducive to social harmony. However, given the general trend in Europe to reduce the use of these mechanisms, in the light of their high cost in a context where there are problems financing retirement and the desire to raise the levels of employment of older workers, the question of the future of older employees is now raised in particularly sharp form.[15]

That being the case, there needs to be a major reassessment of the policies required to meet the risks of employment precarity and long-term unemployment which can push such vulnerable groups towards exclusion.

Changing Approaches to Protection

There has been a major change in the predominant character of support measures since the beginning of the 1980s. Previous to this, the so called 'passive'[16] measures could be separated into the guarantee of financial resources, on the one hand, and the provision of ways of withdrawing from the labour market (mainly pre-retirement) on the other. The excessive cost of withdrawal from the labour market, whether in financial terms or in terms of the social loss caused by premature eviction of valuable human resources, has caused these policies to be increasingly condemned and replaced by a search for measures designed to support the unemployed in their efforts to achieve economic and social reintegration. This recent evolution could be the sign of a change towards a more general model for job protection with new types of exemplary practice.

Guaranteed Resources: From Financial Compensation to Withdrawal From the Labour Market

In general, the guarantee of financial resources through unemployment insurance is an essential element in the fight against social exclusion, with unemployment insurance extended in most countries

---

[15] 'Age et emploi en 2010', *Semaine sociale* Lamy, 12 November 2001, N°°.1050.

[16] The so called 'passive' policies consider the level of employment as taken for granted. Their only objective is to fix a socially acceptable income or to reduce the number of people out of work by encouraging that active part of the population to retire.

by assistance measures. But as these mechanisms are not specific to economic redundancy we will not dwell on them here.[17] However, it is precisely because economic redundancy depends on a motive that is external to the person concerned, that there exist in every regulatory system financial measures that are specific to employees made redundant for economic reasons. These are of two major types.

In the first place they take the form of compensation for the damage caused by the loss of employment. In fact there is a double loss: on the one hand the loss of the job in itself, for which amends is made by severance pay, and on the other, the loss of income which is compensated for by unemployment benefit. For both, there exist in each country, specific measures in cases of economic redundancy.

When the employer pays severance pay, it is first and foremost to compensate for damages, but it can also fulfill the role of guaranteeing resources. The situation varies from one country to another. It is in Spain that this compensation plays the most important role, and indeed, in large companies it is the most important part of the support given to employees who are laid-off. In Germany where there is no legal severance pay as such, the main thrust of a planned redundancy scheme is to negotiate very large compensation payments. Conversely, both legal and conventional severance pay is relatively low in France and Italy.

In all countries, through different measures, employees who have suffered economic redundancy get severance pay that is higher or lasts longer than is the case where the work contract has been broken for other reasons.[18] This is linked to special mechanisms designed to cover those made economically redundant, such as the retraining convention in France, the special retraining allowances in Spain, or the mobility lists in Italy. It can also derive from the use of structural short-time work as in Germany.

The second major type of special measure for those made economically redundant is management of the labour market. The mechanisms for facilitating withdrawal from the labour market concern older workers for whom the possibilities for reintegration can be particularly difficult. These mechanisms have been and still are widely used in all countries for economic redundancies and, in a wider

[17] Other chapters in this publication and especially Chapters 5 and 8 deal with unemployment benefit policies and their conjugation with active policies for fighting social exclusion.

[18] Nevertheless, there has been noted in France, a trend towards uniformization of unemployment benefits, regardless of the type of redundancy.

context, for corporate restructuring. They are universally accepted in companies and have allowed provision of a replacement income for older employees up to the age of retirement, while at the same time giving them the possibility of withdrawing from the labour market. They have taken various forms according to the country. In Germany, those who have taken early retirement are financed by special severance pay schemes which extend up to retirement age; in France, there are special early retirement schemes financed for the most part using public money. In addition, especially in Germany and Italy, disability pensions are used as a way into early retirement.

Once again, economic redundancy is most definitely setting the example. While access to early retirement or to a disability pension is not fundamentally linked to economic redundancy, these measures have figured prominently among the tools used by public authorities to facilitate restructuring.

Nevertheless, demographic changes have raised the issue of whether there are real possibilities of maintaining 'older' employees as part of the work force.[19] This cannot be achieved simply through the protection of income. Furthermore, the cost of compensation policies, and especially those concerning early retirement, has led to the reinforcement of financial support measures by active support measures on the labour market. For example, there has been a debate in Germany which has centered around the need to go from a redundancy system based on compensation, which in effect shifts the responsibility for reintegrating redundant workers into the hands of the public authorities, to one where people are supported to remain in the workforce.

Support Measures on the Labour Market: From Job Placement to Employment Trajectory Security

Two preliminary remarks need to be made. The first concerns the evolution of the types of measures that have existed in the past. These have been principally measures, for which the employer was responsible through the 'social plan', for finding alternative

[19] Thus, in France, the Employment Minister has since 1999 appreciably limited the budget for early retirements financed within the framework of the National Employment Fund. The recent summit in Barcelona, 15–16 March 2002, by taking the decision to raise the average age of retirement to 63 years, presupposes the setting up of schemes to maintain older workers in employment.

jobs. But in France as well as in Germany (albeit in different forms) responsibility for employees in a situation of collective redundancy is also now being assumed by new support systems that are developing with the assistance of the different social actors. These are particularly interesting as they aim to ensure the security of labour market transitions.

Second, it must be emphasized that these new mechanisms are restricted to large companies and to situations of collective redundancy. In all countries, the employees of small and medium-sized companies or of firms in difficulty are in fact, if not by law, excluded from taking advantage of these support measures.[20] Employees in these firms therefore benefit only from the minimum legal protection provided in the case of redundancy due to economic circumstances. This is a major breach in the protection afforded by redundancy regulation, with its effectiveness ultimately depending on the size and means of the company. This breach becomes a paradox when one realizes the very large number of economic redundancies occurring in small companies or those in difficulty. Is it not exactly here that special protective measures should be devised?

Job Replacement Within Planned Redundancy Schemes
The European Directive of 24 June 1992 placed the examination of support measures to mitigate the consequences of redundancies at the centre of the consultative process with workers' representatives. In this way, the idea of the planned redundancy scheme made a conspicuous entry into European norms. But how has this scheme been taken on board in national laws?

In Germany, the employer has an obligation to find alternative jobs prior to a redundancy, but this becomes an issue for discussion during the consultation process on restructuring and for the negotiation leading to a compromise with the works council, which is concerned primarily with the economic impact of the redundancy. Agreement on a 'social plan' makes it possible to decide the fate of those for whom redundancy is inevitable.

The law of 1998 significantly enriched the contents of the 'social plan'. Previously it was primarily concerned with financial compensation; indeed, this was the case for the contents of more than

---

[20] There is a reservation for France in that since 1986 there exists a general mechanism of retraining agreement conventions with the proviso of employee seniority.

85 per cent of such plans in the first half of the 1990s. From 1998, the social partners could, if they so wished, ask for public money to be spent in an effort to favour external placement of employees. This model is characterized by support measures that take place while the work contract is still in place, rather than after it has been broken, which obviously increases the company's responsibility. The measures to facilitate occupational reorientation are made during the redundancy notice period, which may be quite extended (up to 6 months). The aim of granting public money to the planned redundancy scheme is to encourage partners in the negotiation to provide for active job replacement measures in addition to, or as a substitute for, severance pay. However, this policy has come up against the deeply rooted attachment of employees, unions, and works councils to financial compensation practices, slowing down the development of the active promotion of employment. Moreover, even if the company has more than twenty employees and a works council, the contents of negotiations in a planned redundancy scheme are in no way obligatory. They depend on the decision of the social partners, which determines whether or not effective use is made of grants for active measures to help employees (Kirsch and Knuth, 2001).

In France, for a collective redundancy in a company with at least fifty employees, the employer must present a 'social plan', which, following the 2002 reform, has become a scheme to save jobs, putting the accent firmly on preventing redundancies. Greater efforts and precision are now demanded of companies to maintain jobs or facilitate new job placement, whether the latter is external or internal. In particular, large companies are now obliged to contribute to the redevelopment of local labour markets and the employee can take advantage of a period of leave for retraining starting during the redundancy notice period.[21]

In Italy and Spain, to a great extent the employer's social responsibility still lies in his financial liability. The employer is not obliged to set out a planned redundancy scheme in Italy; he is encouraged, however, by financial measures to hire redundant workers from the 'mobility lists'. Finally in Spain, even if officially a planned redundancy scheme must be presented, its contents often translate into the payment of substantial compensation.

---

[21] Application decrees for the social modernization law published in the Official Journal, 5 May 2002.

*Support Measures to Boost the Security
of Employment Trajectories*
These consist of transition mechanisms offered to people who have
broken their links with their original company. Both Germany, with
its transfer companies still known as employment training companies (SPE), and France with its retraining agreement,[22] have set up
personalized support measures for the economically redundant, to
help them find another job. These schemes are particularly interesting as exemplary measures in that they represent two different types
of model: in Germany, support for redundant staff follows a
contractual model within the framework of the work contract,
whereas in France, the retraining agreement comes within the scope
of a personalized support model.

The 'within the work contract' model: Germany. In Germany, it
has been possible since 1998 to use the provisions for 'short time
working for structural reasons' within the framework of an employment training company. Those employees who are surplus to requirements have their contract transferred to an employment training
company. To replace their normal salary, they receive a short-time
working allowance, paid by the employer but reimbursed by unemployment insurance. For the duration of the contract, the employee
benefits from personalized support resembling that found in the
French retraining agreement. The new contracts are limited to a
maximum of 24 months, but the payment of a short-time working
allowance is only continued after 6 months if job placement measures (training or others) are planned.

The great advantage of this mechanism is that it maintains the
employee as a salaried worker, by transferring the work contract to
an employment promotion company over the period.[23] The fact that
'employee' status is maintained means that the entry into unemployment is delayed. This is a more advantageous transition mechanism
in the short term for those concerned. But the impact of the measure

---

[22] The retraining agreement convention has been withdrawn since 1 July 2001
because of the new unemployment insurance convention of 1 January 2001. In spite
of the disappearance of this mechanism, it is still useful to describe it briefly for two
reasons: the first is because labour and management have sought, via the employment assistance scheme (PARE), to generalize this mechanism for all those out of
work, and the second is because of the fact that the retraining agreement conventions will not be withdrawn definitively . . . and could come back into the limelight.

[23] Here, the French social modernization law, by creating job placement leave,
drew its inspiration from this experience.

has been limited by the fact that it tends to require the presence of a relatively assertive works council.

The individualized support model: the French retraining agreement. In parallel with the suppression of administrative authorization for lay-offs, retraining provisions were created, under the terms of the collective agreement between labour and management of 24 October 1986, covering all employees who had been made redundant for economic reasons with at least 2 years' length of service.

Access to this mechanism, which was triggered by a request from the employee, resulted in an immediate break in contract without notice being necessary. Under the terms of an employer/unemployment insurance agreement, the employer and the employee both contributed to financing the arrangement. The beneficiary then received increased 'unemployment' compensation payments for the duration of the retraining period (a maximum of 6 months), and had the advantage of individualized support services (evaluation of abilities, possibility of training) organized by a job centre unit (ANPE) specialized in job placement. The beneficiaries of this convention no longer had the status of employee but neither were they considered to be unemployed. Legally, they enjoyed the distinctive status of members of the retraining agreement provisions.

The advantages of this mechanism were on two levels. The first was rapidity: the employee did not need to go through a notification period, but was immediately taken in hand by the technical units for job placement. It is of fundamental importance for the job chances of those made redundant to start looking for another position without delay. The second is its general nature, since it targeted employees from all companies, small or large, and all economic redundancies whether individual or collective. The mechanism was automatically applied if the employee accepted it, and thus depended neither on the employer's goodwill nor on the existence or otherwise of staff representatives within the company, and even less on negotiations between labour and management.

However, the system had one major drawback in terms of the legal status of the person concerned; it did not allow a delay to the moment of entry into unemployment. In spite of this, the results of the retraining provisions in terms of job acquisition, taking account of duration of unemployment, have been relatively satisfactory.[24]

---

[24] On average, one member out of two finds a job 8 months after entry into the retraining agreement convention. Source: DARES, *Premières synthèses*, N°°.40.2, October 2000.

The recent trend in France has been to extend to everyone, regardless of why they are unemployed, the mechanisms hitherto reserved for those made economically redundant.[25] The new unemployment insurance convention signed in 2001, provides for all persons signed up as job-seekers, who ask for an unemployment insurance allowance, to be part of the re-employment assistance scheme (PARE). Unemployment compensation and help with re-employment are thus very closely linked in this new scheme which results in a personalized action project (PAP) and, if need be, assistance from ASSEDIC (French Association for industrial and commercial employment) concerning training, geographical mobility, etc. In theory, the employee is not obliged to sign a PARE; however, a refusal results in a progressive reduction in unemployment benefits and loss of assistance from ASSEDIC.

The implementation of these provisions nonetheless still left some measures that were distinctive to those who experienced collective redundancy. For instance, the law on social modernization has instigated retraining leave (without breaking the work contract) to ensure people's job placement. And although this mechanism only concerns large companies, for smaller firms there is the possibility of benefiting from the PARE even before the end of the notification period, which is also a way of extending the retraining agreement provisions.

Although the mechanisms of labour market support in collective redundancy provisions set a sufficiently good example to warrant their use for all the unemployed, they do not eliminate the need to develop new measures to reduce the risk factors leading to social exclusion.

Conclusion: Towards a New Conception of Employment Protection

Economic redundancy protection means specific rights for employees who have been laid-off. The risk created by the loss of employment calls for special compensatory measures. But, over and above such measures, protection against economic redundancy continues to have

---

[25] Nevertheless, it remains distinctive in that it is possible for economically redundant staff to benefit from the PARE mechanism in anticipation, during the period when they have been given notice (pre-PARE).

an exemplary function in that it constitutes the point of departure for defining new issues and for formulating new conceptions of protection of much wider relevance.

As has been seen, the trend towards the coexistence of employment protection legislation and active labour market policies tends to favour measures offering support on the labour market rather than those that guarantee financial resources and social protection. However, the elaboration of policies to prevent the risks of a downward trajectory and to ensure security for these particularly vulnerable populations should be built around two considerations. In the first place, it is necessary to combine and inter-relate active and passive measures in the best possible way, while maintaining the essential framework of agreement and social dialogue. At the same time, it essential to establish and develop support measures that are appropriate to a vulnerable or precarious target population.

Actions and Institutions Must be Complementary

The evolution of the concept of guaranteed employment, away from job stability within a company to the provision of secure labour market trajectories for individuals, underlines the necessity of having complementary measures to both guarantee financial resources and to offer support on the labour market, especially for those employees most at risk (Evans-Kloch et al. 1999a).

The need for this policy mix is underlined by the failures to achieve job placement in situations where there are only financial compensation measures, even when these are relatively generous. Yet, particularly in France, negotiations on planned redundancy schemes very often focus on the amount of the leaving bonuses that are to be added to the legal severance pay. The 'golden handshake' is very often the employee's main claim, much more than job placement measures. But, these bitterly negotiated bonuses do not provide an adequate solution. They reduce the tension and impact of a planned redundancy scheme but 'anaesthetize' employees by not stimulating them to look immediately for another job. They also allow some companies to leave job placement as entirely the responsibility of employees.[26] Recent examples of planned redundancy schemes clearly illustrate these placement failures. Thus,

---

[26] At least this is the conclusion arrived at through the analysis (DARES, Premières Synthèses, N°°.40.2, October 2000) of various planned redundancy schemes.

in the case of the Levi Strauss redundancy plan, after 11 months of unemployment, only 95 of the 536 employees made redundant have found another job (fixed-term, long-term, or interim contracts). One is forced to conclude that large payoffs are not an appropriate response to the needs of all highly vulnerable employees.

In the cases of older employees, those with poor qualifications and those with long employment service, an improvement in financial compensation could be justified given the additional risks attached to people with these characteristics: whether this be of long-term or recurrent unemployment. Indeed, in several European countries, such risks are increasingly being taken into consideration. There is a tendency to increase the duration of the compensation period and to increase the level of benefits for older workers. In the same spirit, the suppression in France of a scale of payments that reduces over time is particularly beneficial for this group.

With respect to labour market support measures, the need to take account of the specific difficulties of such groups has led to the introduction in planned redundancy schemes of special targeted measures, tailor-made for each individual, whereas previously there were only collective measures. This individualization is all the more necessary for unskilled workers, whose involvement in job placement schemes is often very weak.

But there still remains the important question of what is the most appropriate status for those made redundant during this job placement period, either the retention of a work contract with support from a company, or a special transition status between job loss and redundancy. Germany gives priority to links with a company, France only does this for the largest scale cases. For a long time Italian law prioritized the maintenance of links with a company (Cassa Intégrazione e Guadagni) before setting up a special transition status with mobility lists.

The evolution in the concept of guaranteed employment calls, in parallel, for a redefinition of the general framework in which the main players in the economic redundancy process interact. It is certain that the objectives of prevention and support of employees need a context of dialogue and joint regulation, as is suggested in European law, which roots the protection of workers involved in restructuring in the obligatory consultation with employee representatives. This recommendation would seem to us to be open to improvement through a quadripartite procedure, making it possible to balance the interests of the employer, the employees concerned by the redundancy, those who remain in the company, and the public authorities. It would then be a process in which the official staff representative bodies would play a central role. The underlying principle of an agreement between the parties under the control of a third person, would tend to favour joint responsibility between the players and greater implication in the follow-up of support measures.

Finally, there is another domain in which negotiation must have an active role and this concerns the company's territorial responsibility, with a view to minimizing the negative consequences of restructuring on the local labour market. This is less a question of compensating for the number of jobs lost and more one of creating conditions for industrial diversification and economic redeployment in the local labour market. The approximate cost of this sort of action would be less than 10 per cent of the global cost of a planned redundancy scheme. It is a matter of providing incentives for companies to do this and to increase the costs of redundancy for those who do not (Thierry, 2001). The principles underlying this type of intervention are interesting: they imply that only the joint utilization of public and private resources in a local area can provide the capacity to develop rather than to destroy. In other terms, it starts from the view that economic renewal cannot be carried out in the middle of a situation of catastrophic collapse, but rather requires advanced planning.

The Necessity to take Account of Risks of Precarity Throughout the Restructuring Process

Longitudinal analysis of the process of economic redundancy and the study of the subsequent working life of the employees has shown that the security of the trajectories people followed was built prior to the redundancy, and through the way it was handled, as much as in the support given to people once they had lost their jobs (LIRHE, 1997). To act effectively against the difficulties of reintegration of populations at risk, it is necessary to pay attention to the risks of precarity throughout the restructuring process in an effort to protect, monitor, and provide support.

First, the objective of prevention involves, above all, a concern to keep jobs. In this perspective, the principle of economic redundancy as an *ultima ratio* could be made stronger by increasing the responsibility of the employer to find alternative work within the firm. Falling back on social buffers such as short-time working must be encouraged in the sense that at the best of times they avoid, and at the worst they retard, entry into unemployment, on the understanding that this period should be used profitably to begin active measures.

Efforts aimed at prevention must next take into account the particular vulnerability of older workers to long-term exclusion from the labour market, a vulnerability that has now become accentuated by the general desire of public authorities to slow down policies of subsidized early retirement or disability. But if the reasons for this policy are well known, the question of how best to maintain these employees in jobs is a difficult one. The main obstacle is to be found in an early retirement culture that is widespread in Europe and that is backed up as much by employees' aspirations as by employer's prejudices concerning the lower productivity, resistance to change, and mobility of older staff. In this area, employment policies rapidly find their limits. Thus, the French attempts to raise the cost of making employees redundant above a certain age have generated, like all measures targeting a particular category, adverse side effects, in this case a slow-down in hiring new staff.

A comprehensive employment and work policy needs to be created around the issues of an ageing work force and the management of different age groups. It is also necessary to create regulations which favour the employment of older people by modifying the mechanisms which put obstacles in the way of continuing to work, such as the rules forbidding the concurrent drawing of work and retirement income or the mechanism giving exemption to job seeking. But maintaining older people in employment depends above all on the company's human resource management practices, which must be rethought in order to have the capacity to better adapt jobs to ageing employees. These reforms include encouraging lifelong in-service training, valuing experience which has been acquired over time and modifying the organization and conditions of work. To provide a fresh dynamic to people's careers, it is important to reward skills, to provide promotion ladders for older workers, and to ensure that there are opportunities for skill development. If it is not possible to provide opportunities for advancement, companies need to consider restructuring work posts. This is not a matter of creating special 'jobs for the old', but of initiating a policy of horizontal mobility (Bernard, 2001).

Here, the experience of the United States, where older employees constitute a labour reservoir that is increasingly in demand, is interesting. Companies there readily acknowledge the professionalism, relational qualities, low absenteeism, and company loyalty of older workers. But it is also true that the context of full-employment and of anti-discrimination legislation that effectively transforms the over forties into a protected category of personnel, have made an important contribution to this. The recent European directive on the fight against discrimination[27] and the writing into the French work regulations of the principle of equality of staff treatment, forbidding discrimination based on age,[28] should also bring about changes.

Second, in order to control the process of economic redundancy, two issues seem crucial. The first concerns the ground for redundancies and the way these are monitored. The legitimacy of the reason for economic redundancy is assessed in different ways according to the particular country and there are differences in the extensiveness of controls, even if the general trend is towards a posteriori judicial control. This has led to considerable legal debate in France. The second issue concerns monitoring of the terms of individualization of redundancies, since, this engenders many of the risks of precarity and exclusion. The same is true for other practices that end up isolating the redundant employee in their search for another job, such as the resort to individual transactions, even when linked to high severance pay, or the resort to redundancies 'in small slices'. On all these points, strong involvement of staff representatives will facilitate control.

Third, there is still a great deal to be done to further the objective of developing measures of labour market support for employees, with the aim both of correctly identifying the situations where there is a risk and improving existing mechanisms for handling these risks.

The protection of employees that have been made redundant is strongly dependent on the company's size and financial standing. The employees of small companies are clearly at a disadvantage, either because they fall outside the field of reference of the regulations on economic redundancy, or because the procedures are, either legally or in practice, simplified, or finally because the support measures just do not exist. Thus, in Germany, only 5 per cent of companies with more than twenty employees produced a planned redundancy scheme. In France, economic redundancies made under the aegis of a planned redundancy scheme account for less than 15 per cent of the total. Employees made redundant in companies in

---

[27] Directive2000/78/CE, Conseil du 27 November 2000 portant création d'un cadre général en faveur de l'égalité de traitement en matière d'emploi et de travail, *Liaisons sociales*, no.8163, 6 March 2001.
[28] Article L122-45, Code du Travail.

difficulty or receivership suffer the same inequalities, because in such a context support measures are not a priority. Re-establishing parity between the economically redundant, quite apart from considerations of social justice, should in this way contribute to a better anticipation of the risks of exclusion.

As for the support measures provided for those made economically redundant, the developments cited earlier have proved their effectiveness but also their limits. First of all, support measures must be given back their primary function which is that of finding new jobs for people, whereas very often they find themselves knowingly diverted from their original objective. This is the case with all mechanisms—SPE in Germany, retraining agreement conventions in France, mobility lists in Italy—once they concern older workers. They merely become holding solutions until retirement.

Next, the importance of the time factor in the success of job replacement efforts should not be underestimated. It is essential to set the support measures in motion as early as possible and to this end, using a period where notice is given of impending change as in Germany, seems to be particularly favourable to rapid reintegration. The duration of the support is also crucial, especially where long-term retraining is concerned. It is the youngest, most qualified, most mobile who find a placement quickest, whereas the others, older, less polyvalent, find reintegration long and difficult. All this presupposes a real investment on the part both of companies, and of the social partners, not only at the point of negotiation but also during the implementation and follow-up of the support measures.

Finally, the question of the respective contribution of each of the players remains crucial. In France, for example, voices have been raised in favour of increasing the responsibility of companies and social partners by 'moving from a means driven to a results driven way of thinking' (LIRHE, 1997). Such a recommendation is based on the view that 'we need to escape from the collective complicity of an obligation to provide resources, which always ends up more or less by negotiating payoffs for the prejudice sustained. A good planned redundancy scheme is just that, where nobody spends his days at the Job Centre (ANPE)' (LIRHE, 1997). The ways in which the public authorities intervene could also be revised in terms of greater participation. For instance, the French State intervened on several occasions concerning large restructuring projects, naming a mediator to oversee job placements and the re-industrialization of local labour markets.

Nonetheless, although the success of job placement depends on the involvement of numerous players in a facilitating role, the employee is the principal person in charge of his own destiny. Although generally agreed, this point has recently opened up a much wider and controversial debate, as to just how much the employee is liable. This can be seen particularly sharply when the public authorities or professional bodies seek to make compensation payments conditional on acceptance of support measures (training, entry into reintegration schemes, or Workfare).

The second debate concerns the adaptation of the employee to job evolution. The chances of an employee finding another job in the wake of restructuring are closely linked to the extent to which he has previously adapted to job change, since this constitutes key evidence of his capacity for professional reintegration. On these questions, the recent decision by the European Commission (15 January 2002)[29] is of interest. With the aim of launching an official consultation between social partners across Europe concerning the way in which companies and employees can anticipate and manage the social consequences of transnational restructuring, the Commission has set out a certain number of principles. Among the themes for consultation proposed is, 'the capacity for professional integration and the capacity for adaptation'. In this respect, the Commission underlines the role of training to avoid job losses, and when that is not possible, to attenuate the consequences and facilitate job change. It adds 'that it is the responsibility of each worker to actively maintain the level of his qualifications and to accept offers from his employers to develop them'. This is not really a one-sided obligation, but rather a reciprocal one, covering training and adaptation.

Economic redundancies have also probably an exemplary value on this point, not so much because protection is strengthened, but because the confrontation between the economic logic of the firm and the employment logic which it implies, is one of those moments where new forms of job security can be invented. But if the employee taken individually is thus invited to take his part, this presupposes that he can. And this is probably one of the main challenges to systems of protection from economic redundancy.

[29] *Liaisons Sociales*, 18 January 2002, N°°.13.566, Bref social, p. 1.

CHAPTER 8

The Development of Workfare within Social Activation Policies

Ivar Lødemel

Introduction

A striking feature of the 1990s was the rapid spread of social activation policies in Europe for recipients of means tested social assistance. These had major implications for the experiences of the unemployed, in particular for the long-term unemployed. This chapter is concerned with assessing the extent to which such policies have come to incorporate principles of 'workfare', in which the receipt of benefit is made conditional upon the acceptance of work. It compares the major programmes set up within different European societies, to see how similar they were and how closely they related to the type of 'workfare' experiments launched in the United States.

The development of social activation policies has to be seen in the broader context of the changing debates about welfare provision. While in earlier decades these revolved primarily around issues of spending priorities, the 1990s witnessed the development of a more fundamental challenge to welfare as a modern project. Attention shifted from debates about the level of welfare expenditure to questions about the desirability and usefulness of welfare payments (although the former contributed to the latter). This new orientation was applied to a range of welfare programmes, but was particularly focused on social assistance provision for able-bodied people who were judged to be available for work. While until recently the policy ambitions of most Western governments have been towards a reduction in overall levels of social assistance payments, selectivity and targeting within social assistance are now being restored as desirable features of welfare provision (Lødemel, 1997). Changes in the organization of working life and the threat of rising welfare expenditure in a climate of increased global competition led to a desire to make the welfare state more effective in terms of limiting spending and improving outcomes.

Nowhere was the spending reduction objective clearer than in the United States where welfare provision arrangements underwent a revolution in the mid-1990s. A cross-party consensus developed around the ambition of 'ending welfare as we know it', so that the Republican and Democrat parties only differed in the extent to which they supported the balance of measures to achieve change. In north-western Europe, support for some form of welfare provision has proved more solid, and a willingness to depart from established principles regarding rights to welfare is less evident. However, on both sides of the Atlantic a new 'wisdom' regarding the role of welfare emerged. The new wisdom asserted that traditional cash benefits fail to support a proportion of recipients in becoming self-sufficient. European and American policy-makers began to turn to new policies, which sought to improve the skills and capabilities of people who have been unable to find work, while reducing disincentives to take work (Heikkilä, 1999).

The chapter draws on research into the nature and implementation of activation in the six European countries that introduced major programmes in the 1990s—France, Denmark, Germany, the Netherlands, Norway, and the United Kingdom—as well as the programmes in the three US states of New York City, Wisconsin, and California, which are often taken as typifying the development of workfare in the United States.[1] It first addresses the question of how 'workfare' should be defined within the context of the more general development of social activation policies; it then turns to consider the development of the programmes, examining the similarities and differences in these programmes in different countries; it addresses the issue of the extent to which the introduction of workfare represents a convergence of national social assistance schemes; and finally, discusses the relative importance of policy inheritance and political

---

[1] The chapter relies heavily on research carried out under the EU-funded project 'Social integration through obligations to work. Recent European workfare initiatives and future directions'. The main publication of the research is: *An Offer You Can't Refuse. Workfare in International Perspective* (Lødemel and Trickey, eds, 2001). The author is indebted to the contributors to that volume.

choice in accounting for the similarities and differences found among national programmes.

From Passive to Active Policies

On both sides of the Atlantic, the latter part of the 1990s witnessed a shift away from 'passive' measures towards a more 'active' use of funds with a view to improving the availability of state training and experience programmes and furthering 'self-help' towards work among individual recipients. In Western Europe during the last decade, 'activation' is the key concept that describes this trend. In contrast, this term is seldom used in the United States, although US commentators talk about a move towards an 'enabling state' (e.g. Gilbert and Gilbert, 1989) to describe a similar process.

The origin of the present emphasis on 'active labour market policies' (ALMPs) in Europe has been traced to Scandinavian countries (Wilensky, 1992), and in particular, Sweden where active policies have long been used to stimulate both the demand and the supply of labour in times of economic restructuring. The rapid diffusion of active policies in recent years was facilitated by the support that they have attracted from key international organizations. In 1992, the Organization for Economic Cooperation and Development (OECD) formulated a number of recommendations for member countries to reform social and labour market policies with a view to furthering integration into work as well as into other institutions in society (OECD, 1994b). In 1995, a meeting of European ministers responsible for social welfare stressed the importance of active social policies, feeding their support for active policies into the 1995 United Nations Summit in Copenhagen. The European Union has adopted activation as the cornerstone of social policy development. In 1997 the EU Luxembourg Jobs Summit laid down three objectives: first, to guarantee training or other employability measures to unemployed individuals who had 6 months of unemployment; second, to repeat intervention with such measures after 12 months of unemployment and, finally, to increase the use of ALMP measures so that they affect at least 20 per cent of unemployed people at any one time (European Council, 1997). The Luxembourg Summit established 'Employment Guidelines', agreed annually by member states and calling for annual 'National Employment Action Plans', whereby member states report on their progress against the guidelines (European Commission, 1998a). The Amsterdam Treaty gives the European Commission powers to make recommendations to the European Council on member states' employment policies. These non-binding international policies together form the 'Luxembourg process'.

An important aspect of the new policies is an extension of their reach beyond those closest to the labour market (unemployed people with good insurance contribution records) to other groups. Policy changes were based on a perceived need to 'build bridges back to work' for out-of-work groups who could benefit from 'soft landings on the side of active society' (Larsson, 1998) and include the development of ALMPs specifically designed for such groups. The activation approach can be linked to similar approaches applied to clients within general social and rehabilitation work (Hvinden, 1999) in the sense that the aim is to help clients to change their circumstances through participation. However, typically the use of the term in the context of labour market policy is narrower, in that an 'active' labour market measure is generally specifically intended to bring individuals into work. It is important to note that, in the context of labour market policy, the term 'active' is usually understood to mean 'economically active'.

Active labour market policies, including workfare, are characterized by the use of a mixture of *incentives* and *disincentives* ('carrots' and 'sticks') to achieve desired aims. Such measures are based on the assumption that individuals respond rationally, at least in aggregate, to cues that help them to maximize their income. The use of this approach within the new policies has been described as demonstrating a 'fundamental shift in policy-makers' beliefs about 'human nature and behaviour' and 'the victory of rational choice thinking' (Le Grand, 1997).

Workfare as a Distinctive Form of Activation Policy

Workfare constitutes a specific type of activation measure (Heikkilä, 1999; Torfing, 1999). As an ideal type, it can be viewed as a form of activation policy that places particularly great emphasis on disincentives in the form of the threat of sanctions (Hvinden, 1999; Abrahamsen, 1998). At present no consensus exists regarding its definition. The use of the term varies over time and between countries (Peck, 1998) and the language of workfare is at least as hazy today as it was more than a decade ago (Standing, 1990).

There are two main reasons for this. First, it has always been a politically charged term. When it was coined during the Nixon administration in 1969, it was used to market work-based programmes as a positive alternative to the passive provision of social assistance. However, despite support for the idea of work-based programmes, the term workfare has not caught on internationally, and is now seldom used to describe policies other than by those who oppose work requirements, which they perceive to be eroding rights-based entitlement to assistance (Shragge, 1997). In Europe, the word workfare is often used by policy-makers as a foil, to explain what the new policies are *not*. Only the political Right in the United States still uses the term to describe policies that they advocate.

Second, in comparison to other social policies, workfare policies are not easily defined either in terms of their purpose (e.g. as compared to rehabilitation policies) or in terms of their target group (e.g. as compared to pension provision schemes). This lack of a clear definition has not, however, prevented the term from increasingly penetrating public and academic discourse. In the three largest US newspapers *(New York Times, Washington Post, Wall Street Journal)*, more references were made to workfare in the year 1995 than in the entire period from 1971–80 (Peck, 1998), a trend also witnessed in academic literature. Only eleven of a total of ninety articles describing workfare were published before 1990 (Social Science Citation Index). The use of the term in the academic literature reflects its ambiguity as well as the blurred boundaries between workfare and related policies.

A review of the literature reveals that a key distinction can be made between *aims-based* (Nathan, 1993; Evans, 1995; Morel, 1998) and *form-based* definitions (Walker, 1991; Wiseman, 1991; Jordan, 1996; Mead, 1997a; Shragge, 1997) of workfare. Aims-based approaches to definition tend to distinguish between programmes which are intended to be more or less overtly punitive. For example, Morel (1998) compares the French 'insertion approach' within social assistance, with a US 'workfare approach'. She suggests that the key difference is that the 'workfare approach' is concerned with a fight against dependency, whereas the insertion approach is intended to counteract social exclusion.

In this chapter, workfare is viewed as an ideal policy *form*, as opposed to a policy that results from a specific set of aims. A form-based definition facilitates investigation of how, why, and for which populations, workfare policies are used; and how and why policies vary in relation to different policy contexts. It is defined as a: 'programme or scheme that requires people to work in return for social assistance benefits'. The definition sets out an 'ideal type' programme and one that strongly diverges from the traditional social assistance contract. The definition has three elements—that workfare is *compulsory*, that workfare is *primarily about work*, and that workfare is essentially about policies tied to the *lowest tier of public income support*. Each of these three elements conditions the way social assistance is delivered. Used in combination, the introduction of work and compulsion tied to the receipt of aid represents a fundamental change in the balance between rights and obligations in the provision of assistance. Prior to the introduction of workfare social assistance was awarded as a right, although the extent of entitlement varied among the countries. In the next three sections each element is briefly discussed.

Compulsion

Previous form-based definitions have focused on compulsion as workfare's key distinguishing feature (e.g. Walker, 1991; Wiseman, 1991; Jordan, 1996; Shragge, 1997). 'Compulsory' means that non-compliance with work requirements carries the risk of loss of or reduced benefits, even if such sanctions are not automatic under the rules of a particular programme. In some cases (e.g. in Denmark), programmes are presented to social assistance recipients as a new offer, and the compulsory character is only revealed when this is not accepted. Because economic necessity often makes clients unable to reject the 'offer' of participation, it is perhaps best described as a 'throffer', combining offers and threats in one package (Steiner, 1994; Schmidtz and Goodin, 1998).

Compulsion is important for two reasons. First, it has a serious impact on the rights of those compelled, and second, it reveals an underlying assumption among policy-makers that the problem of worklessness is not merely a problem of a lack of adequate jobs. Compulsion suggests that policy-makers assume that some unemployed people choose to be dependent on assistance ('rational dependency'), or have become so distanced from the labour market that they cannot, or will not, voluntarily re-enter ('irrational dependency') (Bane and Ellwood, 1994). Compulsion is deemed necessary for at least a portion of the client group. Neither paid work in the regular labour market nor the work scheme itself are considered to offer sufficient incentives or opportunities for all target group members to make use of them as a matter of choice. According to Mead, the main argument for compulsion is that it is effective in integrating participants in the labour market (Mead, 1997a). In his view, it is therefore an essential part of the 'new paternalism', which he justifies on grounds of furthering social citizenship through imposing the duty to work (Mead, 1986, 1997*b*).

Compulsion has been the most controversial feature of workfare. Critics who otherwise support 'activating' measures challenge the justification for compulsion both on the basis of normative considerations and of the likelihood of undesirable outcomes. Benefits, it is argued, must be unconditional in order to serve their function of a residual safety net (Schmidtz and Goodin, 1998). Whereas the entitlement to a guaranteed minimum income expresses the role of welfare as a guarantee of social citizenship (Marshall, 1985), conditionality undermines this. Further, it has been argued (e.g. Grimes, 1997) that compulsion is counterproductive since it undermines consumer feedback, with the result that other people are unable to reject poor quality programmes. Moreover, voluntary programmes are likely to be more motivating and therefore yield better results in terms of integration into work. Finally, Jordan (1996) argues that, the combination of compulsion and poor quality programmes may lead to a 'culture of resistance' where participants use 'the weapons of the weak; malingering, absenteeism, defection, shoddy workmanship and sabotage' (p. 208).

The Primacy of Work

Workfare is distinguished from other compulsory schemes through its primary emphasis on work rather than training or other forms of activation. Although work and other forms of activity operate together within workfare programmes, work is the primary component and unsubsidised work the official desired outcome. The distinction between work and other kinds of activity (particularly forms of 'on-the-job' training) is obviously problematic. However, it is considered to be important because of the different implications for the risk of displacement in the regular labour market and the use of workfare to fill 'regular' jobs or to carry out 'public work'. Unlike compulsory training programmes, clients who enter workfare schemes are compelled to supply their labour in exchange for financial assistance from the state—or, in the words of Laurence Mead, to 'work off the grant' (Mead, 1997*a*, p. viii).

Workfare is a part of social assistance. In the definition adopted, workfare is tied to the receipt of social assistance. In general, the term 'social assistance' is used to refer to last-resort income support programmes, which in all seven countries have means-tested eligibility requirements (as a modern heir to previous poor law arrangements,

Lødemel, 1997). Most other form-based discussions of workfare focus on programmes tied to social assistance. The term workfare is used more uniformly by US writers than European writers, referring to programmes tied to means-tested 'welfare' benefits, especially cash-based social assistance (Shragge, 1997). However, some European commentators have tended to take a broader view and to define programmes based both on social insurance and social assistance as workfare. This reflects the different composition of *the unemployed* in Europe compared to the United States (generally a greater number of people with insurance entitlement) and follows from a focus on 'compulsion' as the key factor. For instance, Standing (1990) focuses on compulsory 'work-related activities' so that his overview of workfare programmes includes those for insured and uninsured recipients.

Programmes and Timing of Legislation

The introduction and evolution of workfare programmes in Europe has been primarily a 1990s phenomenon. However, as can be seen from the timeline in Figure 8.1 below, in some countries its antecedents can be traced considerably earlier. While the United States is often seen as the originator of workfare policies, having a history of programmes going back to the early 1970s, compulsory work-for-benefit measures also have a long history within post-1945 Europe. In Germany a provision for workfare was included in the 1961 social assistance legislation, although the policy was largely dormant until the onset of mass unemployment in the 1970s. Denmark has taken a pioneering role in the more systematic application of compulsory activation policies.

The countries that introduced workfare principles differed in the length of time over which they had adopted activation measures. In the early 1990s Norway and Denmark were leaders in the move towards ALMPs, whereas the United Kingdom and United States had relatively low levels of activation. The different levels of ALMP development in the mid-1990s may have had an effect on the role that compulsory work policies played towards the end of the decade, as consensus around the importance of ALMPs developed. The compulsory policies introduced by UK and US governments of the late-1990s were key components of the drive to a more activating approach in these countries, that lagged behind in the development

Denmark	98	**ACTIVE SOCIAL POLICY ACT—** Activation policy
France		**ANTI-EXCLUSION ACT—**TRACE programme
The Netherlands		**JOBSEEKER'S EMPLOYMENT ACT—** JEA programme
United Kingdom		New Deal for Yong People (and New Deals for others)
France	97	**JOBS FOR YOUTH ACT—***Emploi Jeunes*
United States	96	**PERSONAL RESPONSIBILITY AND WORK OPPORTUNITY RECONCILIATION ACT**
United Kingdom		*Project Work*
United Kingdom	95	**JOBSEEKERS' ACT—**Compulsory short programmes for jobseekers
Norway	93	*A-tiltak programme*
The Netherlands	92	**YOUTH EMPLOYMENT ACT—***YEA programme*
Norway	93	**SOCIAL SERVICES ACT—**Local authority workfare schemes
	91	**SOCIAL SERVICES ACT**
France	89	**SOLIDARITY JOB CONTRACTS ACT—** CES programme **MINIMUM INCOME AND INSERTION ACT—** *Insertion contracts*
United States	88	**FAMILY SUPPORT ACT—***State requirements for caseload activation*
France	84	**COLLECTIVE UTILITY WORKS ACT—** *TUC programme*
United States	81	**OMNIBUS BUDGET RECONCILIATION ACT—** *Allows CWEP programme for AFDC recipients*
Denmark	78	**LOCAL AUTHORITY EMPLOYMENT SCHEME ACT—***Employment projects*
Federal Republic	61	**SOCIAL ASSISTANCE ACT (BSHG)—** *HZA schemes* of Germany

Key: **Bold caps** = Legislative changes permitting/extending workfare; *Italics* = Extinct, or subsequently superseded, workfare programmes; Normal type = Current programmes/schemes

Figure 8.1 *Key legislative changes and policy developments a timeline for the introduction of compulsory work-for-benefit programmes in the last decades of the twentieth century.*

Source: From Lødemel and Trickey (eds) (2001), chapter 1.

of ALMPs more generally. The policies adopted in each country were certainly quite distinctive.

France

Insertion programmes and schemes operating under the Minimum Income and Insertion Act (1989). Unlike the other nations in this study, France did not have in place a general social assistance scheme prior to the introduction of *Revenu Minimum d'Insertion* (RMI) in 1989. The scheme was introduced by the Rocard socialist government after rising unemployment in the 1980s made the lack of a national safety net more apparent. The RMI has been described as a 'double right', a right to a minimum income and a right to 'insertion'. The nature of the law must be understood as a political compromise between right-wing parties, who stressed the need for compulsory participation in programmes and left-wing parties which argued that the minimum income should be unconditional. Other programmes which have developed as part of activation policy in France, but which will not be considered in the following comparison include the Solidarity Job Contracts Act (1989), and the Jobs for Youth Act (1997). These are large-scale programmes with a focus on creating work-and-training opportunities for people who are excluded from the labour market.

Germany

Help towards work policies, based on the Social Assistance Act (1961). Germany is the only nation considered here which carried over the work-requirement from the preceding Poor Law into the first modern social assistance scheme. The *Help towards work* programme has constituted a separate form of aid (rather than, as for example in Norway, a condition tied to general cash assistance) since 1961, but remained a 'sleeping clause' until the onset of mass unemployment in the 1980s. After that time, local authorities have developed two forms of programme. The *Regular Job Opportunities* programme consists of contracts which resemble those of the regular labour market, including wages (instead of benefits) and the rights which come with regular employment. The typical contract lasts for 12 months, the necessary period for establishing a right to state federally financed unemployment benefits. This creates a strong incentive for local authorities to use this type of measure to shift the financial responsibility for the unemployed to the federal government.

The *Community and Additional Work* programme differs in that participants work for benefits and do not become entitled to unemployment assistance after participation.

The Netherlands

The programme outlined in the Jobseeker's Employment Act (1998). The introduction of the Youth Employment Act (YEA) represented a paradigm shift in Dutch social protection policies away from an emphasis on protection and towards an emphasis on promoting participation. Prior to 1992 social assistance in the Netherlands had come very close to being awarded as an unconditional (guaranteed) minimum income. The shift took a new turn in 1998 when the YEA was merged with previously non-compulsory training and employment programmes for older unemployed persons to form the *Jobseeker's Employment Act*. This programme also included a larger number of opportunities for recipients. These options include subsidised work, schooling, training, and work in the voluntary sector. The discussion later in the chapter will focus on the 1998 Act.

Norway

Local schemes resulting from the Social Services Act (1991). Workfare was introduced into Norwegian social assistance with the passing of the Social Services Act in 1991. The enactment was part of a general shift from a 'social security approach' to a 'work approach' which includes both carrots and sticks designed to further employment instead of facilitating exit from the labour force. The Labour Party was the key actor in introducing this shift. In 1991, however, the party was not ready to accept a workfare component in social assistance. Instead the Labour government was overruled by a non-socialist majority in Parliament which proposed and later enacted the new regulation. Unlike the other nations, workfare in Norway can hardly be described as a programme. Instead it was introduced as an additional part of the clause which regulates the conditions that apply when awarding financial assistance. In accordance with the preamble to the Act, compulsory work should further the overarching objective of 'help towards self-help' through rehabilitation. In line with Norwegian tradition, however, the design of projects and activities was left to the local authorities.

Denmark

Programmes and schemes operating under the Active Social Policy Act (1998). Denmark preceded the other European nations by introducing the first compulsory programmes in 1990. The Youth Allowance Scheme required 18–20-year old claimants to participate in 'activation' in exchange for social assistance. This was later extended with the Active Social Policy Act, which required all social assistance claimants to participate after a set time on benefits. In line with the Danish 'active line' (which is broader than the neighbouring Norwegian approach), this programme is both universal and offers a range of defined options for participants. With the 1998 legislation Denmark was also the first nation to widen the scope of workfare by including programmes for people with few opportunities to move to the regular labour market, known as 'social activation'.

United Kingdom

The new deal programmes for 18–24-year olds. The 'New Labour' government, which came to power in 1997, introduced wide-ranging reforms of the social security system. Perhaps the greatest changes can be found in the New Deal schemes targeted at the unemployed. Prior to this time, social assistance was among the most right-based schemes anywhere, with clear entitlements and few conditions for recipients. With New Deal, participation in activities extended to all recipients of working age. While some of these programmes were provided on a voluntary basis (for single parents, the disabled, and the partners of unemployed persons), all able-bodied recipients were made subject to compulsory participation. In line with British tradition the new programmes were centralized on a national level as well as being universal in coverage. Similar to the Dutch and Danish programmes New Deal also offers a range of options for participants. The later comparative discussion in the chapter focuses on the New Deal for young people.

United States

Programmes in New York City, Wisconsin, and California resulting from the Personal Responsibility and Work Opportunity Reconciliation Act (1996). In contrast to the European nations the United States has seen a gradual transition in social assistance over the last three decades from a focus on the alleviation of need towards an emphasis on the obligations of recipients. With the legislation in 1996 the United States introduced a welfare reform which involved drastic changes for those dependent on last resort assistance from the state. While the legislation devolved responsibility from federal government to the states, it also imposed new principles which were to apply everywhere. Already, social assistance entitlement was, for the most part, restricted to families with children. With the new Temporary Assistance for Needy Families (TANF), which replaced the former Aid for Families with Dependant Children (AFDC), states may not use federal funds to provide aid to a family that includes an adult who has received benefits for more than 60 months. Moreover, entitlement can be withdrawn if people fail to comply with new requirements to participate in activities. This workfare component consists of a variety of placements and programmes, including private sector employment for wages and community service programmes in exchange for cash benefits. In the following comparison we consider only the programmes of two states (Wisconsin and California) and one city (New York).

Comparing Programmes

An examination of the principles underlying the European programmes shows that they were far from being mere replicas of the US model of workfare. Further, there were clearly marked differences between them. A key dimension of difference lay in the extent to which their strategies were orientated to rapid placement of people in jobs or to general skill development. Programmes can be classified as being more centred on Labour Market Attachment (LMA) or on Human Resource Development (HRD). This distinction is drawn from a qualitative assessment of the ideological underpinnings of programmes. A LMA-approach is closest to the ideal-type definition of workfare, and is motivated by an understanding of benefit dependency as the main obstacle to work. The emphasis is on prevention through curtailment of entitlement and the use of sanctions. By contrast, the HRD-approach is associated with a more structural understanding of lack of work. As the name suggests, it focuses more on the development of human resources and opportunities.

The strategic orientation of the programme was in turn closely related to the extent to which it was applied universally and controlled by central government. As we can see from Figure 8.2, the

Administrative framework and strategy

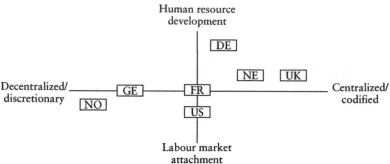

Key:
Y-axis: overall qualitative assessment of the strategy embodied by individual programmes, ranging from
'labour market attachment' to 'human resource development'.
For ease of presentation programmes are denoted by the initial letters of the country in which they operate.
This positioning should not be taken to represent the totality of compulsory work programmes within each country.
DE– 'Activation'
FR – 'RMI based Insertion'
GE – 'Help Towards Work'
NE– 'Jobseekers Employment Act' for young people
NO– Local authority based workfare schemes following the 1991 Social Assistance Act
UK– 'New Deal for Young People'.
US– State programmes following from PRWORA,

Figure 8.2 *Types of programme.*

programmes closest to the HRD approach are more centralized than
programmes closest to the LMA-approach.[2] One group of programmes
might be labelled 'European centralized programmes'—represented
here by activation (Denmark), the Jobseeker's Employment Act for
Young People (the Netherlands), and the New Deal for Young People
(United Kingdom). These are situated within the top right hand cor-
ner of the figure; they are both centralized and emphasize human
resource development. This reflects a strong funding base enabling
more resource-intensive forms of assistance.

These centralized compulsory work programmes also have a
broader target population, are more visible, and so aim to appeal to
a broader electorate. A key factor is their 'universal' rather than
'selective' status. While in these countries the taxpaying public may
accept that *some* people choose not to work, they are less likely to
accept that this is the cause of unemployment for the vast majority of
the target population. The architects of these *'European centralized
programmes'* acknowledged a wide range of 'causes' of worklessness
and, as a result, devised a broad range of strategies to deal with the
problem. The programmes have a wide range of placement options

---

[2] The figure is from Lødemel and Trickey, 2001 (chapter 9).

available, including options which emphasize 'human capital development' as well as 'labour market attachment'.

Of the three centralized European programmes, Danish activation is more integrative than the others, and places a particularly strong emphasis on human resource development. This may be due to two factors. First, the target population for the Danish activation programme is broader than for the Dutch and British programmes for young people, and includes a higher proportion of individuals who are not 'job-ready'. Second, the Danish activation programme has grown out of a rights-based voluntary scheme.

The remaining programmes are less easily grouped. The German and Norwegian programmes are similar in that they are decentralized. Nonetheless, in localities where the German Help Towards Work programme is more centralized, the programme is often more integrative, more human resource development oriented, and more formalized with regard to sanctioning policy. The most decentralized programme—Norwegian Workfare—also demonstrates the relationship between centralization and other factors. Being a decentralized, broadly preventive-oriented programme with a strong focus on labour market attachment objectives, administrators have a high degree of discretion over sanctioning policy.

The French and US programmes are notable in that they have stronger ideological roots than was the case with others. The US programmes combined a moderately centralized approach with an emphasis on preventing claims rather than integrating clients, on labour market attachment rather than human resource development, a limited range of short-term solutions, and strong sanctioning policy. The difference is certainly linked to the strong individual-focused ideology behind US welfare policy-making. In striking contrast, as a result of the Republican ideology of the architects of French social policy, French insertion policies stand out in the strength of their emphasis on the structural causes of unemployment and on the responsibility of society to solve the problem of 'worklessness'. In principle, at least, sanctioning plays a very limited role.

Workfare Programmes and Convergence of National Social Assistance Schemes?

The idea that welfare states would become more similar, or converge, as they developed was first put forward in the 1950s. Among others, Wilensky (1975) maintained that the welfare state is an integral part of modern capitalist society and that nations at similar levels of development will feature similar arrangements. Critics have argued that this assertion ignores the role of politics (see, for example, Mishra, 1977; Castles, 1981). While the importance of politics dominated academic discourse in the 1980s and early 1990s, discussions about convergence have recently returned to the centre of academic social policy discourse, in part reflecting the growing popularity of theories of globalization (Mabbet and Bolderson, 1999: 49). Heightened international competition could be seen as placing increasingly similar constraints on state welfare activity. At the same time globalization involves a more rapid diffusion of ideas between countries. These are arguably factors that underlay the widespread development of new activation policies. But did activation policies, with their emphasis on obligations as well as entitlements, also lead to greater convergence between national systems of social assistance?

Seeliger makes a distinction between two different levels of convergence. If a country adopts a policy when previously there was none, and another country had the same policy in place at $t1$, this can be described as 'nominal' convergence (Seeliger, 1996: 289). For present purposes, the introduction of workfare is viewed as a new policy, and the extent of nominal convergence is made with reference to differences between $t1$ (the early 1990s) and $t2$ (the present day) in the seven countries. In order to discuss the extent of the second form— 'qualified' convergence—it is necessary to apply 'a second set of scaled measurements' (Seeliger, 1996: 289). Our limited discussion of qualified convergence focuses on the extent to which the introduction of workfare has altered key characteristics of national social assistance schemes. We will consider first, convergence in terms of the introduction of social activation programmes and then convergence in terms of the longer-established social assistance schemes.

Convergence in the Introduction of Social Activation

The introduction of compulsory programmes in very different welfare states clearly is a sign of *nominal* convergence. At the beginning of the 1990s, only the United States and Germany had in place workfare programmes as defined here. A decade later, the five other countries discussed had introduced such programmes. During this decade policy-makers in all seven countries shifted their focus towards a greater emphasis on the obligations of the recipients of assistance.

The fact that these programmes were either introduced or greatly expanded within only one decade is also suggestive that this convergence may have resulted from a rapid diffusion of ideas across nations. Commenting on the development of social insurance, as recently as 1973, Heclo (1973: 11) concluded that: 'despite what is declared to be an accelerating rate of diffusion in technical innovation, the rate of diffusion of these social innovations appears to have changed little in the last century. Between 50 and 80 years is the likely diffusion time for all such programs'. But the intensity of legislative activity in seven nations during such a short time period suggests that globalization, resulting from economic interdependence, information technology, and the ease of travel (Midgley, 1997), has resulted in faster diffusion today than was considered possible only a few decades ago.

The starting point of the diffusion of workfare principles is usually taken to be the United States. But if diffusion from the United States has had an impact in Europe, it is likely that this influence may have been primarily in terms of the understanding of worklessness, and of the corresponding need to re-balance rights and obligations in the provision of welfare. Our main finding is that, regardless of this limited convergence in underlying principles, EU countries pursued substantially different strategies from the United States in the design of their workfare programmes. This suggests, first, that understandings of the causes of unemployment other than dependency have guided the design of programmes and, second, that cross-Atlantic diffusion has been a proliferation of *ideas* about the need to re-balance rights and obligations more than an application of *lessons learnt* from United States programmes.

The European Union and the OECD are also likely to have been important influences stimulating the diffusion of ideas on social activation particularly in the countries with 'centralized' programmes and in France. While the European Union has influenced the focus on the problem of social exclusion, the OECD and, later the European Union, have both promoted policies which combine 'carrots' and 'sticks' with the view to promote more active social and labour market policies (Lødemel and Trickey, 2001). Recent developments suggest that the influence of the European Union on policies targeted at young unemployed people in the member states is increasing. One of the objectives in the Employment Guidelines is of particular relevance: 'every unemployed young person is offered a new start before reaching six months of unemployment, in the form of training, retraining, work practice, a job or other employability measure' (European Commission, 1998a: 4). A new system of coordination (in EU documents termed 'open coordination') involves, among other things, the use of 'benchmarks' as a basis for evaluating national success in achieving the aims of the guidelines. The convergent developments found in the United Kingdom, Denmark, and the Netherlands, may be associated with those countries' efforts to achieve the aims of these guidelines. The much more active approach of the United Kingdom to EU social policy, following the change of government in 1997, suggests that the United Kingdom is now more open to participation in policy-making on a European level. Moreover, the United Kingdom has played an instrumental role in working out the tools for implementing the Employment Guidelines. The introduction of 'benchmarking' is, for example, a UK export.

Convergence in the Forms of Social Assistance Schemes?

There are two aspects inherent in all workfare programmes which are likely to have a direct impact on national social assistance schemes. These are the combination of case-work with the provision of financial aid (cash and care) and the fact that the implementation of workfare programmes is always subject to local variation. Perhaps the major distinguishing factor, when comparing social assistance schemes cross-nationally, has been the extent to which the provision of financial assistance is separated from case-work interventions (Jones, 1985). Without exception, the implementation of workfare programmes involves case-work. Whether the case-work is carried out by those who allocate the benefits or by separate agencies, cash is tied to care and, in turn, both are tied to some form of control due to the conditional nature of workfare. National social assistance schemes are also distinguished by the extent to which they are centralized or decentralized in terms of regulation. Workfare programmes, on the other hand, are implemented at the local level leading to variation resulting from local differences in programme design, in the problems addressed, and in the range of placement options available.

Workfare principles were then grafted onto very different social assistance programmes and similar workfare programmes appear to have had very different influences depending on the characteristics of the social assistance schemes to which they were attached. In practice there were three outcomes of this interaction with respect to convergence, affecting different groupings of countries. The first was *qualified* convergence, whereby social assistance schemes that were dissimilar became more similar after the introduction of workfare. The second was a situation in which social assistance schemes that were different continued to have different characteristics (*non-convergence*).

The third was where schemes that were similar became more dissimilar as a result of the introduction of workfare principles, a case of *divergent* development.

The three countries with European centralized programmes—Denmark, the Netherlands, and the United Kingdom—represent the clearest case of the introduction of workfare principles leading to 'qualified convergence' in social assistance. This resulted from their shared HRD-approach to the design of workfare programmes in a context of marked differences in their social assistance schemes prior to the introduction of workfare. Denmark and the Netherlands had in place similar social assistance schemes which were less centralized and combined cash and care to a greater extent than the UK scheme. However, the *workfare* programmes in all three of these countries are distinguished by being more centralized than elsewhere. While the New Deal is the most centralized programme of the seven countries considered here, it is more subject to local variation than the highly centralized social assistance found in the United Kingdom in the early 1990s. Convergence took the form then of centralization in Denmark and the Netherlands and a turn towards a more decentralized and cash-care multifunctional assistance scheme in the United Kingdom. This suggests that an HRD-approach *centralizes* local assistance schemes and *decentralizes* those which were highly centralized prior to the introduction of workfare.

A possible *qualified* convergence of a very different type can also be found among the two countries with the strongest LMA-approach to workfare—Norway and the United States—which had very different social assistance schemes in the early 1990s. In the United States, the AFDC scheme was centralized and the provision of cash was not generally conditioned on case-work interventions (Eardley et al., 1996a: 118). With the expansion of workfare, and accompanying changes, social assistance for workfare recipients in the United States has become both more decentralized and increasingly tied to case-work interventions. In Norway, the administration of social assistance was local and the provision of aid was cash-care multifunctional. The impact of workfare on these two aspects of social assistance was therefore limited. While the Norwegian schemes remain unchanged in respect of these two dimensions, there *is* evidence of change in the US programmes. This suggests that an LMA approach is closely linked to *decentralized* cash-care multifunctional social assistance schemes, and is likely to decentralize a previously centralized system.

The comparison of France and Germany is an example of non-convergence, despite some important similarities in the activation programmes they introduced. While the schemes in these two countries have both been described as belonging to a 'dual social assistance regime' (Gough et al., 1997: 36), Germany can be viewed as closer to a 'corporatist regime' and France to a 'Latin regime' (Lødemel and Schulte, 1992: 533–4).[3] We found that the strategy pursued within the RMI and the Hilfe zur Arbeit was similar, although the French programme had more centralized delivery than the German programme. This reflects the different degree of centralization in the overall social assistance schemes of the two nations (Lødemel and Schulte, 1992). Moreover, because both countries combined the provision of financial aid with case-work in social assistance, the introduction of workfare is not likely to have impacted on these two aspects of the French and German social assistance schemes.

Finally, perhaps the clearest sign of *divergence* in national social assistance schemes is demonstrated by the developments in Denmark and Norway. At the beginning of the 1990s social assistance in Denmark was described as belonging to a Nordic model of decentralized and residual social assistance (Lødemel, 1992). Later comparisons suggest a change towards a scheme more akin to that found in the Netherlands, for example (Bradshaw and Terum, 1997; Gough et al., 1997). The development of a European centralized programme in Denmark may therefore be a sign of a further departure from the Nordic model of social assistance.

In conclusion, the rapid spread of a new emphasis on matching entitlement to obligations in the provision of social assistance may have been facilitated by the diffusion of ideas from the United States to policy-makers in the six European countries studied. However, if we look beyond the introduction of such general principles, it is clear that the cross-Atlantic diffusion of ideas has not been matched by the import of US-style programmes in Europe. This was true even for the United Kingdom where the influence from the United States has received the greatest political and academic attention. In spite of widespread assumptions about the diffusion and the shared turnaround in the administration of social assistance, these two countries

---

[3] Gough et al. (1997) focus on the shared characteristic of a dual system whereby 'categorical assistance for specific groups are supplemented with a general safety-net' (p. 36). Lødemel and Schulte (1992) focus on two criteria—whether or not social work measures are attached to the receipt of assistance—and the degree of centralization. On this basis they find that the German system is less focused on social work and less centralized compared to France.

pursue very different strategies in their workfare programmes. Moreover, comparing the EU countries, the introduction of workfare principles clearly led to very diverse developments—increasing similarity between certain countries, but decreasing between others. Moreover, because workfare programmes target only a proportion of social assistance recipients, the changes in administration they caused may not have greatly altered the broader social assistance regimes prevalent in the mid-1990s.

Policy Inheritance Versus Political Choice in the Design of Social Activation

There has been a long-standing debate in the literature about the relative importance of policy inheritance and political choice or ideology in accounting for the form taken by 'new' social policies. In particular, policy inheritance might be expected to influence two aspects of programme development: the extent of centralization and the strategies pursued in programmes.

There are certainly countries in which an analysis in terms of policy inheritance would appear to be fruitful. The fact that the German programme was introduced much earlier than the other six programmes (1961), and that it has recently been expanded rather than introduced anew, suggests that, in Germany, policy inheritance is an important explanatory factor. Unlike Norway, where, in principle, all unemployed people have access to ALMP, access for social assistance recipients in Germany can only be secured by participants in one specific form of programme. Those selected for participation in these 'contract' programmes must remain in work for one year for a transfer to state programmes to be achieved. Because successful completion of this contract involves a substantial saving for the local authorities (because the responsibility for both benefits and training is transferred to Federal government), it is in the interests of local authorities to 'cream' participants who are closer to the labour market. As a result, we find a strong social division of programmes, first within towns which organize both contract and non-contract programmes, and, second, between those towns which have both types of programme in place and towns which only have non-contract programmes.

In Norway, the local workfare schemes represent a continuation of the history of a localized, relatively generous social assistance scheme exhibiting strong social control of recipients. The wider context of workfare has added to the importance of policy inheritance as a decisive factor. Among the seven countries, ALMP programmes were more extensive in Norway than elsewhere. The fact that recipients of social assistance were eligible to participate in labour market programmes designed for the insured impacted on workfare in two ways. First, in this situation, local authority workfare plays a residual role, selectively targeting people who are both distant from the labour market and who have failed to benefit from the opportunity to participate in ALMP or achieve entry into a tight labour market, with relatively good job opportunities for people with few skills. As a result, we can see that a 'negative social construction' of the target group has been created, which has led to an emphasis on corrective measures rather than investment through an HRD approach. This implies that, in Norway, policy inheritance is the factor structuring both the target group and the principles underlying strategy.

In spite of the high political profile surrounding the introduction of New Deal in the United Kingdom, and the fact that its introduction involves a departure from the key characteristics of pre-workfare social assistance, it is still arguable that policy inheritance, rather than politics, may offer an explanation for the strategies pursued in workfare programmes. In the words of Rose and Davis (1994) the recent development in the United Kingdom may be described as a version of policy inheritance: 'change without choice'. While the political reorientation of the UK government after 1997 cannot be ignored, and has facilitated the introduction of workfare, it is arguable that other factors better explain the strategy pursued in New Deal. Social assistance has been more centralized in the United Kingdom than in any of the other six countries. The tradition of universally applied policies (a result of centralization), the marginalization of unemployment insurance, and the poor development of ALMP have created a broad target group. This has, in turn, resulted in the development of an HRD strategy. The re-balancing of rights and obligations, however dramatic, has been contained by the fact that there is a broad risk group. The fact that the scope of ALMPs includes groups with some political weight is likely to have resulted in a more 'positive construction' of the target group.

Even in France, where ideology is sometimes thought to be a particularly important driving force, there are grounds for thinking that policy inheritance weighed heavily in the form policies actually took. For it is far from clear that the ideological aims of policy were reflected in the implementation of the programmes. The emphasis on combating social exclusion was not accompanied by any real fulfillment of the 'guarantee' of an insertion contract. This may be because the strong centralization in the provision of cash benefits has not been followed in the provision of insertion opportunities which remains a local responsibility. It may be understood as an unwillingness or inability by local departments to organize and finance programmes, and thereby meet their obligations to the state and to recipients.

However, despite the evident weight of past policy inheritance on the form taken by social activation policies in many of the countries, it is clear that it was not necessarily determinant. Denmark and the Netherlands did not fit the assumption of the dominant effect of policy inheritance. They are the countries in which political choice appears to have had the strongest impact on the strategy pursued in workfare programmes and in which policy inheritance appears to have the most limited influence. The development of activation policies represented a marked departure from previous traditions of social assistance. Policy-makers in the Netherlands and Denmark designed programmes with a strong HRD strategy in spite of their tradition of relatively decentralized social assistance schemes. Contrary to expectations from policy inheritance, the introduction of workfare in these two countries has contributed to a centralization of social assistance, at least for the target group of workfare. The departure from inheritance was particularly marked for Denmark. Unlike neighbouring Norway, in Denmark an already developed ALMP was more integrated with workfare, thereby establishing a broad risk group that led to the avoidance of a 'negative social construction' of the target group. The recent extension of programmes to also include people with little prospect of labour market integration strengthens the impression of Denmark as a country which goes beyond an emphasis on work and thereby addresses the wider problems associated with social exclusion.

The three US programmes represent a similar departure to the United Kingdom from a rights-oriented social assistance scheme with relatively low benefits, to social control with the introduction of workfare. In other aspects, the experience in these three states is exceptional in our overall findings and the departure from policy inheritance appears to be more politically motivated in the United States than is the case in the United Kingdom. There are five main reasons why this departure resulted in a LMA strategy. First, and most important, the target group is different from those found in Europe. In the European programmes single parents' participation in programmes is either voluntary, or they are not singled out as a target group at all. Although we have not pursued this aspect further, this highlights a strong trans-Atlantic difference in how single parents are viewed, and its implication adds an important gender dimension to workfare in the United States. Moreover, the workfare discourse in the United States is much more racialized than it is in Europe (Deacon, 2000). Second, the widespread assumption that dependency is the main problem of this group, rather than lack of income, work opportunities, and childcare, further strengthens the trans-Atlantic difference, and shows an ideological dimension to the political choice of an LMA strategy in workfare programmes. Third, the focus on dependency and the associated negative social construction of the target group is further facilitated by the policy context of workfare. This results both from a limited development of ALMP and from changes in other areas of social assistance. Most importantly, among these changes is the strong reduction in the coverage of General Assistance which, in most US states, excludes single workless people (the main target group in the six European programmes) from more than rudimentary entitlement to aid. Fourth, these three states have experienced a tight labour market, with job opportunities available for people with low skills. This has resulted in a relatively small-scale problem, and has strengthened an individual rather than a structural understanding of worklessness. Fifth, because the target group here are parents, the high labour market participation among mothers in two-parent households in the United States has also contributed to a negative social construction of the target groups. These factors have all facilitated a pendulum swing from entitlement to obligations rather than a re-balancing of these two aspects of the contract between the state and people in need.

In short, the relative significance of policy inheritance and political choice varied considerably between countries. The relationship between the degree of centralization, target group, and strategy suggests that, when national programmes were found to be similar in terms of strategy, they may have arrived at that point for very different reasons.

Conclusion

The research reported in this chapter made an attempt to survey a relatively unchartered area for comparative studies. Given the multiplicity of definitions in everyday usage, it was necessary to provide a working ideal-typical definition of workfare that could be the basis of a comparison between systems. Workfare was defined as a 'programme or scheme that requires people to work in return for social assistance benefits'. The 'workfare' schemes that were actually implemented in the 1990s differed substantially in the extent to which they approximated this ideal-type. The closest programmes were those implemented in the United States and in Norway. But many of the European programmes, motivated by a concern to combat social exclusion or to enhance social integration, took a much broader view of programme development, emphasizing the need to develop human resources and to provide assistance to those who were still far from ready to take up a job.

While on both sides of the Atlantic we are witnessing a redirection of welfare provision with the aim of furthering integration and inclusion, at the moment we can distinguish between two different experiments taking place. In Europe—particularly among the European centralized programmes—the experiment involves a move away from entitlement to conditional aid and, perhaps, towards a new kind of entitlement more suited to the risks and changes in modern society (Leisering and Walker, 1998). In the United States the experiment is more dramatic. By combining an end to entitlement and an accompanying emphasis on harassment rather than help, the nation goes beyond the principle of the 1834 UK Poor Law and, instead, follows the advice provided by Malthus at that time: 'if welfare is the root of exclusion, the best way to inclusion is to do away with welfare' (Malthus, 1998 [1798]).

There was little sign that workfare was leading to any overall convergence in national systems of social assistance, and certainly no convergence on a specifically US model of workfare. While there was some convergence between particular countries, there was divergence between others. There was convergence between the previously highly centralized system of the United Kingdom and the more decentralized systems of Denmark and the Netherlands as they developed models of activation that emphasized human resource development. The United States and Norway became more similar as they came to share a strategy that gave priority to 'labour market attachment' which encouraged decentralized cash-care multifunctional social assistance schemes. But in sharp contrast, the impact of the introduction of workfare principles led to a sharp divergence between Norway and Denmark which had been characterized in the past by highly decentralized social assistance provision.

It is clear that in many countries the form taken by activation policies was heavily influenced by past policy inheritance. But two EU countries in particular (Denmark and the Netherlands) did not fit these assumptions. Policy-makers in the Netherlands and Denmark designed programmes with a strong HRD strategy in spite of their traditions of relatively decentralized social assistance schemes. Contrary to expectations, the introduction of workfare in these two countries has contributed to a centralization of social assistance, at least for the target group of workfare.

It will take time, and more long-term evaluation will be necessary, before we can begin to assess the success of either experiment (Lødemel, 2002). On both sides of the Atlantic, changes in policy may contain elements of a new way to conceptualize social security as well as elements of the old. The LMA strategy can be interpreted as an 'old' form that can be assessed in traditional terms of 'less or more' (the workhouse test). However, the HRD strategy partly intends to substitute an old form of more security with a new form— based on opportunities for participation in 'social production' rather than merely opportunities to participate in consumption (by providing income). Evaluation in this case depends on the extent to which this strategy succeeds in providing individuals with the new opportunities which are needed to compensate for providing 'less' in a traditional sense.

CHAPTER 9

The Experience of Activation Policies

RIK VAN BERKEL AND IVER HORNEMANN MØLLER

Introduction

This chapter will deal with an important development taking place in the welfare states of the European Union: the gradual 'paradigm shift' in the main objectives of social policies from protection to participation (van Berkel et al., 1999; Rosanvallon, 2000). In the context of this development so-called active policies are introduced and income protection entitlements of unemployed people are made increasingly dependent on their willingness to participate in activation measures (e.g. Lødemel and Trickey, 2001; van Berkel and Hornemann Møller, 2002). The chapter will be based upon results of a research project that took place in the context of the European Union's TSER research programme. It involved six EU countries that roughly represent the various types of welfare state regimes as these have been distinguished, among others, by Esping-Andersen (1990) and Gallie and Paugam (2000). Denmark is a social-democratic welfare state, the United Kingdom a liberal welfare state, Belgium a conservative welfare state, Portugal and Spain Southern European, 'family-based' welfare states, and the Netherlands a hybrid welfare state combining social-democratic and conservative elements. The core of the project's empirical work were national case studies into various types of work in order to investigate the inclusionary and exclusionary potentials of these types of work. The underlying aim of these case studies and the project in general was to make a critical assessment of some of the assumptions often taken for granted in social policies, that is, that employment or having a regular job equals inclusion, and unemployment equals exclusion. It was the theoretical starting point of the project that the differentiation processes taking place in the world of work—both paid and unpaid work—as well as the heterogeneity and individualization of people's needs and preferences in modern society make simple, uniform policy assumptions like the ones mentioned before increasingly inadequate. These processes strengthen the discrepancies between social reality as perceived by policy-makers and social reality as experienced and lived by policy users, and contribute to the ineffectiveness of social policies in terms of combating exclusion and promoting inclusion. Against this background, we expected to find that different (sub)types of work offer people various opportunities and resources for inclusion and for meeting their needs and preferences in terms of inclusion.

Some of the case studies that were carried out in the context of the research project focused on activation programmes in the countries involved in the project, either training and education programmes (Denmark, Belgium, Portugal) or temporary or permanent subsidized employment (Denmark, Belgium, Portugal, the Netherlands; the special nature of the Spanish programme is described later). One activation scheme aimed at promoting inclusion by involving unemployed people in unpaid activities (the Netherlands). Apart from the Spanish scheme, all of them are targeted at vulnerable groups on the labour market: long-term or very long-term unemployed, low-skilled unemployed, or unemployed people in economic need (in the Portuguese case). They can involve both the insured and the uninsured unemployed, although some countries (e.g. Denmark) have slightly different programmes and policies for these groups. The subsidized employment programmes differ in various respects. Apart from temporal characteristics (the permanent or temporary nature of participation) mentioned above, they can differ with respect to the sector where subsidized jobs are created (e.g. private or public sector, social economy), the institutional context of the work environment ('regular' companies or more 'sheltered' working environments), income regulations (e.g. benefits, benefits + constructions, wage), the institutional context of programme implementation (the degree of involvement of social partners, local and community organisations etc.), the use of obligations and sanctions, etc. Put differently, the introduction of activation programmes is itself part of the process of the differentiation of work and of the creation of forms of atypical or non-standard employment (Lind and Hornemann Møller, 1999).

This chapter will deal with these activation programmes and mainly the experiences of participants in these programmes. Given the diversity between national activation schemes, precise comparison between countries of the effects of schemes is difficult. It is, however, possible to examine whether broadly similar conclusions emerge from the range of different schemes.

The chapter will discuss the following issues. First, we will deal with the question as to what degree participation in activation programmes can be said to improve the situation of unemployed people. Policy-makers are inclined to consider this question super-fluous: in their perception, it goes without saying that activation is to be preferred over unemployment. But how do the participants themselves see this? And, in the context of a multi-dimensional con-ceptualization of inclusion and exclusion, does being involved in activation programmes impact inclusion in other respects, that is, in other domains of society? Second, we will address our attention to one type of activation programmes: subsidized employment programmes for (long-term) unemployed people. Based on our case studies into this type of programmes, we will discuss the inclusion-ary and exclusionary potentials of this type of work. Finally, we will reflect on the issue of the 'residue' of unemployed people for whom the mainstream of current activation programmes is not effective because they never manage to enter these programmes or drop out from them. In our view, tackling this issue requires a reformulation of the problem: rather than focusing on the 'unem-ployability' of this 'residue', attention should be directed at the degree to which social policies manage to match people's situations and possibilities with the inclusion opportunities of (types of) work.

Activation: Does it Help the Unemployed?

In answering the question whether people participating in activation programmes are 'better off' in terms of inclusion than unemployed people, in general two approaches can be used. One approach is to compare a group of activated people with a group of unemployed people on several indicators of, in the context of this chapter, inclu-sion and exclusion. In doing this, one should, of course, keep in mind that activated people cannot be considered to be a random sample of unemployed people. Even though efforts are being strengthened to target activation at all unemployed people, selection processes occur, both at the levels of policy design and policy delivery, and in terms of self-selection. The second approach would be to do longitudinal research and compare people's situation in activation programmes with their situation as unemployed, that is, before they participated in activation programmes. Of course, here again one needs to keep in mind that the experiences of activated people cannot be generalized to all groups of unemployed people who will or might enter activation programmes in the future. The first approach, comparing a group of activated people with a group of unemployed people, was not part of the common objectives of the research project. The Danish partners, however, were able to make a comparison of a group of activated people with a group of long-term unemployed people, who are the primary target group of activation policies. The results of this comparison, presented below, can be regarded only as tentative, since the Danish case study was not designed as an attempt to 'isolate' effects of activation. That is, differences between both groups in terms of inclusion and exclusion cannot be simply interpreted as effects of participation in activation programmes, among others, because it cannot be taken for granted that the activated are a random sample of the long-term unemployed. As far as the second approach is concerned, the case studies did not involve longitudinal research of the kind mentioned above. Nevertheless, a retrospective approach is possible, since several case studies offer data on how activated people compare their experiences in activation to their situation when unemployed. We will discuss results from both approaches subsequently.

Comparing Activated and Unemployed People

The Danish partner in the project compared situations of inclusion and exclusion of a group of activated and a group of unemployed people. The activated were participating in a variety of activation schemes, both work and education oriented ones, and involved social benefit and social assistance recipients. Following the project's conceptualization of inclusion and exclusion (see van Berkel et al., 2002), the Danish team distinguished five domains of inclusion and exclusion: the domain of work, including paid and unpaid work; the domain of income and consumption; the domain of social networks; the domain of leisure; and the domain of politics. Furthermore, both 'objective' and 'subjective' indicators for inclusion and exclusion were used. To take the domain of work as an example, we were not only interested in whether or not people are participating in work, but also in their experiences with participation or non-participation in work in terms of inclusion and exclusion. We will highlight some of the results here.

First, a majority of both groups turned out to be excluded from several kinds of non-occupational work activities, that is, voluntary work, moonlighting work, helping friends, and do-it-yourself activities. A larger proportion of the activated than of the unemployed were involved in voluntary work: 22 and 12 per cent, respectively. Non-participation in non-occupational work amounted to 52 and 57 per cent, respectively. With respect to 'regular' paid work, the Danish case study focused on work attitudes. Among both groups, the researchers found a high work ethic, although there were some small differences in aspects of the work ethic considered to be of importance. Activated people were more inclined to emphasize non-monetary advantages of working (work as important for one's self-respect, work as a way to combat social isolation), whereas the unemployed more often valued work mainly as a way to earn money. Similar differences were found in answers to the question whether the respondents would work if they could receive a basic income. Activated people more often answered 'yes, certainly' to this question than the unemployed did.

A second domain of inclusion and exclusion concerns social life. Here, we will focus on social life outside work. A composite indicator for inclusion in, and exclusion from, social life was constructed, including frequency of contacts with family and friends (an 'objective' variable) and satisfaction with the social network (a 'subjective' variable). The researchers found only minor differences between the activated and the unemployed, pointing at slightly higher levels of exclusion among the latter: 18 per cent of the activated and 20 per cent of the unemployed were excluded.

Differences were somewhat larger when inclusion in, and exclusion from, the domain of income/consumption are concerned. Here, exclusion was defined in terms of a household income under a certain threshold (790 euros for singles and 1840 euros for couples) and dissatisfaction with standard of living. Using this indicator of exclusion, 9 per cent of the activated people were excluded, compared to 19 per cent of the unemployed.

The fourth domain that was distinguished was the political domain. Here, exclusion was defined in terms of passive or non-membership of certain organizations or associations, and in terms of the experience of having insufficient influence on issues that are of concern to respondents' lives. On the one hand, compared to the other domains, we find the highest levels of exclusion for both groups in the political domain. On the other hand, differences between both groups are smallest (24 per cent of the activated and 26 per cent of the unemployed are excluded).

The fifth domain concerns the domain of leisure activities. Here, only an objective measure (time spent in leisure activities) is available. Once again, there are only small differences between both groups in terms of the occurrence of exclusion from this domain. And again, the activated are slightly better off than the unemployed: of the former, 19 per cent are excluded, compared to 23 per cent of the unemployed.

When we use this approach of comparing unemployed and activated people, we have to conclude that differences between both groups are modest and that the activated people as a group are only slightly better off than the unemployed (see Table 9.1 for a summary of findings). Based on the results from this approach, and with the limitations of this comparison outlined above in mind, one could reach the tentative conclusion, that activation does not change much in people's lives. Of course, this conclusion should be interpreted in the context of the Danish welfare state and society. For example, in the case of the income/consumption domain, income improvement as a consequence of participation in activation programmes is limited, which is related to the relatively generous level of income provided by social benefits. This is very different from the situation that was found in the Portuguese case studies, where participation in activation for some people was the only way to obtain any (formal) income at all.

Table 9.1 *Exclusion from several domains, activated and unemployed people, data from Danish case studies*

Domain	Percentage of unemployed who are excluded	Percentage of activated who are excluded
Work (non-participation in non-occupational activities)	57	52
Social life (composite indicator)	20	18
Income and consumption (composite indicator)	19	9
Politics (composite indicator)	26	24
Leisure (time spent in leisure activities)	23	9

The Activated on Experiences of Activation

For all case studies into activation programmes, which involved both subsidized employment and education/training programmes, we have information on how activated people compare their current situation with the preceding period of unemployment. In general, a majority of our respondents experience their participation in activation as progress in relation to unemployment. This does not mean, however, that they are in general satisfied with their activation programme. As we will elaborate in more detail in the next section with respect to people participating in subsidized employment, there is quite some criticism among participants in subsidized employment with respect to their current status and situation as workers and with their future prospects.

With respect to income improvement, we already saw that the situation is different in different welfare states. In countries such as Denmark and the Netherlands, that provide the unemployed with relatively generous benefits, participation in activation involves modest income improvement at most. Nevertheless, the Danish study shows that effects can be different for different groups. For example, young activated people often report an improvement in their economic situation as a consequence of activation, whereas older activated people actually report that their economic situation has become worse. In contrast, in Portugal, where part of the unemployed do not receive any benefits and rely on the family or on informal income sources, income improvement as a consequence of activation can be significant and can be experienced as by far the most important effect of activation.[1]

The Spanish case study investigated a work-oriented activation programme that, in comparison with many other activation programmes in the European Union, is quite exceptional and cannot be conceived of as a subsidized employment programme in the common sense of the word. This activation programme, the Capitalization of Unemployment Benefit scheme, offers unemployed people the opportunity to capitalize their unemployment benefit entitlements and invest this money in a social economy company, of which they then become a co-owner. Compared to participants in other activation schemes, their labour-market situation seems to be less

---

[1] With the recent introduction of a General Minimum Income scheme in Portugal, income entitlements have been made conditional to participation in activation.

precarious: they often have experienced short periods of unemployment only, and for them, the relevant comparison is not so much 'in activation versus unemployment', but rather 'co-owner versus worker'. In this case, income improvement is very much dependent on the functioning of the company. Initially, many of the participants earn a smaller income than they were used to, but this may change once the company manages to become successful. But also in situations where participation in activation does not lead to significant income improvement, inclusion in the domain of income can increase due to the fact that people reach economic independence and are no longer dependent on social security agencies. Of course, this effect of activation only takes place in the programmes where participants receive a wage. In these instances, economic independence or 'earning your own income' are experienced as an increase of autonomy and status.

Respondents also mention other more non-material advantages of activation in comparison with unemployment. Many report increased self-esteem and self-respect (70 per cent of the Belgian activated respondents, 61 per cent of Danish activated respondents), although there can be significant differences in this respect between various activation schemes. These differences occur when we compare different types of activation programmes (subsidized employment versus education/training), but also when we compare various schemes within either of these types. As an example of the former, Danish participants in educational programmes reported increased self-respect more often than those in work-oriented activation schemes. As an example of the latter, the Belgian case studies into work-oriented activation schemes revealed significant differences with respect to their inclusionary potentials.

Participation in social networks is another area where respondents experienced positive effects of activation. Participants experience themselves as being part of society to a higher degree now than when they were unemployed. Positive effects of activation were also mentioned with respect to (participation in) informal social networks. For example, two-thirds of the Belgian respondents in training and subsidized work programmes reported that their social networks enlarged, and 44 per cent of the Danish activated people reported that their social life had improved. Also, it was reported that increasing self-confidence and feeling relieved from feelings of shame or marginalization related to unemployment, may positively influence peoples' social interactions with others. However, negative experiences were reported as well, for example by subsidized workers who themselves, or whose social environment, look at this type of employment as 'inferior' work. Furthermore, participation in activation may be experienced as leaving people too little time or energy (e.g. in cases where people reported health problems) to engage in social networks of family or friends. Lack of time and energy to spend time with relatives or friends as a consequence of 'over-inclusion' in the domain of work was also reported by some respondents of the Spanish case study, who, due to their commitment with and responsibility for their company, spend lots of extra hours at work, especially in the initial phase of the company. Of course, people's household situation matters here as well. Whereas in the Northern European countries many activated people live alone or are single parents, most activated respondents from Spain and Portugal lived with a partner, with or without children.

Another positive impact of activation can be seen in the realm of what we might call personal development. In various ways, respondents mentioned positive experiences in this respect. For example, a majority of the respondents from the Belgian training and work-oriented activation programmes felt more positive, were less confronted with boredom or feelings of uselessness, and felt better able to contribute to society. A majority of Danish respondents evaluate their participation in education or subsidized work positively with respect to issues such as feeling more responsible (57 per cent), having a more exciting life (67 per cent), and having new possibilities for self-expression (52 per cent). Also, 70 per cent of the Danish activated respondents reported that their skills were being better utilized; although, as we will see in the next section, this does not necessarily imply a good match between skills and jobs. Dutch respondents also felt more self-confident and assertive compared to when they were unemployed, and to have increased their functional and social skills. Part of the Spanish respondents attributed an important part of the inclusionary potential of the capitalization scheme to the fact that with acquiring the status of co-owner, they also acquired more autonomy and responsibility than they were used to having as 'regular' workers.

In sum, generally speaking most activated respondents evaluate their status as 'activated persons' positively when comparing this situation with their experiences of unemployment. At the same time, these positive evaluations have to be interpreted in the context of developments taking place in European welfare states that increasingly put pressure on the unemployed to conform to the norms of 'being independent economically' and 'being included in the labour market'.

Participation in Subsidized Employment Programmes

Subsidized employment programmes now constitute an important part of the activation programmes in practically all EU countries. In 1996, the EU countries spent 25 per cent of their activation expenses on subsidized employment programmes (Martin, 1998). In the context of these programmes, subsidized jobs or work-experience opportunities are created which are aimed at vulnerable labour-market groups, such as the long-term unemployed and the low-skilled.[2] As we pointed out before, the variety of these programmes is large.

Among the various activation programmes, subsidized employment programmes are probably the most contested. Proponents of these programmes argue that subsidized employment can be a stepping stone towards regular labour-market participation—for example, by providing work experience opportunities—or can offer permanent employment to persons who are very unlikely ever to find jobs on the regular labour market. Others are very critical about subsidized employment. Among other instances, they criticize subsidized employment for the following reasons: subsidized jobs concern 'artificial' and 'unreal' jobs; subsidized workers have a marginal position on the labour market; subsidized jobs lead to displacement and substitution effects and weaken the negotiation position of 'regular' low-paid and low-skilled workers on the labour market; and subsidized jobs may increase market inefficiency, because they interrupt people's job-search activities (e.g. Standing, 1999).

Here, we are concerned with the effects of participation in these programmes on inclusion and exclusion, rather than with their more macro-economic effects. Nevertheless, several of the arguments put forward by proponents and critics of subsidized employment programmes are reflected in the experiences of subsidized workers. In the former section we saw already that subsidized employment may provide resources and opportunities for (partial) inclusion. Of course, since the former section focused on comparing activation with unemployment, it presented a one-sided picture of activation programmes biased towards their inclusionary rather than exclusionary potentials. At the same time—and we will elaborate this in more detail in this section—these programmes may also involve serious risks for unwilling exclusion. Furthermore, whether or not participation in these

---

[2] Because of the exceptional character of the Spanish Capitalization of Unemployment Benefits scheme, we will leave this scheme aside in the discussion in this section. For more information, see Gómez, 2002.

programmes will contribute to inclusion, not only depends on the programme in question, but also on the needs and preferences of the participants themselves with respect to inclusion and (voluntary) exclusion. This leads us to the conclusion that simple statements about 'the' inclusionary or exclusionary potential of subsidized work programmes are impossible. Not only because these programmes vary considerably: subsidized employment programmes have different opportunity and risk profiles and operate in different welfare state contexts; but also because participants in them may have a variety of inclusion (and voluntary exclusion) preferences.

In terms of the inclusionary potential of subsidized employment, we already pointed at the fact that subsidized employment programmes may offer people access to an income independent from benefit transfers; or even any income at all in cases where participants are not entitled to benefits or social assistance. In some cases, subsidized employment can also provide people with some income improvement. Of course, social policies matter here: both income regulations of subsidized workers and the generosity of social security systems are important in this context. Whereas for the Portuguese respondents the remuneration they received for participation in the scheme was an important if not the most important effect of participating, only about 30 per cent of the Danish participants reported income improvement. A group of approximately similar size reported that their income situation actually deteriorated. What matters here as well, is whether participation in subsidized employment schemes is temporary or permanent. In our research we studied two examples of permanent schemes, one in the Netherlands and one in Belgium. A considerable proportion of the respondents in these case studies longed for a job on the regular labour market (72 per cent of the respondents in the Dutch case study) or for some other job (30 per cent of the respondents in the Belgian case study). Participants in these schemes reported experiences of exclusion related to their weak or marginal position in the labour market and also to a lack of income improvement opportunities. For example, in the case of the Dutch permanent scheme, participants reached the income ceiling of the scheme after 5 years of participation, on average. From then on, no income improvement is possible, not even by working overtime.[3]

---

[3] Recent adjustments of the scheme have raised the income ceiling from 120 to 130 per cent of minimum wage.

234 Rik van Berkel and Iver Hornemann Møller

The temporary or permanent character of subsidized employment programmes is an important issue in other respects as well. In the case of temporary measures, what happens after the termination of participation is, of course, vital for participants' opportunities for realizing (sustainable) inclusion. Since these schemes are designed to be stepping stones to the regular labour market, their inclusionary potential is highly dependent on the realization of regular labour market entry. When participants do not manage to enter the regular labour market, risks of marginalization and of feelings of stigmatization and exclusion increase significantly. The fear of being trapped in an 'activation recycling' process was present, especially among participants that had already been participating in other schemes. In the Belgian case study into this type of schemes, 50 per cent of the respondents had been enrolled in other activation schemes before entering the current one. And although 82 per cent of the Belgian participants in work-related activation schemes consider their activities as useful for getting a job, 80 per cent think it will be difficult to find a job in the future. Many of the respondents from the Portuguese case study reported similar experiences. Of the respondents that had finished participation in the activation scheme already when we interviewed them, 60 per cent were still unemployed. Becoming involved in a revolving 'training-go-round' process can raise problems of demoralization, loss of prospects, and stigmatization. At the same time, the Portuguese case study showed that prior labour market experiences may influence the evaluation of temporary activation schemes. For some of the respondents who had a work history characterized by a succession of bad jobs and spells of unemployment, the precariousness of the subsidized employment programmes was more acceptable.

From this point of view, one could expect that permanent schemes offer more sustainable forms of inclusion. For 'objectively', these schemes offer participants permanent employment. However, participants do not necessarily experience these permanent jobs as sustainable forms of inclusion, especially not after a prolonged period of participation. The lack of income improvement prospects is one reason for this. But other aspects are involved as well, as we shall describe later.

The former section showed that most of the respondents reported several non-material positive consequences of participation in the schemes. Participation sometimes improves inclusion in social life, and some participants also report improvement of feelings of well-being, personal development, and personal capital. However, subsidized employment schemes also involve exclusion risks in these respects. This is the case, for example, where the status of the participants is concerned. Whereas for participants in temporary schemes, status differences may be acceptable because there is—or rather, in case there is—the prospect of a regular job in the near future, status differences for permanent scheme participants may at some point become unacceptable. If this occurs, escaping marginal-ization can become an important motive to leave the subsidized employment scheme and find a regular paid job. Our case studies of permanent schemes revealed several aspects of this status issue. For example, only a minority of the Belgian respondents reported that recognition from their social environment had increased as a consequence of their participation in subsidized work. Some of the respondents from the Dutch case study told us that they decided not to inform people in their social networks about their participation in the scheme, because of the low status attributed to the programme. Participants in this scheme, who are working alongside 'regular' employees, also reported 'in-company' status differences, which were experienced as particularly unjust in cases where participants have the idea that they are doing similar tasks and share similar responsibilities as some of the regular workers. At the micro-level of social interactions with regular colleagues, a third of the respondents from the Dutch scheme report that they are confronted with condes-cending and stigmatizing comments, are treated with contempt, and asked to do tasks that are considered inferior. In both permanent schemes, participants have the experience that they are employed in jobs that offer little prospects. When they realize that opportunities of participation in the regular labour market are extremely rare, participation in subsidized employment leaves them with a feeling of resignation.

Another frequently mentioned exclusion hazard concerns the match between people's skills, abilities and ambitions on the one hand, and the characteristics of their jobs and career prospects on the other. In the Belgian case, for example, nearly half of the respond-ents reported that they were doing tasks which did not correspond to their level of qualification. This may be one of the reasons why 41 per cent of the Belgian respondents from subsidized work schemes said that they do not want to stay in their present type of job forever. The same complaint of 'under-utilization' of skills was heard by Dutch respondents. Furthermore, a majority of them were critical with respect to the degree of development offered to them in the context of the scheme. Many reported lack of opportunities to realize their participation ambitions, either in the context of the scheme or by finding regular employment. For them, subsidized employment programmes run the risk of becoming participation traps rather than stepping stones towards fuller forms of inclusion.

Thus, although subsidized employment programmes do have an inclusionary potential, many of the participants in temporary and permanent schemes also are confronted or threatened with forms of exclusion. What could be expected and is clear when we compare this and the former section, is that the picture looks more positive when subsidized workers are asked to compare their situation with their former situation of being unemployed, than when they use 'regular' workers or their own perceptions of their skills, ambitions, abilities, etc., as point of reference.

Partly, aspects of marginalization and stigmatization are institutionalized in the design of subsidized employment schemes. Partly, they are a consequence of the delivery of these schemes, that sometimes seem to be oriented at realizing placements in the short term ('plug-and-play' as one of the respondents called it), rather than at offering opportunities and support for more long-term, sustainable activation and inclusion processes. Partly, they are the result of personnel policies of the companies for whom subsidized workers are working. These companies sometimes hardly invest in people's human capital, for example, by offering subsidized workers opportunities to enlarge their skills or by supporting them to find a regular job. Both Dutch and Portuguese respondents reported that once they were placed in the scheme, no one seemed to care for them anymore: policy deliverers have 'scored' by realizing a 'successful' placement, companies have managed to hire cheap labour, and the experiences of the subsidized workers with the programme do not really seem to matter.

The 'Residual'

Up until now, our attention has been focused on participants of activation programmes, that is, the unemployed who are targeted and actually reached by these programmes, manage to enter them and are considered to be, from an institutional point of view, the successfully activated. Activation targets of the EU countries have become more and more ambitious over the years. Ever larger proportions of the unemployed population have become target groups of activation policies and programmes. In order to realize these ambitions, activation programmes have become more differentiated, and procedures of 'profiling' clients have become more ingenious. The differentiation of activation programmes often takes the form of a 'participation hierarchy' of activation measures that are targeted at groups with various 'labour market distances' or levels of 'employability', and often includes mediation to regular jobs, education, work-experience programmes, temporary subsidized work, permanent subsidized work, and, though exceptional, voluntary work.

In a way, enlarging target groups of activation, programme differentiation, and developing expert systems for refining the assessment of potential programme participants can be seen as attempts to reduce the 'residual' of unemployed who are non-activated or not able to be activated. Partly, the production of residual groups is the effect of the definition of target groups of activation as such, which always leads to the inclusion of some and the exclusion of others (e.g. groups of sick and disabled people, single mothers with young children, etc.). Partly, it is the consequence of creaming off processes taking place during policy implementation and delivery, which includes some parts of the policy target groups and excludes others. That is, for parts of the target groups of activation, activation programmes reproduce exclusion rather than combat it.

There is reason to assume that the emphasis on activation in the EU countries, and the ever larger ambitions EU countries have in this respect, will decrease the first type of exclusion from activation (more and more groups are 'formally' treated as activation's target groups) but will increasingly confront society with the consequences of processes of creaming and the production of residual groups of people who do not manage to enter these programmes, drop out from them, or are considered 'unfit' for activation at the policy delivery level. It is not uncommon for these exclusionary effects of activation to be interpreted in terms of the 'non-employability' of certain parts of policy target groups. Eventually, this may result in a situation in which these groups are excluded from activation on a more or less permanent basis.

Insofar as this scenario implies that, eventually, society will leave groups of unemployed people to their own devices when it comes to realizing forms of participation to prevent exclusion, this may certainly be regarded as a negative scenario. It often implies a 'blaming the victim' perspective: 'personal characteristics' of these groups prevent them from taking part in the resources society offers them for inclusion. However, elements of a more positive scenario can be observed as well. In the context of employment, anti-exclusion or anti-poverty policies, several EU countries are developing initiatives targeted at 'residual groups' or, formulated in a less stigmatizing way, at society's most vulnerable groups. Here, we refer to initiatives that recognize policy design and delivery itself as a crucial factor in excluding parts of policy target groups from activation and in producing a group of 'residuals'. Not the unemployability of these groups of clients, but the activation offers and the activation process are identified as the core issues in explaining the ineffectiveness of activation for groups of clients. Traditional, mainstream social policies are criticized for being top-down oriented: policy-makers determine what problems policy clients are confronted with and what solutions are desirable and feasible; policy-makers develop activation offers without taking notice of policy clients' situation, needs, possibilities and perceptions on problems and solutions; policy-makers treat clients as objects rather than subjects of activation processes; policy-makers see clients as 'calculating citizens' whose behaviour can be fully explained in terms of behaviourist principles and can be influenced by rewards and punishments.

From a more general point of view, these initiatives to combat the most severe problems of exclusion or, put differently, to develop responses to the failures of traditional social policies, can be seen as attempts and experiments to transform what we have elsewhere called orthodox policy approaches into reflexive policy approaches (see van Berkel and Hornemann Møller, 2002, Chapter 10). This transformation process can be seen as an attempt to deal with the implications of processes of modernization in society for social policies (e.g. Leisering and Leibfried, 1999).

The orthodox policy approach is based on a more tough and strict application of policy orientations that have characterized social policies for much of their history: labourism, that is, a fixation on labour market participation, and paternalism, that is, top-down defined means and objectives of social interventions (Standing, 1999). In this perspective, social policies should aim at getting people from benefits into employment. Target groups of social policies are objects rather than subjects of these policies: they have to conform to top-down and uniformly defined notions of 'good citizenship' and will be sanctioned when they do not. In order to reach this objective, income entitlements of the unemployed are made increasingly conditional upon their efforts to enhance their employability and to become independent from welfare state transfers. People's own participation strategies, which may partly be directed at coping with unemployment and risks of exclusion and can involve, for example, participation in unpaid work or paid and unpaid informal work, are ignored or counteracted.

In reflexive social policies, inclusion and participation are understood in a broader sense than employment only; in the same way, exclusion is not treated as synonymous to unemployment (or welfare-state dependency). They do not focus on problems of unemployment and welfare state dependency only or predominantly, but also focus on other problems, such as housing, poverty, physical and psychological health, social isolation, addiction, etc. Reducing the situation of vulnerable groups in society to problems of unemployment and welfare-state dependency is seen as one of the examples of growing disparities between policy-makers' perceptions of the life world of policy target groups and the way these people perceive and experience their own situation. Contrary to the labourist orientation of orthodox policies, reflexive policies operate broader concepts of inclusion, work and participation, and concentrate on matching resources of various types of work with the inclusion (and, for that matter, wanted exclusion) preferences of policy clients. Furthermore, they are based on empowering and enabling policy approaches, oriented towards enlarging people's self-confidence, autonomy and independence, rather than on enforcement, paternalism, and discipline. Whereas orthodox approaches see policy clients either as calculating or incompetent, reflexive social policies take the competence and autonomy of clients as starting points. The relationship between the state and its citizens or, in this context, target groups of social policies, is based on reciprocal adequacy (Valkenburg and Lind, 2002). In other words, processes of determining the problems that clients of social policies are confronted with, and of finding solutions that are adequate in their individual contexts, is seen as a negotiation process in which clients and professionals work towards an agreement about the nature and direction of policy intervention. In Scheme 9.1, we summarize some characteristics of these approaches.

Of course, the reality of current social policies is more complex than this rather stereotypical juxtaposition of policy approaches captures. The point we would like to make here is, that even though the orthodox consensus is dominant in present-day social policies, we are witnessing developments that can be interpreted as potential moves towards more reflexive social policies. The initiatives we mentioned before function as breeding grounds where experiments take place with new policy approaches and new interventions aimed at inclusion. They are 'tolerated' by the policy orthodoxy because

Scheme 9.1 *The orthodox consensus versus reflexive social policies approach of some central social policy issues.*

	Orthodox consensus	Reflexive social policies
Dealing with clients	Clients are incompetent or calculating. Heterogeneity of clients is relevant insofar as it influences employability and selection processes with respect to activation offers	Clients are competent and autonomous. Heterogeneity is relevant for the definition of the problems to be solved by policy interventions and for determining their objectives
Dealing with differentiation of work/participation	Mainly relevant as far as employment is concerned; employability determines where in the participation hierarchy individual placements take place	Relevant for the variety of resources different types of paid and unpaid work/participation give access to
Main objective of policy interventions	Matching employability of clients with the corresponding position on the participation hierarchy	Matching individual needs and preferences with resources offered by types of work and participation
Characteristics of policy interventions	Paternalistic or enforcing: rights and obligations are predefined and hardly subject to negotiation	Rights and obligations are negotiable and subject to a process of 'mutual adequacy'
Linking participation and income	Income improvement through labour-market participation; welfare state transfers conditional upon participation in activation	Alternative ways of income improvement, unconditional (income as a basic citizens' right), or conditional (income as a reward for participation and contributing to society)
Informal, non-labourist inclusion strategies	Neglected or counteracted (penalized or criminalized)	Recognition and facilitation

mainstream policies are unable to tackle the problems of the most vulnerable. At the same time, we can see processes in which mainstream policies are 'adopting' elements of these initiatives. For example, concepts such as 'tailor-made' policy interventions, focusing on clients' capacities, competencies and skills instead of deficiencies, decompartmentalization and networking, client-centred approaches of activation, etc., have become part and parcel of mainstream social policy rhetoric. Of course, adopting fashionable rhetoric is evidently something quite different from transforming policy practices accordingly. Nevertheless, active social policies gradually become more hybrid, mixing elements of the two policy approaches distinguished above.

Conclusions

In this chapter, we have tried to interpret the results of our international research project in the light of three questions. First, we have analysed what our data can say about the inclusionary potential of activation: does activation have to offer anything to the unemployed? After comparing a group of unemployed and a group of activated people, we concluded that there were only small differences between both groups in terms of their inclusion in, or exclusion from, several domains of society, indicating that the inclusionary effect of activation is modest. However, when we look at the stories activated people tell us about their activation and experiences of participation in activation programmes, the effects of activation seem to be more significant, at least for most of the respondents. Nevertheless, stating that many respondents of our case studies feel better off in activation than in unemployment is not the entire story. This became clear when we looked at the second question. There we investigated the inclusionary and exclusionary potentials of subsidized employment programmes. We concluded that besides the fact that these programmes do offer unemployed people resources that can help them realize forms of inclusion they strive for, they may also confront them with (unwanted) exclusion. Many respondents in our case studies reported experiences that can be interpreted in terms of marginalization. On the one hand, they are no longer unemployed, which many of them consider as an improvement of their situation. On the other, they lack resources to achieve more full or sustainable forms of inclusion, either in the context of the activation scheme or by finding regular employment. Third, we discussed the issue of the 'residue': people who do not manage (or are not allowed) to enter activation schemes or drop out of them. In our view, the increasing emphasis on, and ambitions regarding, activation will increase the visibility and importance of this problem. A negative scenario could be, that the most vulnerable will be stigmatized as unemployable and left to their own devices where inclusion is concerned. A more positive scenario is that room is created to experiment with new policy approaches aimed at inclusion, which are client centred, give clients voice and choice in defining exclusion problems and inclusion options, aim at matching resources and needs, and are based on broader concepts of inclusion, work, and participation. Current initiatives in this field and their characteristics were analysed as breeding grounds for potential alternatives for mainstream activation policies.

CHAPTER 10

Policy Responses to Marginalization: The Changing Role of the EU

Iain Begg

A social dimension to European integration has long been on the agenda, yet has been slow to emerge and has had to confront sustained resistance from many, if not all, Member States. The reasons are not hard to identify. First, social policy and its institutions are sensitive matters that reflect accommodations painfully reached at national level, and recent welfare reforms that have proceeded at differing paces and in different directions. Second, any suggestion that the European Union should acquire a role in re-distributive policy is anathema to member governments concerned to prevent further 'mission creep' by EU institutions against a backdrop of charges that these institutions are poorly administered. Third, whereas economic integration can, largely, be justified on the grounds that there are resulting gains in the economic efficiency needed as a response to increasingly open markets, the normative and political foundations for a Europeanization of social policy remain to be built. 'Positive' integration (the tying together of social models and distributive aims), as Tinbergen (1954) identified so long ago, is more complicated than the 'negative' integration implicit in reducing the barriers to free movement of goods, services, and factors of production. In particular, it can be argued that cross-border solidarity does

This chapter draws extensively on work produced by the EXSPRO project, funded under the European Commission's *Targeted Socioeconomic Research* programme. The material presented in this chapter summarizes findings produced by the entire project partnership, even though none of the others involved in EXSPRO can be held responsible for the conclusions and inferences.

not stretch beyond the regional development agenda embodied in current EU 'cohesion' policies.

The counter-argument is that, with the long march to economic and monetary union (EMU) now completed for 12 Member States, still on the cards for the remaining three and desired by most of the countries due to accede in 2004, economic integration is now so advanced that a more extensive EU role in social policy must, sooner or later, be defined. In a wider economic space, economic policy decisions taken at EU level clearly have repercussions for all territories, yet their capacity to respond is limited. Problems, such as persistent unemployment, the greater visibility of forms of social exclusion and the apparent fragmentation of societies (Hills et al., 2002), have common causes and, therefore, require either common solutions or solutions embedded within a common framework. Moreover, even if it is accepted that integration yields unambiguous benefits in aggregate, it does so by reallocations of resources that inevitably create new classes of winners and losers.

However, the case for an EU social policy can also be presented in positive terms. That elusive creature, the European social model, is something to be cherished: it may need modernization and recasting, but the values that underpin it are at the heart of the European identity and of the form of capitalism that prevails in the European Union (Begg and Berghman, 2002). Moreover, effective employment policy and social protection systems can enhance the productive potential of an economy, rather than being seen purely as responses to problems with hefty price tags that erode competitiveness (Atkinson, 1999). Indeed, under EMU, the switch to a single monetary policy and the restrictions on fiscal policy autonomy (the demand side of macroeconomic policy) mean that significantly more of the burden of economic adjustment must fall on supply-side policy. Measures to boost productivity by reviewing regulatory frameworks, boosting rates of innovation, and developing the knowledge-intensive economy (in EU-speak, the Cardiff and Lisbon processes) have an obvious part to play, but the labour market is, arguably, at the heart of the supply-side agenda (Bertola et al., 2001).

At present, the policy framework in the European Union is a curious hybrid, with the supranational level subservient to the Member States in certain respects, while in others there is a more familiar, top-down hierarchy of the sort seen in most countries. Overt federalism (as in the United States or Germany) is a distant prospect and there is a marked reluctance in many national capitals to see further powers transferred to the European Union. This structure is likely to come under strain as EMU is consolidated, and can be expected to prompt calls for a rethinking of the boundaries between national and EU policy-making, yet without further transfers of formal competence. To satisfy this latter condition, the compromise answer that seems to be emerging, notably in the Constitutional Treaty based on the 'Giscard' convention, is a reinforcement of policy co-operation and the development of new approaches to coordination.

Efforts to coordinate economic policy across the European Union were enhanced under the various 'processes' named after the European Councils at which they were agreed (for a concise description, see European Commission, 2002). Beyond macroeconomic coordination, notably as embodied in the Stability and Growth Pact, the area of policy that is most developed in this regard is employment. The first steps towards a concerted policy response were taken at the 1994 Essen Council, but it was only following the Amsterdam Treaty, agreed in 1997, that concrete measures were taken to establish what is now known as the European Employment Strategy (EES).

Within this broad framework, policy on dealing with marginalization has to be seen not as a sideshow, but as a core element of a remodelled policy system. Social exclusion can be a consequence of economic integration, but it can also be a factor inhibiting productivity growth or an increase in the employment rate, especially if excluded groups lack the opportunity—or capabilities—to take advantage of jobs that may be offered. This chapter looks, first, at the interplay between macroeconomic developments and different forms of marginalization, especially in relation to EMU. The next section traces how EU policy in the social arena has evolved and how it fits in with other policies that act on marginalization. This is followed by an appraisal of the open method of coordination (OMC), a system of governance that has emerged in recent years. The chapter then turns to whether the outcome is, or could become, a coherent EU approach to marginalization.

Macroeconomic Influences on Marginalization in the European Union

The availability of jobs is heavily influenced by the overall performance of any economy. Although social exclusion manifestly has complex roots and consequences, the macroeconomy clearly has a potent influence in determining social outcomes, and a direct link to the level of unemployment can readily be demonstrated. Macroeconomic factors are thought to affect social exclusion in three main ways. First, the *increased pace of structural change* stemming from factors such as globalization is, arguably, likely to result in existing skills becoming redundant more rapidly in future. Although there is, as yet only limited evidence that this phenomenon is occurring, it is in the knowledge-intensive industries, above all, that it is expected (Rodrigues, 2002). This prospect could engender the unemployment of some individuals and the economic decline of some areas. If these influences do work in the manner described, notably by increasing the vulnerability of hitherto more secure individuals, there could be an increase in the rate at which social exclusion is generated, with no indication that it might be reversed.

Second, it is clear that the process of continuing change is *asymmetric* in the sense that an adverse shock of a given size in terms of income and wealth tends to result in more unemployment and social exclusion than a favourable shock of the same size reduces them. Thus, to prevent social exclusion from remaining at higher levels, a disproportionate response is required (Mayes and Viren, 2002). If this does not occur through favourable macroeconomic shocks or macroeconomic performance, then offsetting microeconomic measures will be required. Third, major *regime* changes that alter the nature of the economy affect the scope for macroeconomic adjustment. EMU is a prime example of such a change, through having a single currency and monetary policy, regulating competition in the Internal Market, establishing rules for the conduct of fiscal policy through the Stability and Growth Pact, and coordinating other structural policies.

The move to the single currency will have a variety of repercussions on how policy is conducted and will have an impact on the prospects for dealing with the different manifestations of marginalization. With a common monetary policy and restrictions on fiscal policy, other macroeconomic policy instruments will be needed to assure economic adjustment and, in particular, to resolve economic 'shocks' that have a more pronounced effect on some regions, sectors, or social groups than on others. Equally, the promise of EMU is that it will mean a more stable macroeconomic context that is expected to allow more rapid aggregate economic growth.

While a link between the macroeconomy and marginalization exists, therefore, the precise nature of the relationships remains unclear. This ambiguity is especially apparent on the demand side of the economy, when we consider the extent to which the macroeconomic development of the euro area will of itself allow the Member States to 'grow' out of their social problems. Investigation of this as part of our research programme found that even if unemployment continues its downward trend, either a significant increase in the sustainable rate of economic growth or a significant further decrease in the level of unemployment consistent with that growth rate appears to be unlikely. The possibility remains, however, that the process of reacting to the favourable shocks that have stimulated the euro economy from closer integration of recent years and from the adoption of Stage 3 of EMU itself have yet to work their way fully through the system.

In parallel, the European Union is confronted by a number of longer run trends that will bear on the incidence of, and capacity to respond to, social problems. Thus, the imminent enlargement of the European Union will bring in new Member States with significantly lower labour costs, and even if the enlargement is ultimately of mutual benefit, it can be expected to have local and sectoral impacts that will constitute new causes of unemployment with the attendant risk of intensified social exclusion. Ageing of the population because of its demographic profile is a well-documented trend that will simultaneously increase the proportion of the traditionally vulnerable elderly in the population and lower the tax-paying base of working individuals. In addition, and notwithstanding the recent bursting of the 'dotcom' bubble in the United States, the phenomenon of the new economy will continue to reshape productive processes.

Implications for EU Macroeconomic Policy

At issue is whether these trends will affect unemployment and social exclusion in a predictable and manageable way. EMU is only gradually evolving towards a coherent policy system and, even though the longer-term trends are well-known, it can be argued that policy has been slow to react, partly because the time horizons are beyond the usual political cycle. New skill demands and work patterns take time to be recognized, let alone to be dealt with, and there are clearly implications for the character of social protection and activation systems.

Many of the responses will come from the evolution of institutional behaviour, which is traditionally very slow. Evidence of a 'new economy' effect is contested, even in the United States, where there has been a substantial increase in the underlying growth rate in recent years (even though the recession of 2000–2 saw a reversal). More encouragingly, neither enlargement of the EU/euro area nor the ageing of the population need have particularly adverse effects on unemployment. To the extent that enlargement stimulates economic growth in the accession countries, it will raise demand both in these countries and in EU-15. Similarly, there will be new demands—for example, for care and leisure services—from an elderly population that will be financially more secure than predecessor generations. Nevertheless, ageing is bound to increase the potential problems of social exclusion, particularly where people have not planned for it in advance. It is also conceivable that adverse movements of capital and labour could make the impact of enlargement on exclusion much harsher than anticipated.

These macroeconomic limitations imply that public policy will have to shoulder some of the burden if unemployment and social exclusion are to be tackled effectively. Many of the proposals for action in this regard require increases in public expenditure, at least during the period in which social exclusion, especially, is being reduced (as opposed to the longer run where it is to be kept at low levels). In this regard the scope for such increases—funded by taxation—will be rather limited at current euro area tax rates, as balanced increases in public spending tend to have detrimental effects on overall activity (Karras, 1996; Mayes and Viren, 2001). On the contrary, it is reductions in the general level of public spending that are likely to increase wealth faster. Hence, public expenditure will need to be focused clearly on activities that will expand human and physical capital and the determinants of inclusion if the expenditure itself is not to be a 'dead-weight' loss and a partial contribution to the problem.

Worries about the adverse impact of the macroeconomic structure of Stage 3 of EMU may have been exaggerated. First, it appears likely that the euro economy will continue to respond fairly rapidly and substantially to variations in its exchange rate with respect to the rest of the world. Although the euro area may increasingly become a more closed economy as it matures, that is not likely to happen overnight. Second, counter-cyclical policies will be less difficult to implement under EMU than has often been imagined. As things stand, policies do seem to respond quite rapidly and effectively to shocks although there is clear non-linearity to the response (Mayes and Viren, 2002). Moreover, contrary to widely-held beliefs, and the positions adopted by France and Germany in their dispute with the Commission in late 2003 over their deficits, simulation work found little evidence that the Stability and Growth Pact (SGP) will act as a restraint on prudent policy responses to future shocks. 'Automatic stabilizers'—the combination of increased public expenditure on benefits triggered when unemployment increases and the fall in tax receipts when there is an economic downturn—appear to be quite quickly acting and it is open to question whether discretionary fiscal action will have short-run positive benefits that would outweigh its longer-term negative consequences. The coordinated automatic stabilization inherent in the Pact will also tend to ease problems of response in the future even in the case where the shocks are confined to just a few Member States.

Even so, it is clear that the euro area countries are currently very different in key macroeconomic respects and will hence continue to be somewhat subject to asymmetric shocks and asymmetric responses to symmetric shocks. However, the normal experience is, on the one hand, for these differences to diminish over time and, on the other, for new mechanisms to develop to offset the remaining problems. It is not as if these problems themselves are new. These asymmetries are just as big within the Member States, even the smaller ones. It is just that national governments have learnt over the years how to cope, whereas under EMU they are faced with a new system. Certainly, the elaboration of the European Employment Strategy since the signing of the Amsterdam Treaty represents a major development of the economic policy framework within the European Union. How well-integrated it is with the core macroeconomic policies of the euro area is, however, unclear. Although there are growing institutional links through the macroeconomic dialogue, the Economic Policy Committee, and the Economic and Financial Committee, it is not easy to judge the weight given to employment in, for instance, the elaboration of the Broad Economic Policy Guidelines (BEPGs)—see Begg, 2002.

In dealing with shocks, the response of the labour market will be critical and it is clear that, in a variety of ways, EMU is engendering change in this area (Boeri, 2001). On the one hand, with a common monetary policy and the loss of exchange rate flexibility, it is in the labour market that much of the adjustment to economic fluctuations will have to take place. On the other, the scope for the European Union to make progress towards the Lisbon Process target of an increase to 70 per cent (from around 62 per cent in 2000) in the employment rate will depend crucially on how effectively EMU functions as a policy system. Reforms of welfare systems (Scharpf and Schmidt, 2000) will also be important.

Thus, even though fears of overly harsh macroeconomic developments can probably be discounted, it would be unrealistic to expect that stable and sustained economic growth will go far enough to address current and forthcoming problems of marginalization. While there is a clear role for greater voluntary macroeconomic coordination for which the incentives exist (see Issing, 2002 for a discussion of the macroeconomic issues), dealing with social exclusion is going to remain fundamentally a detailed, localized, and complex problem for which active targeted policies are required. Equally, all countries and federal arrangements have systems for transferring resources from the gainers to the losers on a scale not contemplated by the European Union, suggesting that, in time, some such redistributive system may be required to complement local action.

Social Policy in the Post-EMU Policy Framework

Social protection outlays averaging 28 per cent of GDP in the European Union are bound to play an important role in the economy. They not only have an impact on stabilization of aggregate economic activity by acting as automatic stabilizers, but also help to equilibrate regional imbalances. These, however, are essentially passive, albeit substantial macroeconomic effects in so far as they provide incomes, but do not necessarily contribute to resolving the root causes of social exclusion. A more active role for social policy can be envisaged in the context of supply-side reforms, implying that social policy—with distinctive aims and ambitions—should be seen as a vital complement to employment policy (van Berkel and Hornemann Møller, 2002).

Social policy is apt to be judged primarily on whether it succeeds in alleviating the immediate social problem it is designed to address, such as reducing homelessness or providing income support to vulnerable groups. The argument here is that appropriately configured social policy can also contribute to the solution of macroeconomic adjustment problems. It is in this context that the scope for social protection to have productive effects is critical. In the emerging EMU policy framework, different policy areas will combine to determine the overall macroeconomic impact. The challenge will be to ensure that the trajectory for demand management is not set so as to exacerbate social exclusion, but equally that the package of social measures is consistent with stable growth.

The Evolution of the Social Dimension of Integration

Coordination of social policies has been an issue in European integration ever since the negotiations leading up to the Treaty of

Rome in 1957 and, according to Scharpf (2002), could well have taken an entirely different direction if French preferences had been followed. At the time, it was perceived as a call for 'harmonization', more specifically the need to approximate the rates of social security contributions between the six founding Member States. But each wave of enlargement raised new barriers to harmonization, the first taking place in 1973 with Denmark, Ireland, and the United Kingdom joining. The member countries differed not only as regards the contribution rates but also in terms of the underlying principles of their welfare systems. Over time, harmonization came to be regarded as impossible as well as unnecessary (Chassard, 2001).

The European Union's position on social policy has also been shaped by the *Internal Market Programme*. Competition policy and rulings by the European Court of Justice (ECJ) concerning completion of the Single Market may, in fact, have had a stronger influence on social matters than explicit attempts at social policy coordination. From the perspective of competition policy, national bodies that exclusively administer social security schemes are suspected of abusing their dominant position. But from a social insurance point of view, a dominant position may be required to insure individuals effectively against risks that private companies could not profitably provide. The case law created by the ECJ's rulings over the years now differentiates between voluntary schemes and compulsory schemes. The latter include the growing number of supplementary retirement schemes based on collective agreements between the social partners, which are compulsory for the individual employee. Compulsory schemes are considered to be compatible with the internal market if the insurance bodies in question pursue a social objective for which compulsion is required to realize the principle of solidarity as well as financial viability.

The social dimension of integration has evolved around the concept of 'Convergence of Objectives', as in the two 1992 Council Recommendations on, respectively, 'Convergence of social protection objectives and policies' and 'Common criteria concerning sufficient resources and social assistance in the social protection systems'. Thus, rather than being rooted in either supranational competence or binding legislative instruments, 'soft' policy coordination has been the norm in social policy. The principal exception has been where differences were thought to offer opportunities for unfair advantage in the context of the single market, as in the case of health and safety or conditions of employment, with action justified not on social but on competition grounds.

Changing Policy Principles

Since the mid-1990s, a number of novel orientations in European Union and Member State policies aimed at dealing with marginalization can be discerned. The first is the shift away from direct job creation through either public sector employment or explicit labour subsidies towards a focus on activation and employability, on the one hand, and preventative measures on the other. Despite initial resistance from some Member States and the suspicions of many union leaders, employability was given pride of place as the first 'pillar' of the guidelines agreed at EU level as the basis for coordinated employment policy in the EES. Inspection of successive National Action Plans for employment (NAPempls), which all countries are required to develop to demonstrate how they will meet these guidelines, suggests that most Member States have fully embraced this pillar (see Madsen and Munch-Madsen, 2001; Raveaud, 2002). In parallel, the NAPempls reveal a widespread shift towards more active labour market polices aimed at overcoming the tendency of passive replacement income policies to engender welfare dependency.

The preventive approach was first seen when 'adaptability' was introduced as a new Objective (4) for the Structural Funds for the 1994–9 programming period and was subsequently also incorporated as the third pillar of the EES from 1998–2002, and has resurfaced in the recast EES now in force. Its essence is to provide scope for workers at risk to be more easily redeployed. It is important to note that it sits side-by-side with flexibility in the EES, because the approach being employed is one which is not purely about labour market deregulation, US-style, but also about anticipating and preventing loss of skills and motivation. Thus, the combination of employability and adaptability is intended to activate those not currently employed, while providing for those who are employed, but who might be at risk from structural change and other macroeconomic trends.

Social inclusion has come, progressively, to be seen as a core aim of the European Union. Although economic and social cohesion are written in to Article 2 of the Treaty as fundamental objectives of the Union—ostensibly on the same plane as monetary union and the single market—it would be fair to say that they have not hitherto received equivalent attention. Lately, however, a number of policy statements and initiatives have stressed the importance of social inclusion, both as an objective in its own right and as a political necessity for garnering popular support for what the European Union tries to do.

Recent Developments in Social Policy: Opportunities and Constraints

An EU level input into the fight against social exclusion is written into the Amsterdam Treaty explicitly as a fundamental aim of the EU (Article 136), even though the means for pursuing this aim remain slender. Indeed, it is followed in the Treaty by Article 137 which re-affirms the primacy of Member States, although a limited range of initiatives under the European Social Fund have explicitly targeted social exclusion. The continuing resistance of a number of Member States meant, however, that the veto on allowing more social policy to be subject to qualified majority voting was not relaxed at the December 2000 Nice European Council, despite the advocacy of the French Presidency.

A major social policy initiative was, however, launched at Nice, with the agreement to ask Member States to develop National Action Plans for promoting social inclusion (NAPincls). The model for these was, clearly, the European Employment Strategy. The approach underlying both policy areas has come to be known as the open method of co-ordination since the expression was coined at the Lisbon European Council in March 2000. It represents a new form of policy integration in which the role of the European bodies is to set the framework and objectives, and to orchestrate the monitoring and review of the Plans, while leaving Member States free to decide on detailed policies and their implementation (Hodson and Mahler, 2001; Telo, 2002; see Appendix for a description of how the OMC functions).

There are many constraints on the scope for a more extensive EU social policy, the most obvious of which is the European Union's very limited formal competence in these matters. Social security issues are still to be decided unanimously by governments. Policy coordination using the OMC in employment and social policies gives the lead role to national governments. From a strictly legal point of view, the European Union can still promote social cohesion, but mainly as a means to promote economic cohesion. This is why the internal market programme acts as a vehicle to push for social policy reforms at the national level. But this may not necessarily be consistent with declared goals of combating marginalization. Other constraints reflect more fundamental issues.

The directives that grant freedom of movement apply only to employed workers, not to job-seekers. On the one hand, this is legally at odds with the promotion of EU citizenship as postulated in the Treaty. But there are, of course, political and economic constraints on a legally more consistent solution. These constraints stem from the public's fear of 'social tourism', that is, marginally employed households migrating to more generous welfare states. Even though there is scant evidence that this phenomenon is significant, the spectre of migration alone alarms the public and, as a result, politicians. This is a particular threat to systems that rely heavily on means-testing, that is on non-contributory benefits.

A major difficulty is the very fact that the European welfare states are so different (Scharpf and Schmidt, 2000). Problems of compatibility arise for instance with respect to means testing. A tax-payer who has faithfully contributed to finance social security in his or her country has no acquired rights when moving to a country where contribution-based benefits prevail. Another prominent example for compatibility problems is related to the extension of privately funded pensions. In contrast to statutory social protection programmes, supplementary pensions are not covered by Community regulations on coordination. With reforms tending towards partial privatization of social protection, this is likely to become a more important issue. Yet despite these constraints, as Begg and Berghman (2002) argue, there are core, common values that—far more than the machinery of the welfare state—constitute the bases for the European social model.

Open Coordination

Since the Amsterdam Treaty was agreed in 1997, it is clear that new approaches to economic integration are being sought and favoured, and that further thought will be given to these issues despite the fact that the convention on the future of Europe only reached an unsatisfactory compromise. In particular, the open method of coordination can be seen as an innovative attempt to advance integration more subtly than by transferring competence. Soft law is manifestly being preferred to hard law by the Member States, at least in the social domain. This raises a core question about social policy at EU level: is the informal approach sufficient to ensure that social issues are given the importance they deserve? Equally, the view might be taken that there is really no alternative in the current political setting.

OMC's principal advantages are that it provides the means to move towards common solutions to common problems without demanding the sort of harmonization that would be anathema to many governments, and that it can be implemented by governments without recourse to major and potentially contested legislative change. Moreover, by allowing countries to shape national programmes within common guidelines, governments have the flexibility to weight their policy packages appropriately. Such *differentiated policy harmonization* represents an artful compromise between policy integration and subsidiarity. Politically, the mere fact of being seen to 'do something' is likely to be appealing to governments. The question that then arises is whether this outcome is one which goes far enough to resolve problems common to all Member States.

Early critics of the OMC as applied to the European Employment Strategy—even predating the invention of the term (see, for example, Goetschy, 1999)—expressed concerns that the looseness of the method, the absence of enforcement mechanisms, and the lack of formal EU level competence would add up to ineffective policy and other criticisms have since been added. The potential drawbacks of OMC can be grouped under four headings: legitimacy, monitoring, enforcement, and effectiveness. The legitimacy of OMC is dubious. This is despite the fact that the intimate involvement of national government in the process seems to provide the legitimacy of the nation state. This, it can be argued, is little more than a veneer, as the OMC does not answer the fundamental criticisms of EU governance: elitism and opacity (Hodson and Maher, 2001). The democratic legitimacy of guidelines drawn up by unaccountable officials and agreed by representatives of national government in closed sessions is questionable. This will be especially true in politically sensitive policy areas such as social and employment policy, however well-intentioned the proposals and the underlying diagnoses. Decisions in areas like employment have always been reached through a delicate process of mediation between national interests, so that if guidelines are issued by 'Brussels' that call for unpopular or controversial reforms, they risk being seen as unacceptable (Chassard, 2001). A risk in this regard is that the European Union could be used as a scapegoat. Indeed it might be argued that this could provide part of the motivation for Europeanization, for example governments try to push through unpopular measures such as pension reforms at the European level to circumvent a lack of domestic support.

Then, there are the issues of monitoring and enforcement of policy. Here, there is a tension at the heart of OMC. The more strictly any targets are monitored, the less the discretion available to a Member State in shaping programmes. At the same time, if there is no sanction (or, as was the case for the EMU convergence criteria, a reward) for failing to adopt suitable measures, let alone meeting targets, the attempt to coordinate could prove to be empty. The degree to which the OMC genuinely leads to policy innovation rather than repackaging of existing policies is germane. In the EES, the evidence from the first three annual cycles is that policies have evolved and that governments have learned from their counterparts. Countries differ significantly in how they implement the OMC, especially the degree of involvement of non-governmental actors including, notably, the social partners (de la Porte and Pochet, 2002). But there is growing evidence that the need to prepare National Action Plans—both for employment and inclusion—and to respond to evaluations of policy has informed and influenced national policy discourse.

A final drawback is that the OMC could be used as a pretext for avoiding hard decisions about the appropriate recasting of policy competencies in the EU policy framework, bearing in mind the salience of the integration of monetary policy. Thus, the EES may give the impression that an effective European response is emerging to employment problems when in reality little is changing.

OMC: A Tool for Effective Integration of Social Policy?

Yet, despite these misgivings, the OMC has, plainly, served to promote fuller integration of policy areas such as employment or social inclusion. For employment policy, especially, there is growing evidence that the annual cycle with its guidelines, identification of best practice, benchmarking, peer review, and recommendations is leading to a convergence of policy. The extensive engagement of government ministers and civil servants in the process will also produce a convergence of the ideological underpinnings of the policy, which will—in circular fashion—reinforce the convergence of policy. This increasing convergence will highlight the problems associated with the lack of a common policy. When sufficient convergence of policy and ideology is achieved, it could be argued that the case for Europeanization of the policy, with competence shifted upwards, would be the next step. The elites involved in the process will initiate the process of developing new EC legislation and of legitimating EU policy in the Member States. Although superficially this might seem to be the direction the EES is taking, the reality is more complex.

This complexity is the result of the profound difference in employment policies that have their roots in different histories and ideologies and are intimately related to the society in which they exist (Esping-Anderson et al., 2001). Part of the difference between Northern and Southern Europe in this area is the result of the much greater reliance on family networks in the Southern welfare systems. This explains why youth unemployment remains so high in Southern Europe in the absence of social entitlements. Young people live at home and their geographical mobility is limited because, if they are to move, they require a wage and security in employment sufficient for them to live independently. Seen in this wider context the imperatives for Europeanization do not seem as persuasive.

In practice, the Employment Strategy seems to have worked better than might have been envisaged, with Member States taking their obligations seriously and real signs that policy learning has been encouraged. But what will be crucial as to whether or not the approach is successful in its application to social policy is not so much the mechanics as the political will. An 'open' method is precisely that: one that allows for experimentation, learning, and the development of new procedures, not a precisely defined approach. If the various actors want it to work, it will allow the European Union to have a meaningful role in a manner much less threatening to' Member States, yet break the logjam that has bedevilled EU social policy for decades.

A reasonable verdict on OMC was delivered by Social Affairs Minister Frank Vandenbroucke (a notable convert to OMC) at a conference on EU social policy held under the auspices of the Belgian Presidency in October 2001. He said, 'Without considering it as a magic formula, I am convinced that the open method of coordination can be extremely useful in this field, as well as in others. But we have to make sure that we deal with this method in a well-considered way.' It has been argued, amongst others by Frank Vandenbroucke, that the application of the OMC was facilitated by the preponderance of centre-left governments in power at the turn of the millennium. To the extent that the 'social' focus of the OMC, as applied to employment and social inclusion, chimes with the interests of such governments, it may indeed have been helpful. But it also has to be recognized that the use of the method for stability orientated macroeconomic policy through the BEPGs provides counter-arguments. Moreover, as Scharpf (2002) shows, there is scope for embedding the use of the method in a firmer legal setting that would, arguably, allow it to lose any such sensitivity to ideological balances.

A Coherent and Distinctive EU Policy Approach?

The problems of marginalization need us to invent new forms and mixes of public and private action. In particular, fresh thought is needed on the relationships between long-term unemployment (more so than temporary or frictional unemployment), social exclusion, and the 'new' requirements of the workplace in terms of flexibility and employability while maintaining security or protection against social risks. A social exclusion approach also (see Hills et al., 2002) encourages a potentially richer policy mix in dealing with the wider societal processes that give rise to exclusion, some of which (health, educational attainment, or housing) have not always been adequately dealt with in the poverty literature (see Fouarge, 2002). Other chapters in the present volume take up some of these matters in greater depth, but it is clear that an effective integrative response (demand and supply oriented) has to bring in local actors: social partners, firms, municipalities, institutions, and social groups, that is those who are most aware of the problems and ways to solve them (see Muffels et al., 2002, for an EXSPRO contribution). Yet at the EU level a broader framework is also required both to give strategic direction and to create a process in which countries and regions can learn from one another. Peer review and benchmarking should be seen less as means of apportioning blame and criticizing the efforts of others, than as an opportunity for the exchange of 'best-practices' and learning experiences and a way to improve policy competition in a 'race-to-the-top' process of upward convergence.

Why Europeanize?

With the advent of monetary union, there is a good case for looking at the scope for the EU level to play a more extensive role in social policy, particularly in developing an over-arching framework within which local actors can deal with social exclusion. It might, however, be asked why Europeanization of social policy should be contemplated, given that national traditions and priorities are so diverse. Certainly, the preference in recent years has been to maintain the status quo, but it can be argued that shared values embedded in the European social model—whichever variant we consider—justify greater EU involvement. A commitment to 'minimum guaranteed resources' or to solidarity are examples. Attempting to take isolated policy elements developed for the specific set of institutions in which they appear to succeed in one Member State and transfer them to other social environments would run a high risk of being unsuccessful. Equally, some factors could also be relevant in other contexts. For example, the Danish experience points to the importance of the macroeconomic environment. Labour market policies cannot generate ordinary jobs by themselves and sufficient pressure from the demand side is a prerequisite. On the other hand, once the upswing is under way, labour market policies play an important role in securing the supply of skilled labour and avoiding bottlenecks.

Some of the specific elements of national labour market policies particularly in Denmark and the Netherlands in recent years, such as the idea of decentralization, the strong involvement of the social partners, the idea of an individual action plan, and the concepts of job rotation and leave schemes, are important. Both systems also try to achieve 'flexicurity' (Ferrera et al., 2000), the combination of flexible employment relationships with good coverage by the unemployment benefit system and the principle of the right and duty to activation. What matters is that the EU system should, somehow, facilitate the transfer across jurisdictions of such experience and thus promote policy innovation.

The deepening of European integration could itself justify a rethinking of the assignment of policy competencies. One reason to do so is that there are manifestly common problems. Despite the decline in the headline total of unemployment since it peaked in the mid-1990s, all Member States bar Luxembourg have pockets of persistent unemployment, a significant proportion of which result from EU-wide structural changes. Similarly, although the EXSPRO research shows the diversity in ways that social exclusion manifests itself in different countries, there are systematic processes in all countries that engender exclusion. Therefore, just as the recognition of a common problem motivated the employment strategy, it can be argued that the fight against social exclusion should similarly be a shared endeavour.

A particular concern under the EMU umbrella is that too much of the policy agenda is predicated upon a narrow definition of remits, with anti-exclusion policy falling almost exclusively under the 'welfare' label, while macroeconomic policy is not required to pay heed to social inclusion. Employment policy is gradually becoming better integrated with fiscal and monetary policy, the two conventional poles of macroeconomics, but it has been a slow and tortuous journey and it is only from 2003 that the timetables for the EES and the BEPGs will be aligned. Yet the nature and evolution of employment regimes have a marked impact on social cohesion. A conclusion, therefore, is that an excessive compartmentalization of policy is not only unhelpful, but also leads to poorly informed choices. This is more than a plea for more 'joined-up' government in responding to social exclusion. The complementary challenge is to develop a conceptual model of policy-making that recognizes the interplay and reciprocal impact of policy areas in shaping social outcomes.

The relevant question here is, thus, not 'whether the EU should do more', but rather 'what is the most desirable distribution of competencies between different levels of governance?' In this regard, the potential for local actors, working in partnership with the national and EU levels, to be more involved (as they are in Denmark, for instance) should not be overlooked. For too long the debate has been conducted purely in defensive terms: what we have, we keep. Several justifications for a more extensive role for the EU can be put forward (see, for example, Vleminckx and Berghman, 2001).

Defining an EU Role

There are several options for altering the EU role in social policy, involving differing degrees of integration of policy formulation and the implementation of any measures agreed. The two extreme cases are no change, that is, leaving competence for dealing with social exclusion entirely with Member States, and Treaty changes that transfer at least some competencies to the EU level. In between, there are various possibilities either for new directives that increase the scope of EU rules or for enhanced coordination of policy. Significant Treaty change is probably not a realistic option for the next few years, although minor amendments may surface in the Constitutional Treaty due to accompany the 2004 enlargement. Although some proposals for directives are working their way through the legislative process, there is little sign that major new initiatives will surface.

If a Treaty change is implausible and Member States continue to be reluctant to countenance new directives in the social policy field, a concerted response to social exclusion at EU level will have to be developed through the coordination of national policies. The blessing given to the open method of coordination by successive European Councils suggests that OMC is not only a viable option for an EU role in the combating of social exclusion, but would also stand a good chance of finding political favour from Member States, because this form of 'back-door' is not threatening to their sovereignty. Clearly, the decision to develop NAPincls and their incorporation into regular procedures is a signal of how things might evolve.

The Way Forward?

Although EU welfare states plainly face difficult times (Pierson, 1998), there is no compelling reason to believe that they need to be either dismantled or radically reined back. Certainly, further modernization is required, although as Esping-Andersen et al. (2001) show, much has already been achieved. Consolidation of the EMU policy framework will also draw attention to new challenges (Buti et al., 1999; Begg, 2002). This chapter has argued that part of that modernization should be to extend the role of the European Union in social policy. Responses to marginalization, in particular, seem to warrant a concerted, EU-wide response.

   The EES has shown that a common approach can successfully be pursued without trampling unduly on national sensitivities—a reconfiguring of regimes and boundaries (Teague, 1999). In this way, it may serve as a pointer to what might be achieved in the still more sensitive areas of social policy that seek to deal with marginalization. Our contention is that the OMC provides a valid way of reconciling these competing demands and, as such, should be embraced as the way forward for EU social policy. OMC is not, however, a panacea, although as a novel approach to integration it has the potential to be developed in diverse ways. Given the lack of alternatives, the challenge may be to work out 'how' rather than 'whether' to use OMC.

   A robust response to unemployment, social exclusion, and other facets of marginalization would entail going beyond the agreement reached at Nice on national plans to combat poverty and social exclusion to develop more explicit and forceful guidelines for national policies (Begg and Berghman, 2001). One potential benefit would be to persuade public opinion that the EU was adopting a constructive approach to the promotion of social inclusion. At the same time, a coherent response will help to complete the EMU policy framework in a manner consistent with the underlying values of the

European social model. These are ambitious aims that deserve serious attention.

Appendix: An Overview of how the Open Method of Coordination Functions

The OMC functions through non-binding recommendations to Member States which are designed to encourage the pursuit of common aims, to achieve policy coordination and to enhance the effectiveness of national policies. The implementation of the guidelines is monitored by the European Commission, with 'peer pressure' from other Member States supplementing policing by the Commission as the principal means of assuring compliance. In contrast to rule-based coordination (such as the Maastricht convergence criteria and their extension to the Stability and Growth Pact), which seeks to impose discipline on national policy, reinforced by possible sanctions, the OMC is aimed more at stimulating policy learning, adoption of best-practice and the development of a comprehensive strategy. The OMC therefore fits into the broader framework of policy coordination called for in Article 99 of the Treaty (see European Commission, 2002; Begg, 2002).

Variants of the OMC are now being used in the *Broad Economic Policy Guidelines*, the EES and, since the Nice European Council, in relation to social inclusion and have latterly also been adopted for other areas, such as pensions policy. Part of the attraction of the OMC is, precisely, that it does not impose a single administrative 'model', but some key characteristics can be discerned in the use of the method for the BEPGs, the EES, and social inclusion. These can be summarized as follows: The *European Commission* proposes a set of guidelines that interpret the overall aims for the policy area decided by the Heads of State and of Government. These are then amended and agreed by the *Council of Ministers*. For some objectives, explicit targets are set, while for others only a statement of intent is provided. Some Member States have been reluctant to agree to formal targets, fearing the adverse publicity that might arise from publication of 'league tables'. *Member States* then develop plans for meeting the guidelines, containing detailed descriptions of the policies that will be implemented, reports. For employment and social inclusion, the *National Action Plan* is submitted to the *Commission* for comment and approval. Economic policy is, similarly, set out in *Stability Plans* (for euro area members) or *Convergence Plans* (for others). The *Commission* draws up a report on the implementation of the plans and assesses the success of the policy, both overall and in each Member State. The *Council* then considers and amends the report which then becomes the basis for the elaboration of guidelines for the next cycle. The *Employment Guidelines* provide a good illustration of how the system operates. After the so-called 'Luxembourg Process' was established in 1997, they were grouped under four 'pillars' within each of which there are several guidelines, albeit with variations from year to year in the numbers, although since 2003 the EES has been reshaped to be more strategic. The four pillars were:

- *Employability* which covers a range of measures aimed at increasing the likelihood that an individual will be equipped to take-up available jobs. Particular attention is paid to segments of the labour force with poor employment prospects, such as the long-term unemployed or youths.
- *Entrepreneurship* focuses on initiatives to increase the supply of jobs, principally in small and medium-sized firms, and on encouraging self-employment, and new business starts.
- *Adaptability* which refers to equipping the labour force to cope with inevitable economic restructuring that requires redeployment and re-skilling.
- *Equal opportunities* with an emphasis, above all, on gender equality.

For assessments of the OMC, see Hodson and Maher, 2001; de la Porte and Pochet, 2002; Telo, 2002.

REFERENCES

Aberg, R. (2001). 'Equilibirum unemployment, search behaviour and unemployment persistency', *Cambridge Journal of Economics*, 25: 131–47.

Abrahamsen, P. (1998). 'Efter velf3/4rdsstaen: ret og plikt til aktivering', *Nordisk Sosialt Arbied*, 3: 133–44.

Acemoglu D. and Shimer, R. (1999). 'Efficient unemployment insurance', *Journal of Political Economy*, 107, 5: 893–928.

Alphametrics (2002). 'Analytical and statistical tools for monitoring EU tax-benefits systems', *Unpublished report*, Alphametrics Limited.

Anxo, D., Carcillo, S., and Erhel, C. (2001). 'Aggregate impact analysis of active labour market policy in France and Sweden: A regional approach', in Jaap de Koning and Hugh Mosley (eds.) *Labour Market Policy and Unemployment. Impact and Process Evaluations in Selected European Countries*. Cheltenham: Edward Elgar.

Arulampalam W. and Stewart, M. B. (1995). 'The determinants of individual unemployment durations in an era of high unemployment', *The Economic Journal*, 105, March: 321–32.

Ashton, D. N. (1984). *Unemployment under Capitalism: The Sociology of British and American Labour Markets*. Brighton: Wheatsheaf Books Ltd.

—— Davies, B., Felstead, A., and Green, F. (1999). *Work Skills in Britain*. Oxford: Centre for Skills, Knowledge and Organisational Performance.

Atkinson, A. B. (1989). *Poverty and Social Security*. London: Harvester Wheatsheaf.

—— (1999). *The Economic Consequences of Rolling Back the Welfare State*. Cambridge, MA: MIT Press.

—— (2000). *The Consequences of Rolling Back the Welfare State*. Oxford: Oxford University Press.

—— —— (1985). *Unemployment Benefits and Unemployment Duration*. London: Suntory-Toyota International Centre for Economics and Related Disciplines, London School of Economics.

—— —— (1991). 'Unemployment compensation and labour market transitions: A critical review', *Journal of Economic Literature*, 29: 1679–727.

Autor, D. H., Katz, L. F., and Krueger, A. B. (1998). 'Computing inequality: Have computers changed the labor market?', *Quarterly Journal of Economics*, 113: 1169–213.

Bakke, E. W. (1940a). *Citizens without Work. A Study of the Effects of Unemployment upon the Workers' Social Relations and Practices*. New Haven, CT: Yale University Press.

—— (1940b). *The Unemployed Worker: A Study of the Task of Making a Living without a Job*. New Haven, CT: Yale University Press.

Baktavatsalou, R. (1996). 'Licenciements économiques au début des années 90', in *Données sociales*. INSEE.

Bane, M. J. and Ellwood, D. (1994). *Welfare Realities. From Rethoric to Reform*. Cambridge, MA: Harvard University Press.

Banks, M. H. and Ullah, P. (1988). *Youth Unemployment in the 1980s: Its Psychological Effects*. London and Sidney: Croom Helm.

Bean, C. (1994). 'European unemployment: A survey', *Journal of Economic Literature*, 32: 573–619.

Begg, I. (ed.) (2002). *Europe Government and Money—Running EMU: The Challenges of Policy Co-ordination*. London: The Federal Trust.

—— and Berghman, J. (2001). 'The future role of the EU in the fight against social exclusion: Problems and perspectives', in D. G. Mayes, J. Berghman, and R. Salais (eds.) *Social Exclusion and European Policy*. London: Edward Elgar.

———— (2002). 'Introduction: EU social (Exclusion) policy revisited?', *Journal of European Social Policy*, 12: 179–94.

Berger, P. A., Steinmueller, P., and Sopp, P. (1993). 'Differentiation of life-courses? Changing patterns of labour-market sequences in West Germany', *European Sociological Review*, 9(1): 43–65.

Berman, E., Bound, J., and Machin, S. (1998). 'Implications of skill-biased technological change: International evidence', *Quarterly Journal of Economics*, 113: 1245–79.

Bernard, Q. (2001). 'Age et emploi en 2010', *Conseil économique et social*, October.

Berthoud, R. (1999). *Young Caribbean Men and the Labour Market: A Comparison with Other Ethnic Groups*. Joseph Rowntree Foundation Report No. 69. York: York Publishing Services.

Bertola, G., Boeri, T., and Nicoletti, G. (eds.) (2001). *Welfare and Employment in a United Europe*. Cambridge, MA: MIT Press.

Biermann, I., Schmerl, C., and Ziebell, L. (1985). *Leben mit kurzfristigem Denken. Eine Untersuchung zur Situation arbeitsloser Akademikerinnen* [Life with Short-term Thinking. A Study on Unemployed Female Academics]. Weinheim: Beltz.

Björklund, A., Haveman, R., Hollister, R., and Holmlund, B. (1991). *Labour Market Policy and Unemployment Insurance*. Oxford: Oxford University Press.

Blau, F. and Kahn, L. (1996). 'International differences in male wage inequality: Institutions versus market forces', *Journal of Political Economy*, 104: 791–837.

Blossfeld, H. P. and Shavit, Y. (1993). *Persistent Inequality: Changing Educational Attainment in Thirteen Countries*. Boulder, CO: Westview Press.

Bluestone, B. and Harrison, B. (1988). *The Great U-Turn: Corporate Restructuring and the Polarizing of America*. New York, NY: Basic Books.

Blundell, R. (2001). 'Welfare-to-work: Which policies and why?'. Keynes Lecture in Economics 2001. Institute of Fiscal Studies.

—— Costas Dias, M., Meghir, C., and van Reenen, J. (2001). *Evaluating the Employment Impact of a Mandatory Job Search Assistance Programme*. IFS Working Paper. WP01/20. Institute of Fiscal Studies.

Boeri, T. (2001). 'Introduction: Putting the debate on a new footing', in G. Bertola, T. Boeri, and G. Nicoletti (eds.) *Welfare and Employment in a United Europe*. Cambridge, MA: MIT Press.

Boheim, R. and Taylor, M. P. (2000). 'Unemployment duration and exit states in Britain'. ISER Working Papers Number 2000–1. Colchester: University of Essex.

Bonjour, D., Dorsett, R., Knight, G., Lissenburgh, S., Mukherjee, A., Payne, J., Range, M., Urwin, P., and White, M. (2001). 'New deal for young people: National survey of participants: Stage 2'. Employment Service Report ESR44. Sheffield: Employment Service.

Borghi, V. and Kieselbach, T. (2002). 'Disoccupazione grovanile e lavoro irregolare: Nord e Sud Europa a confronto', In V. Borghi (ed.) *Vunerabilita, inclusione sociale e lavoro: contributi per la comprensione dei processi di osclusione sociale e delle problematche di policy*, 175–86. Milano: FrancoAngeli.

—— —— (2003). 'The submerged economy as a trap and a buffer: Comparative evidence on long-term youth unemployment and the risk of social exclusion in southern and northern Europe', Paper presented at the EU-Workshop 'Informal/Undeclared Work', European Commission (DG Research), Brussels.

Borjas, G. and Ramey, V. (1995). 'Foreign Competition, Market Power, and Wage Inequality,' *Quarterly Journal of Economics*, 110: 1075–1110.

Bradshaw, J. and Terum, L. I. (1997). 'How Nordic is the Nordic Model? Social Assistance in a Comparative Perspective', *Scandinavian Journal of Social Welfare*, 6: 247–56.

Buck, N. (1992). 'Labour market inactivity and polarisation: A household perspective on the idea of an underclass', in D. J. Smith (ed.) *Understanding the Underclass*. London: Policy Studies Institute.

Buti, M., Franco, D., and Pench, L. (eds.) (1999). *The Welfare State in Europe: Challenges and Reforms*. Cheltenham: Edward Elgar.

—— ——(2000). *Reconciling the Welfare State with Sound Public Finances and High Employment*. Working Paper, Forward Studies Unit, European Commission.

Callan, T., Nolan, B., and O'Donoghue, C. (1996). 'What has happened to replacement rates?', *The Economic and Social Review*, 27: 439–56.

Card, D., Kramarz, F., and Lemieux, T. (1999). 'Changes in the relative structure of wages and employment: A comparison of the United States, Canada and France', *Canadian Journal of Economics*, 32: 843–77.

Carey, D. and Tchilinguirian, H. (2000). *Average Effective Tax Rates on Capital, Labour and Consumption*. OECD Economics Department Working Paper, OECD, 258.

Carle, J. (1987). 'Youth unemployment-individual and social consequences, and research approach', *Social Science and Medicine*, 25(2): 147–52.

—— (2000). 'Method and Research Design', in A. Furlong and T. Hammer (eds.) *Youth Unemployment and Marginalisation in Northern Europe*, Norway: NOVA.

—— and Julkunen, I. (2003). 'Young and Unemployed in Scandinavia—a Nordic Comparative Study', *Nord*, 14. Copenhagen: The Nordic Council of Ministries.

Castles, F. (1981). 'How does politics matter? Structure and agency in the determination of public policy outcomes', *European Journal of Political Research*, 9: 119–32.

Central Planning Bureau (1995). *Replacement rates—A transatlantic view*. CPB Working Paper, No. 80, Central Planning Bureau, The Hague, pp. RR.

Chassard, Y. (2001). 'European integration and social protection: From the spaak report to the open method of co-ordination', in D. G. Mayes, J. Berhman, and R. Salais (eds.) *Social Exclusion and European Policy*. London: Edward Elgar.

Daly, M. (1996). *Social Security, Gender and Equality in the European Union*. European Commission.

Daniel, W. W. (1990). *The Unemployed Flow*. London: Policy Studies Institute.

de Koning, J. and Arents, M. (2001). 'The impact of active labour market policy on job hirings and unemployment in the Netherlands', in Jaap de Koning and Hugh Mosley (eds.) *Labour Market Policy and Unemployment. Impact and Process Evaluations in Selected European Countries*. Cheltenham: Edward Elgar.

—— and Mosley, H. (2001). *Labour Market Policy and Unemployment. Impact and Process Evaluations in Selected European Countries*. Cheltenham: Edward Elgar.

de la Porte, C. and Pochet, P. (eds.) (2002). *Building Social Europe through the Open Method of Co-ordination*. Brussels: P.I.E.-Peter Lang.

Deacon, A. (2000). 'Learning from the US? The influence of American ideas upon new labour thinking on welfare reform', *Policy and Politics*, 28, 1: 5–18.

Department for Work and Pensions. (2003). *New Deal for Young People and Long-Term Unemployed People Aged 25+. Statistics to March 2003*. London: Department of Work and Pensions.

Department of Social Security. (2000). *Income Related Benefits: Estimates of Take-up in 1998–99*. London: DSS Analytical Services Division.

Devillechabrolle, V., Fairise, A., and Landré, M. (2002). 'Les plans sociaux, le case tête des reclassements', *Liaisons sociales Magazine*, January.

Dingeldey, I. (2001). 'European tax systems and their impact on family employment patterns', *Journal of Social Policy*, 30(4): 653–72.

Eardley, T., Bradshaw, J., Ditch, J., Gough, I., and Whiteford, P. (1996a). *Social Assistance Schemes in the OECD Countries*. Vol. 1. Synthesis Report. DSS Research Report 46. London: HMSO.

Eardley, T., Bradshaw, J., Ditch, J., Gough, I., and Whiteford, P. (1996*b*). *Social Assistance Schemes in the OECD countries.* Vol. 11. Country Reports. DSS Research Report 47. London: HMSO.

Ellingsæter, A. (1998). 'Dual breadwinner societies: Provider models in the Scandinavian welfare states', *Acta Sociologica,* 41(1): 59–74.

Erikson, R. and Goldthorpe, J. (1992). *The Constant Flux. A Study of Class Mobility in Industrial Societies.* Oxford: Oxford University Press.

————— (2002). 'Intergenerational inequality: A sociological perspective', *Journal of Economic Perspectives,* 16(3): 31–44.

Ermisch, J. F. and Francesconi, M. (1997). *Family Matters.* Working Papers of the ESRC Research Centre on Micro-social Change. Paper 97–1. Colchester: University of Essex.

————— and Pevalin, D. J. (2002). *Childhood Parental Behaviour and Young People's Outcomes.* Working Papers of the Institute of Social and Economic Research. Paper 2002–12. Colchester: University of Essex.

ESO (1997). *Lönar sig arbete?* Stockholm: Swedish Ministry of Finance.

Esping-Andersen, G. (1990). *The Three Worlds of Welfare Capitalism.* Princeton, NJ: Princeton University Press.

——— (2002). 'A child-centred social investment strategy', in G. Esping-Andersen, D. Gallie, A. Hemerijck, and J. Myles (eds.) *Why We Need a New Welfare State.* Oxford: Oxford University Press.

——— Gallie, D., Hemerijck, A., and Myles, J. (2001). *A New Welfare Architecture for Europe?.* Report submitted to the Belgian Presidency of the European Union, Brussels.

European Commission (1998*a*). *From guidelines to action: The national action plans for employment,* Brussels: DG V.

——— (1998*b*). *Social Protection in Europe 1997.* Brussels.

——— (2000*a*). *The EU Economy: 1999 Review.* Brussels.

——— (2000*b*). *Employment in Europe 2000.* Brussels.

——— (2002). 'Co-ordination of economic policies in the EU: A presentation of key features of the main procedures', Directorate-General for Economic and Financial Affairs, *Euro Papers,* No. 45, Brussels.

European Council (1997).

Eurostat (1998). *Basic Statistics of the Community.* Brussels: Author.

——— (2000). *European Social Statistics: Labour Force Survey Results 2000.* Luxembourg: Eurostat.

Evans, P. (1995). 'Linking welfare to jobs: Workfare, canadian style', in A. Sayeed (ed.) *Workfare: Does It Work? Is It Fair?* Montreal, Canada: Institute for Research on Public Policy.

Evans-Kloch, C., Kelly, P., Richards, P., and Vargha, C. (1999*a*). 'Suppressions d'emplois et licenciements économiques: mesures de prévention et de compensation', *Revue Internationale du Travail,* 138 (1): 49–71.

————— (1999*b*). 'Worker retrenchment: Preventive and remedial measures', *International Labour Review,* 138(1): 47–66.

Fagin, L. and Little, M. (1984). *The Forsaken Families. The Effects of Unemployment on Family Life*. Harmondsworth: Penguin Books Ltd.

Felli, L. and Ichino, A. (1988). 'Do marginal employment subsidies increase re-employment probabilities? Preliminary results on the experiment of the Agenzia del lavoro of Trento (Italy)', *Labour*, 2: 63–89.

Felstead, A., Gallie, D., and Green, F. (2002). 'Work skills in Britain 1986–2001', London: Department for Education and Skills.

Ferrera, M., Hemerijck, A., and Rhodes, M. (2000). *The Future of Social Europe*. Oeiras: Celta Editora.

Fitzroy, F. R. and Hart, R. A. (1985). 'Hours, layoffs and unemployment insurance funding: Theory and practice in an international perspective', *Economic Journal*, 95: 700–13.

Fouarge, D. (2002). *Minimum Protection and Poverty in Europe: An Economic Analysis of the Subsidiarity Principle*. Ph.D. Thesis, Tilburg University, awarded June 2002.

Francesconi, M. and Ermisch, J. F. (1998). *Mother's behaviour and children's achievements*. Working Papers of the ESRC Research Centre on Micro-social Change. Paper 98–3. Colchester: University of Essex.

Freeman, R. B. and Schettkat, R. (2000). *The role of wage and skill differences in US-German employment differences*. National Bureau of Economic Research Working Paper 7474.

Fryer, D. and Payne, R. L. (1984). 'Proactive behaviour in unemployment: Findings and implications', *Leisure Studies*, 3: 273–95.

Gallie, D. (1991). 'Patterns of skill change: Upskilling, deskilling or the polarization of skills?', *Work, Employment and Society*, 5: 319–51.

—— (1999). 'Unemployment and social exclusion in the European Union', *European Societies*, 1(1): 139–67.

—— (2002). 'The quality of working life in welfare strategy', in G. Esping-Andersen, D. Gallie, A. Hemerijck, and John Myles (eds.) *Why We Need a New Welfare State*. Oxford: Oxford University Press.

—— (2003). 'The quality of working life: Is Scandinavia different?', *European Sociological Review*, 19(1): 61–79.

—— and Alm, S. (2000). 'Unemployment, gender and attitudes to work', in D. Gallie and S. Paugam (eds.) *Welfare Regimes and the Experience of Unemployment in Europe*. Oxford: Oxford University Press.

—— and Paugam, S. (2000*a*). 'The Social Regulation of Unemployment', in D. Gallie and S. Paugam (eds.) *Welfare Regimes and the Experience of Unemployment in Europe*. Oxford: Oxford University Press.

—— —— (eds.) (2000*b*). *Welfare Regimes and the Experience of Unemployment in Europe*. Oxford: Oxford University Press.

—— —— (2003). *Social Precarity and Social Integration*. Luxembourg: Office for Official Publications of the European Communities.

—— —— and Jacobs, S. (2003). 'Unemployment, Poverty, and Social Isolation. Is there a vicious circle of social exclusion?', *European Societies*, 5(1): 1–32.

—— and Russell, H. (1998). 'Unemployment and life satisfaction. A cross-cultural comparison', *European Journal of Sociology*, 2: 248–80.

Gallie, D. and Vogler, C. (1993). 'Unemployment and attitudes to work', in D. Gallie, C. Marsh, and C. Vogler (eds.) Social Change and the Experience of Unemployment. Oxford: Oxford University Press.

—— White, M., Cheng, Y., and Tomlinson, M. (1994). 'The employment commitment of unemployed people', in M. White (ed.) Unemployment and Public Policy in a Changing Society. London: Policy Studies Institute.

—— (1998). Restructuring the Employment Relationship. Oxford: Clarendon Press.

Gilbert, N. and Gilbert, B. (1989). The Enabling State: Modern Welfare Capitalism in America. New York, NY: Oxford University Press.

Glyn, A. and Salverda, W. (2000). 'Employment inequalities', in M. Gregory, W. Salverda, and S. Bazen (eds.) Labour Market Inequalities. Oxford: Oxford University Press.

Goetschy, J. (1999). 'The European employment strategy: Genesis and development', European Journal of Industrial Relations, 5(2): 117–37.

Gómez, A. (2002). 'Capitalisation of unemployment benefits in Spain: An experience of labour inclusion', in R. van Berkel and I. Møller Hornemann (eds.) Active Social Policies in the EU. Inclusion through Participation? Bristol: The Policy Press.

Gornick, J., Meyers, M., and Ross, K. (1997). 'Supporting the employment of mothers: Policy variation across fourteen welfare states', Journal of European Social Policy, 7(1): 45–70.

Gosling, A., Machin, S., and Meghir, C. (1994). 'What has happened to men's wages since the mid-1960s?', Fiscal Studies, 15: 63–87.

Gough, I., Bradshaw, J., Ditch, J., Eardley, T., and Whiteford, P. (1997). 'Social assistance in OECD countries', Journal of European Social Policy, 7(1): 17–43.

Green, F., Felstead, A., and Gallie, D. (1998). Changing Skill-Intensity: An Analysis Based on Job Characteristics. Working Paper.

—— —— —— (2003). 'Computers and the Changing Skill Intensity of Jobs', Journal of Applied Economics, 35: 1561–76.

Gregg, P. and Machin, S. (1993). 'Is the rise in UK inequality different?', in R. Barrell (ed.) Is the British Labour Market Different?, Cambridge: Cambridge University Press.

—— and Manning, A. (1997). 'Skill-biassed change, unemployment and wage inequality', European Economic Review, 41: 1173–200.

Gregory, M., Zissimos, B., and Greenhalgh, C. (2001). 'Jobs for the skilled: How technology, trade and domestic demand changed the structure of UK employment, 1979–90', Oxford Economic Papers, 53: 20–46.

Grimes, A. (1997). 'Would workfare work? An alternative approach for the UK', in A. Deacon (ed.) From Welfare to Work. Lessons from America. London: Institute of Economic Affairs.

Groot, W. and Maasen van Den Brink, H. (2000). 'Overeducation in the labor market: A meta-analysis', Economics of Education Review, 19(2): 149–58.

Gustavsen, B., Hofmaier, B., Philips, M. K., and Wikman, A. (1996). A Concept-driven Development and the Organisation of the Process of

Change. An Evaluation of the Swedish Working Life Fund. Amsterdam/Philadelphia: John Benjamins Publishing Company.

Hakim, C. (1996). *Key Issues in Women's Work: Female Heterogeneity and the Polarisation of Women's Employment.* The Athlone Press Ltd.

Hammer, T. (1996). 'Consequences of unemployment from youth to adulthood in a life course perspective', *Youth and Society*, 27(4): 450–68.

—— (2003). 'The Probability for Unemployed Young People to Re-enter Education or Employment: A Comparative Study in Six Northern European Countries', *British Journal of Sociology of Education*, 24(2): 209–23.

—— and Julkunen, I. (2003). 'Surviving unemployment, a question of money or families? A comparative study of youth unemployment in Europe', in T. Hammer (ed.) *Youth Unemployment and Social Exclusion in Europe.* Bristol: Policy Press.

Harrison, R. (1976). 'The demoralizing experience of prolonged unemployment', *Department of Employment Gazette*, April: 339–48.

Hartog, J. (1997). 'On returns to education: Wandering along the hills of ORU land', Keynote Speech for the LVIIth Conference of the Applied Econometrics Association, Maastricht.

Haskel, J. (1996). *The Decline in Unskilled Employment in UK Manufacturing.* Discussion Paper No. 1356, Centre for Economic Policy Research.

—— (1999). 'Small firms, contracting-out, computers and wage inequality: Evidence from UK manufacturing', *Economica*, 66: 1–21.

Hauser, R., Nolan, B., Morsdorf, C., and Strengmann-Kuhn, W. (2000). 'Unemployment and poverty: Change over time', in D. Gallie and S. Paugam (eds.) *Welfare Regimes and the Experience of Unemployment in Europe.* Oxford: Oxford University Press.

Heady, P. and Smyth, M. (1989). *Living Standards during Unemployment.* Vol. 1. London: HMSO.

Hecklo, H. (1973). *Modern Social Politics in Britain and Sweden.* New Haven, CT: Yale University Press.

Heckman, J. (1979). 'Sample selection bias as a specification error', *Econometrica*, 47: 153–61.

Heikkilä, M. (1999). 'A brief introduction to the topic', in *Linking Welfare and Work.* Luxembourg: European Foundation for the Improvement of Living and Working Conditions.

Hills, J., Le Grand, J., and Piachaud, D. (2002). *Understanding Social Exclusion.* Oxford: Oxford University Press.

Hobcraft, J. (2003). *Continuity and Change in Pathways to Young Adult Disadvantage: Results from a British Birth Cohort.* CASE Paper No. 66, London School of Economics: Centre for Analysis of Social Exclusion.

Hodson, D. and Maher, I. (2001). 'The open method as a new mode of governance: The case of soft economic policy co-ordination', *Journal of Common Market Studies*, 39(4): 719–46.

Holmlund, B. (1998). 'Unemployment insurance in theory and practice', *Scandinavian Journal of Economic*, 100(1): 113–41.

House, J. S. (1981). *Work Stress and Social Support*. Reading, MA: Addison-Wesley.

Hvinden, B. (1999). 'Activation: A nordic perspective', *Linking Welfare and Work*, Luxembourg: European Foundation for the Improvement of Living and Working Conditions.

IMF (1999). *World Economic Outlook*. Washington.

Immervoll, H. and O'Donoghue, D. (2001*a*). *Towards a Multi-purpose Framework for Tax-Benefit Microsimulation. A Discussion by Reference to MMEANS, a Software System Used for Constructing EUROMOD, a Tax-Benefit Model for the European Union*. EURO-MOD Working Paper EM2/01, Department of Applied Economics, University of Cambridge, available through http://www.econ.cam.ac.uk/dae/mu/emod.htm.

——— (2001*b*). *Welfare Benefits and Work Incentives: The Distribution of Net Replacement Rates in Europe*. EUROMOD Working Paper EM4/01, Department of Applied Economics, University of Cambridge, available through http://www.econ.cam.ac.uk/dae/mu/emod.htm.

—— O'Donoghue, C., and Sutherland, H. (1999). *An Introduction to EUROMOD*. EUROMOD Working Paper EM0/99, Department of Applied Economics, University of Cambridge, available through http://www.econ.cam.ac.uk/dae/mu/emod.htm.

Issing, O. (2002). 'On macro-economic policy co-ordination in EMU', *Journal of Common Market Studies*, 40(2): 345–58.

Jackman, R., Layard, R., Manacorda, M., and Petrongolo, B. (1997). *European versus US Unemployment: Different Responses to Increased Demand for Skill?*. Discussion Paper No. 349, Centre for Economic Performance.

Jackson, P. R., Stafford, E. M., Banks, M. H., and Warr, P. B. (1983). 'Unemployment and psychological distress in young people: The moderating effect of employment commitment', *Journal of Applied Psychology*, 68(3): 525–35.

Jahoda, M. (1979). 'The impact of unemployment in the 1930's and the 1970's', *Bulletin of the British Psychological Society*, 32: 309–14.

—— (1982). *Employment and Unemployment: A Social-Psychological Analysis*. Cambridge: Cambridge University Press.

—— and Rush, H. (1980). *Work, Employment and Unemployment*. Occasional Paper Series, No. 12, SPRU, University of Sussex.

—— Lazarsfeld, P., and Zeizel, H. (1933). *Marienthal: The Sociology of an Unemployed Community*. London: Tavistock.

——————— (2002). *Marienthal: The Sociology of an Unemployed Community (1933)*. With a new introduction by Christian Fleck. New Brunswick: Transaction.

Jensen, P. and Westergard-Nielsen, N. (1989). *Temporary Layoffs*. Labour Economics Group Working Paper, University of Aarhus and Aarhus School of Business, 89, 2.

Jones, C. (1985). *Patterns of Social Policy: An Introduction to Comparative Analysis*. London: Tavistock Publications.

Jordan, B. (1996). *A Theory of Poverty and Social Exclusion*. Cambridge: Polity Press.

Karras, G. (1996). 'The optimal government size: Further international evidence on the productivity of government services', *Economic Inquiry*, 34: 193–203.

Katz, L. F. and Murphy, K. M. (1992). 'Changes in relative wages, 1963–1987: Supply and demand factors', *Quarterly Journal of Economics*, 107: 35–78.

Kaul, H. and Kvande, E. (1991). 'Mestring av arbeidsledighet' (Coping with Unemployment), *Tidsskrift for samfunnsforsking*, 32: 3–21.

Kelvin, P. and Jarrett, J. E. (1985). *Unemployment. Its social psychological effects*. Cambridge, MA: Cambridge University Press.

Kieselbach, T. (1987). 'Self-disclosure and help-seeking as determinants of vulnerability. Case studies of unemployed from social-psychiatric services and demands for health and social policy', in D. Schwefel, P. G. Svensson, and H. F. K. Zöllner (eds.) *Unemployment, Social Vulnerability and Health in Europe*. New York, NY: Springer.

——(1991). 'Unemployment', in R. Lerner, J. Brooks-Gunn, and A. C. Petersen, (eds.) *Encyclopaedia of Adolescence*. Philadelphia, PA: Garland Publisher.

——(1997). 'Individuelle und gesellschaftliche Bewältigung von Arbeitslosigkeit—Perspektiven eines zukünftigen Umganges mit beruflichen Transitionen' [Individual and societal coping with unemployment—perspectives of a future coping with transitions in the working life], in H. Holzhüter, R. Hickel, and T. Kieselbach (eds.) *Arbeit und Arbeitslosigkeit: Die gesellschaftliche Herausforderung unserer Zeit* [Employment and Unemployment: The Societal Challenge of Our Time] (S. 39–64). Bremen: Kooperation Universität – Arbeiterkammer – Bremen.

——and Beelmann, G. (2003). 'Arbeitslosigkeit als Risiko sozialer Ausgrenzung bei Jugendlichen in Europa' [Unemployment as a risk for social exclusion among young people in Europe], *Aus Politik und Zeitgeschichte. Beilage zur Wochenzeitung "Das Parlament"* (B 6–7/2003) v. 3.2.2003.

——(ed.) in collaboration with Heeringen, K. van, La Rosa, M., Lemkow, L., Sokou, K., and Starrin, B. (2000a). *Youth Unemployment and Health. A Comparison of Six European Countries* (Psychology of Social Inequality, Vol. 9). Opladen: Leske + Budrich.

——(2000b). *Youth Unemployment and Social Exclusion. A Comparison of Six European Countries* (Psychology of Social Inequality, Vol. 10). Opladen: Leske + Budrich.

——Heeringen, K. van, Lemkow, L., Sokou, K., and Starrin, B. (eds.) (2001). *Living on the Edge—A Comparative Study on Long-Term Youth Unemployment and Social Exclusion in Europe* (YUSEDER publications, No. 3, Psychology of Social Inequality, Vol. 11). Opladen: Leske + Budrich.

Kilpatrick, R. and Trew, K. (1985). 'Life-styles and psychological well-being among unemployed men in Northern Ireland', *Journal of Occupational Psychology*, 58: 207–16.

Kirsch, J. L. (1999). 'Devenir des bas niveaux de qualification: comparaison des situations nationales' mimeo CEREQ, Marseille.

Kirsch, J. and Knuth, M. 'Restructurations économiques et protection des transitions', *Travail et emploi*, 87: 29.

Knuth, M. and Kirsch, J. (2001). 'Restructurations économiques et protection des transitions: approches contrastées en France et en Allemagne', *Travail et Emploi*, 87: 29–45.

Kronauer, M. (1998). '"Social Exclusion" and "Underclass"—New concepts for the analysis of poverty', in H.-J. Andreß (ed.) *Empirical Poverty Research in Comparative Perspective*. Aldershot: Ashgate.

—— (2002). *Exklusion. Die Gefährdung des Sozialen im hoch entwickelten Kapitalismus* [Exclusion. The Precarisation of the Social in Advanced Capitalism]. Frankfurt: Campus.

Krueger, A. B. and Pischke, J.-S. (1997). 'Observations and conjectures on the US employment miracle', National Bureau of Economic Research Working Paper 6146.

Krugman, P. (1994). 'Past and prospective causes of high unemployment', in *Reducing Unemployment: Current Issues and Policy Options*, Jackson Hole Conference, WY.

Lampard, R. (1993). 'An examination of the relationship between marital dissolution and unemployment', in D. Gallie, C. Marsh, and C. Vogler (eds.) *Social Change and the Experience of Unemployment*. Oxford: Oxford University Press.

Larsson, A. (1998). 'The welfare society: Added value or excessive burden?'. Speech to PES Conference, 'Reform of the welfare state and employment', Brussels, July.

Lawless, P., Martin, R., and Hardy, S. (eds.) (1998). *Unemployment and Social Exclusion: Landscapes of Labour Inequality*. London: Jessica Kingsley Publishers.

Layard, R., Nickell, S., and Jackman, R. (1991). *Unemployment: Macro-economic Performance and the Labour Market*. Oxford: Oxford University Press.

Le Grand, J. (1997). 'Knights, knaves or pawns: Human behaviour and social policy', *Journal of Social Policy*, 26: 149–69.

Leira, A. (1992). 'Welfare States and Working Mothers', Cambridge: Cambridge University Press.

Leisering, L. and Leibfried, S. (1999). *Time and Poverty in Western Welfare States. United Germany in Perspective*. Cambridge: Cambridge University Press.

—— and Walker, R. (eds.) (1998). *The Dynamics of Modern Society: Poverty, Policy and Welfare*, Bristol: The Policy Press.

Leonard, M. (1998). 'Invisible work, invisible workers. The informal economy in Europe and in the US. London: MacMillan.

Lerner, M. J. (1974). 'Social psychology of justice and interpersonal attraction', in T. L. Huston (ed.) *Foundations of Interpersonal Attraction*. New York, NY: Academic Press.

—— (1980). *The Belief in a Just World. A Fundamental Delusion*. New York, NY: Plenum.

Levy, F. and Murnane, R. (1992). 'Earnings levels and earnings inequality: A review of recent trends and proposed explanations', *Journal of Economic Literature*, 30: 1333–81.

Lewis, J. (1992). 'Gender and the development of welfare regimes', *Journal of European Social Policy*, 2(3): 159–73.

Lind, J. and Hornemann Møller, I. (eds.) (1999). *Inclusion and Exclusion: Unemployment and Non-standard Employment in Europe*. Aldershot: Ashgate.

Lirhe. (1997). 'Le processus de licenciement économique', *Commissariat Général du Plan*, March.

Lødemel, I. (1992). 'Sosialhjelpa I europeisk inntektssikring', *Sosiologi I dag*, 2: 57–72.

—— (1997). *The Welfare Paradox. Income Maintenance and Personal Social Services in Norway and Britain, 1946–1966*. Oslo: Scandinavian University Press.

—— (ed.) (2002). 'Workfare in six European nations, findings from evaluations and recommendations for future development', Fafo-paper 24, Oslo: Fafo.

—— and Schulte, B. (1992). 'Social assistance—A part of social security or the poor law in new disguise?', in *Yearbook*, Leuven: European Institute of Social Security.

—— and Trickey, H. (2001). *An Offer You Can't Refuse. Workfare in International Perspective*. Bristol: The Policy Press.

Mabbet, D. and Bolderson, H. (1999). 'Theories and methods in comparative social policy', in J. Clasen (ed.) *Comparative Social Policy: Concepts, Theories and Methods*. Oxford: Blackwell Publishers.

Machin, S. (1996). 'Changes in the relative demand for skills in the UK labour market', in A. Booth and D. J. Snower (eds.) *Acquiring Skills: Market Failures, Their Symptoms and Policy Responses*. Cambridge: Cambridge University Press.

—— and van Reenen, J. (1998). 'Technology and changes in skill structure: Evidence from seven OECD countries', *Quarterly Journal of Economics*, 113: 1215–44.

Madsen, P. K. and Munch-Madsen, P. (2001). 'European employment strategy and national policy regimes', in D. G. Mayes, J. Berhman, and R. Salais (eds.) *Social Exclusion and European Policy*. London: Edward Elgar.

Mallet, L. and Teyssier, F. (1992). *Sureffectif et licenciement Èconomique Droit social*. p. 348–59.

Malmberg-Heimonen, I. and Julkunen, I. (2000). 'Gender, family context and labour-market involvement in six northern European countries', in A. Furlong and T. Hammer (eds.) *Youth Unemployment and Marginalisation in Northern Europe*. Norway: NOVA.

Malthus, T. (1998[1798]). *An essay on the principle of population.* Amherst: Promethus Books.

Manacorda, M. and Petrongolo, B. (1999). 'Skill Mismatch and Unemployment in OECD Countries', *Economica,* 66: 181–207.

Marsh, C. and Alvaro, J. L. (1990). 'A cross-cultural perspective on the social and psychological distress caused by unemployment', *European Sociological Review,* 6(3): 237–55.

Marshall, T. H. (1985). *T. H. Marshall's Social Policy.* London: Hutchinson and Co.

Martin, J. P. (1998). *What Works among Active Labour Market Policies: Evidence from OECD Countries' Experiences.* Labour Market and Social Policy—Occasional Paper, No. 35, Paris: OECD.

Mayes, D. G. and Viren, M. (2001). *Macroeconomic Factors, Policies and the Development of Social Exclusion.* Centre for Research on Europe Discussion Paper, University of Canterbury, New Zealand.

—— Berghman, J., and Salais, R. (eds.) (2001). *Social Exclusion and European Policy.* London: Edward Elgar.

McKee, L. and Bell, C. (1985). 'Marital and family relations in times of male unemployment', in B. Roberts, R. Finnegan, and D. Gallie (eds.) *New Approaches to Economic Life.* Manchester: Manchester University Press.

—— —— (1986). 'His unemployment, her problem: The domestic and marital consequences of male unemployment', in S. Allen, A. Waton, K. Purcell, and S. Wood (eds.) *The Experience of Unemployment.* London: Macmillan.

Mead, L. (1986). *Beyond Entitlement: The Social Obligations of Citizenship.* New York, NY: The Free Press.

—— (1997a). *From Welfare to Work: Lessons from America.* London: Institute of Economic Affairs.

—— (1997b). *The New Paternalism: Supervisory Approaches to Welfare.* Washington, DC: The Brooking Institute.

Mellander, (1999). 'The multi-dimensional demand for labour and skill-biased technical change', Mimeo, Industriens Utredningsinstitut, Stockholm.

Midgley, J. (1997). *Social Welfare in Global Context.* Thousand Oaks, CA: Sage Publications.

Mishra, R. (1977). *Society and Social Policy.* London: Macmillan.

Morel, S. (1998). 'American workfare versus French insertion policies: An application of common's theoretical framework', Paper presented at Annual Research Conference of the Association for Public Policy and Management, New York.

Mortensen, D. (1977). 'Unemployment insurance and job search decisions', *Industrial and Labor Relations Review,* 30: 505–17.

Mortensen, D. T. and Pissarides, C. A. (1999). 'Unemployment responses to skill-biased technology shocks: The role of labour market policy', *Economic Journal,* 109: 242–65.

Moylan, S., Millar, J., and Davies, R. (1984). *For Richer, For Poorer? DHSS Cohort Study of Unemployed Men.* London: HMSO.

Muffels, R., Tsakloglou, P., and Mayes, D. G. (eds.) (2002). *Social Exclusion in European Welfare States*. Cheltenham: Edward Elgar.

Muhlau, P. and Horgan, J. (2001). *Labour Market Status and the Wage Position of the Low-Skilled*. European Low-Wage Employment Research Network Working Paper 5.

Murphy, K. M. and Welch, F. (1992). 'The structure of wages', *Quarterly Journal of Economics*, 107: 285–326.

Murray, A. (1990). *The Emerging British Underclass*. Institute of Economic Affairs, Health and Welfare Unit, London.

—— and Steedman, H. (1998). *Growing Skills in Europe: The Changing Skill Profiles of France, Germany, the Netherlands, Portugal, Sweden and the UK*. Centre for Economic Performance Discussion Paper, No. 399, London School of Economics.

Narendranathan, W. and Stewart, M. B. (1993). 'How does benefit effect vary as unemployment spells lengthen?', *Journal of Applied Econometrics*, 8: 361–81.

Nathan, R. P. (1993). *Turning Promises into Performance. The Management Challenge of Implementing Workfare*. New York, NY: Columbia University Press.

Nickell, S. (1979). 'Estimating the probability of leaving unemployment', *Econometrica*, 47(5): 1249–66.

—— (2003). 'Poverty and worklessness in Britain'. Royal Economic Society Presidential Address at the RES Conference at Warwick University.

—— and Bell, B. (1996). 'Changes in the distribution of wages and unemployment in OECD countries', *America Economic Review*, 86: 302–8.

Nolan, B., Hauser, R., and Zoyem, J.-P. (2000). 'The Changing Effects of Social Protection on Poverty' in Gallie, D. and Paugam, S. (eds.) *Welfare Regimes and the Experience of Unemployment in Europe*. Oxford: Oxford University Press, 87–106.

—— and Whelan, C. T. (2000). *Loading the Dice? A Study of Cumulative Disadvantage*. Dublin: Oak Tree Press.

O'Connell, P. J. (2002). 'Are they working? Market orientation and the effectiveness of active labour-market programmes in Ireland', *European Sociological Review*, 18(1): 65–83.

OECD (Organisation of Economic Co-operation and Development) (1994a). *OECD Jobs Study: Facts, Analysis, Strategies*. Paris: OECD.

—— (1994b). *New Orientation for Social Policy, Social Policy Studies*, no.12, Paris: OECD.

—— (1997a). *Employment Outlook*. Paris: OECD.

—— (1997b). *Making Work Pay. Taxation, Benefits, Employment and Unemployment*. Paris: OECD.

—— (1999). *Employment Outlook*. Paris: OECD.

—— (2002). *Employment Outlook July 2002*. Paris: OECD.

OECD/CERI (1997). 'Literacy skills: Use them or lose them', in *Education Policy Analysis*. Paris: OECD.

Olafsson, O. and Svensson, P. G. (1986). 'Unemployment-related lifestyle changes and health disturbances in adolescents and children in the western countries', *Social Science and Medicine*, 22(11): 1105–13.

Paugam, S. (1991). *La disqualification sociale*. Paris: Presses Universitaires de France.

—— (1996a). 'The spiral of precariousness: A multidimensional approach to the process of social disqualification in France', in G. Room (ed.) *Beyond the Threshold: The Measurement and Analysis of Social Exclusion*. Bath: Policy Press.

—— (ed.) (1996b). *L'exclusion: L'etat des savoirs*. Paris: La Decouverte.

—— (2000). *Le salarié de la précarité*. Paris.

Peck, J. (1998). 'Workfare, a geopolitical etymology', *Environment and Planning D: Society and Space*, 16: 133–60.

—— (1999). 'Workfare in the Sun: Politics, representation, method in US welfare-to-work-strategies', *Political Geography*, 17: 535–66.

Pedersen, P. J. and Smith, N. (2001). *Unemployment Traps: Do Financial Disincentives Matter?* EPAG Working Paper 18. Colchester: University of Essex.

Pierson, P. (1998). 'Irresistible forces, immovable objects: Post-industrial welfare states confront permanent austerity', *Journal of European Public Policy*, 5(4): 539–60.

Raveaud, G. (2002). 'Employability and social exclusion: A capabilities approach', in R. Muffels, P. Tsakloglou, and D. G. Mayes (eds.) *Social Exclusion in European Welfare States*. Cheltenham: Edward Elgar.

Riphahn, R. T. (2001). 'Rational poverty or poor rationality? The take-up of social assistance benefits', *Review of Income and Wealth*, 47(3): 379–98.

Rodrigues, M. J. (ed.) (2002). *The New Knowledge Economy in Europe— A Strategy for International Competitiveness and Social Cohesion*. Gloucester: Edward Elgar Publishing Inc.

Room, G. (ed.) (1995). *Beyond the Threshold: The Measurement and Analysis of Social Exclusion*. Bristol: Policy Press.

Rosanvallon, P. (2000). *The New Social Question. Rethinking the Welfare State*. Princeton, NJ: Princeton University Press.

Rose, R. and Davis, P. L (1994). *Inheritance in Public Policy: Change without Choice in Britain*. New Haven, CT: Yale University Press.

Rouyer, R. (2001). 'Un cadrage macro et méso-économique des licenciements économiques', in G. Schmidt (co-ordinated) 'La gestion des sureffectifs: enjeux et pratiques', *Economica*, September.

Russell, H. (1996). *Women's Experience of Unemployment: A Study of British Women in the 1980s*. D. Phil. Thesis, University of Oxford.

—— and Barbieri, P. (2000). 'Gender and the experience of unemployment', in D. Gallie and S. Paugam (eds.) *Welfare Regimes and the Experience of Unemployment in Europe*. Oxford: Oxford University Press.

Salomäki, A. (2001). 'Net replacement rates of the unemployed: Comparisons of various approaches', in M. Buti, P. Sestito, and H. Wijkander (eds.)

Taxation, Welfare and the Crisis of Unemployment in Europe. Cheltenham: Edward Elgar.

—— and Munzi, T. (1999). 'Net replacement rates of the unemployed: Comparisons of various approaches', *EC DG ECFIN Economic Papers*, European Commission, 133.

Scharpf, F. W. (2002). 'The European social model: Coping with the challenges of diversity', *Journal of Common Market Studies*, 40(4): 645–69.

—— and Schmidt, V. A. (eds.) (2000). *Welfare and Work in the Open Economy*, Vol. 1: 'From Vulnerability to Competitiveness', Vol. 2: 'Common Challenges and Diverse Responses'. Oxford: Oxford University Press.

Schlozman, K. L. and Verba, S. (1979). *From Injury to Insult: Unemployment, Class and Political Response*. Cambridge, MA: Harvard University Press.

Schmid, G., Speckesser, S., and Hilbert, C. (2001). 'Does active labour market policy matter? An aggregate impact analysis for Germany', in Jaap de Koning and Hugh Mosley (eds.) *Labour Market Policy and Unemployment. Impact and Process Evaluations in Selected European Countries*. Cheltenham: Edward Elgar.

Schmidtz, D. and Gooding, R. (1998). *Social Welfare and Individual Responsibility*. Cambridge: Cambridge University Press.

Schmitt, J. (1995). 'The changing structure of male earnings in Britain, 1974–1988', in R. Freeman and L. Katz (eds.) *Changes and Differences in Wage Structures*. Chicago, IL: University of Chicago Press.

Seelinger, R. (1996). 'Contextualising and researching policy convergence', *Policy Studies Journal*, 24(2): 334–7.

Shragge, E. (1997). *Workfare: Ideology for a New Underclass*. Toronto, Canada: Garamond Press.

Sianesi, B. (2002). *Swedish Active Labour Market Programmes in the 1990s: Overall Effectiveness and Differential Performance*. IFS Working Paper. W02/03 London: Institute of Fiscal Studies.

Siebert, H. (1997). 'Labour market rigidities: At the root of unemployment in Europe', *Journal of Economic Perspectives*, 11: 37–54.

Silver, H. (1994). 'Social exclusion and social solidarity: Three paradigms', *International Labour Review*, 133: 531–78.

—— (1995). 'Reconceptualising social disadvantage: Three paradigms of social exclusion', in G. Rodgers, C. Gore, and J. B. Figueiredo (eds.) *Social Exclusion: Rhetoric, Reality, Responses*. Geneva: International Institute for Labour Studies.

Simpson, D., Love, J., and Walker, J. (1987). *The Challenge of New Technology*. Brighton: Wheatsheaf Books.

Snower, D. J. (1996). 'The low-skill, bad-job trap', in A. Booth and D. J. Snower (eds.) *Acquiring Skills: Market Failures, Their Symptoms and Policy Responses*; Cambridge: Cambridge University Press.

—— (1997). 'Evaluating unemployment policies: What do the underlying theories tell us?', in D. J. Snower and G. D. L. Dehesa (eds.)

Unemployment Policy: Government Options for the Labour Market.
Cambridge: Cambridge University Press.

Spiezia, V. (2000). 'The effects of benefits on unemployment and wages: A comparison of unemployment compensation schemes', *International Labour Review*, 139(1): 73–87.

Standing, G. (1990). 'The road to workfare—Alternative to workfare or threat to occupation', *International Labour Review*, 129(6): 677–91.

——(1999). *Global Labour Flexibility. Seeking Distributive Justice.* Houndmills: MacMillan.

Steedman, H. and McIntosh, S. (2001). 'Measuring low skills in europe: How useful is the ISCED framework', *Oxford Economic Papers*, forthcoming.

Steiner, H. (1994). *Essays on Right.* Oxford: Blackwell.

Sutherland, H. (1999). 'EUROMOD data robustness assessment exercise questionnaire', microsimulation unit, Department of Applied Economics, University of Cambridge.

—— (2001). *Final Report. EUROMOD: An Integrated European Benefit-tax Model.* EUROMOD Working Paper EM9/01, Department of Applied Economics, University of Cambridge, available through http://www.econ.cam.ac.uk/dae/mu/emod.htm.

Teague, P. (1999). 'Reshaping employment regimes in Europe: Policy shifts alongside boundary change', *Journal of Public Policy*, 19(1): 33–62.

Telo, M. (2002). 'Governance and government in the EU: OMC', in M. J. Rodrigues (ed.) *The New Knowledge Economy in Europe.* Cheltenham: Edward Elgar.

Thierry, D. (2001). 'Social Plans: how to go from a logic of means to a logic of results!, *Le Monde*, 11.09.01.

Tinbergen, J. (1954). *International Economic Integration.* Amsterdam: Elsevier.

Torfing, J. (1999). 'Workfare with welfare: Recent reforms of the danish welfare state', *Journal of European Social Policy*, 9(1): 5–28.

Valkenburg, B. and Lind, J. (2002). 'Orthodoxy and reflexivity in international comparative analysis', in R. van Berkel and I. Hornemann Møller (eds.) *Active Social Policies in the EU. Inclusion through Participation?* Bristol: The Policy Press.

van Berkel, R. and Hornemann Møller, I. (eds.) (2002). *Active Social Policies in the EU. Inclusion through Participation?* Bristol: The Policy Press.

——Coenen, H., and Dekker, A. (1999). 'Regulating the unemployed: From protection to participation', in J. Lind and I. Hornemann Møller (eds.) *Inclusion and Exclusion: Unemployment and Non-standard Employment in Europe.* Aldershot: Ashgate.

——Hornemann Møller, I., and Williams, C. (2002). 'The concept of inclusion/exclusion and the concept of work', in R. van Berkel and I. Hornemann Møller (eds.) *Active Social Policies in the EU. Inclusion through Participation?* Bristol: The Policy Press.

Vandenbroucke, F. (2001). 'Open co-ordination on pensions and the future of Europe's social model', Closing speech at the Conference. *Towards a New Architecture for Social Protection?* Leuven, October.

Vleminckx, K. and Berghman, J. (2001). 'Social exclusion and the welfare state: An overview of conceptual issues and implications', in D. G. Mayes, J. Berghman, and R. Salais (eds.) *Social Exclusion and European Policy*. London: Edward Elgar.

Vogel, B. (2000). 'Am Rande der Arbeitsgesellschaft' [On the Edge of the Work Society], *Verhaltenstherapie and Psychosoziale Praxis*, 32(3): 359–66.

Wacker, A. (1983). 'Differentielle Verarbeitungsformen von Arbeitslosigkeit—Anmerkungen zur aktuellen Diskussion in der Arbeitslosenforschung' [Differential Coping with Unemployment. Annotations to the Actual Debate in Unemployment Research], *Prokla*, 53: 77–88.

Walker, R. (1991). *Thinking about Workfare: Evidence from the US*. London: HMSO.

Wallace, C. (1987). *For richer or poorer: Growing up in and out of work*. London: Tavistock.

Warr, P. (1987). *Work, Unemployment and Mental Health*. Oxford: Clarendon Press.

—— (1989). 'Individual and community adaptation to unemployment', in B. Starrin, P. G. Svensson, and H. Wintersberger (eds.) *Unemployment, Poverty, and Quality of Working Life—Some European Experiences*. Berlin: Edition Sigma.

—— Cook, J., and Wall, T. (1979). 'Scales for the measurement of some work attitudes and aspects of psychological well-being', *Journal of Occupational Psychology*, 52: 129–48.

Whelan, C. T., Hannon, D. F., and Creighton, S. (1991). *Unemployment, Poverty and Psychological Distress*. Dublin: Economic and Social Research Institute.

White, M. (1983). *Long-term Unemployment and Labour Markets*. London: Policy Studies Institute.

Wilensky, H. (1975). *The Welfare state and equality*. Berkley, CA: University of California.

—— (1992). 'Active labour-market policy: Its contents, effectiveness and odd relation to evaluation research', in C. Crouch and A. Heath (eds.) *Social Research and Social Reform*. Oxford: Clarendon Press.

Wilson, J. (1987). *The Truly Disadvantaged: The Inner City, the Underclass and Public Policy*. Chicago, IL: University of Chicago Press.

Wiseman, M. (1991). *What Did the American Work-welfare Demonstrations Do? Why Should Germans Care?* Bremen: Zentrum für Sozialpolitik, University of Bremen.

Witzel, A. (1987). Das problemzentrierte Inerview. [The problem-focused interview]. In G. Jüttemann (E.), *Qualitative Forschung in der Psychologie*. [Qualitative Research in Psychology] (pp. 227–256). Heidelberg: Asanger.

—— (1995). Auswertung problemzentrierter Interviews: Grundlagen und Erfahrungen. [Analysis o problem-focused interviews: Fundamental principles and experiences]. In R. Strobl & A. Böttger (eds.), *Wahre Geschichten? Zu Theorie und Pracis qualitativer Interviews*. [True stories? Theory and Practice of Qualitative Interviews] (pp. 49–76). Baden-Baden: Nomos.

Wood, A. (1994). *North–South Trade, Employment and Inequality*. Oxford: Clarendon Press.

NAME INDEX

Groot, W. 142
Gustavsen, B. 32

Hakim, C. 82
Hammer, T. 8, 82, 88, 90, 101
Harrison, B. 149
Harrison, R. 58
Hart, R. A. 109
Hartog, J. 142
Haskel, J. 150, 151, 152
Hauser, R. 35, 37
Heady, P. 35
Heckman, J. 116, 118
Heeringen, K. van 61
Heikkilä, M. 198, 200
Hills, J. 244, 258
Hobcraft, J. 31, 32
Hodson, D. 254, 255, 263
Holmlund, B. 29
Horgan, J. 158
Hornemann Møller, I. 223,
    224, 238, 250
House, J. S. 47
Hvinden, B. 200

Ichino, A. 109
Immervoll, H. 10, 110, 118, 119,
    124, 126, 127
Issing, O. 250

Jackman, R. 158
Jackson, P. R. 83, 84
Jahoda, M. 36, 54, 55, 57, 83
Jarrett, J. E. 58
Jensen, P. 109
Jones, C. 214
Jordan, B. 201, 202, 203
Julkunen, I. 82, 83, 88

Kahn, L. 154
Karras, G. 248
Katz, L. F. 149
Kaul, H. 100
Kelvin, P. 58
Kieselbach, T. 3, 5, 7, 56, 61, 72, 75, 79
Kilpatrick, R. 57
Kirsch, J. L. 147, 159, 161, 186
Knuth, M. 186
Kronauer, M. 3, 35, 58, 59
Krueger, A. B. 156
Krugman, P. 154
Kvande, E. 100

Lampard, R. 36
Larsson, A. 200
Lawless, P. 47
Layard, R. 106
Le Grand, J. 200
Leibfried, S. 238
Leira, A. 87
Leisering, L. 221, 238
Lemkow, L. 61
Leonard, M. 76
Lerner, M. J. 56
Levy, F. 149
Lewis, J. 87, 101
Lind, J. 224, 239
Little, M. 36
Lødemel, I. 198, 205, 210, 213,
    216, 222, 223

Maassen van Den Brink, H.
    142
Mabbet, D. 212
Machin, S. 149, 150
Madsen, P. K. 252
Maher, I. 254, 255, 263
Mallet, L. 174
Malmberg-Heimonen, I. 83
Malthus, T. 221
Manacorda, M. 158
Manning, A. 158
Marsh, C. 84
Marshall, T. H. 203
Martin, J. P. 232
Mayes, D. G. 246, 248
McIntosh, S. 14, 146
McKee, L. 36
Mead, L. 201, 202, 203
Mellander 152, 153, 154, 155
Micklewright, J. 10, 107, 111,
    116
Midgley, J. 213
Mishra, R. 212
Morel, S. 201
Mortensen, D. 29, 154
Mosley, H. 27
Moylan, S. 35
Muffels, R. 258
Muhlau, P. 158
Munch-Madsen, P. 252
Munzi, T. 112
Murnane, R. 149
Murphy, K. M. 149
Murray, A. 83, 147, 159

SUBJECT INDEX

activation 20–6, 28, 32, 59, 130, 198–205,
    208, 210–12, 217, 221, 223–42, 247,
    252, 259
  and social inclusion 226–8
  and personal well-being 229–31
  convergence of programmes 212
  Danish programme 211
  policy/policies 1, 20–4, 26–7, 197–8,
    200–6, 212, 219, 221, 223–42
  political choice, effects of 217–20
  programmes 22–3, 31, 211–12, 215–16,
    224–6, 228–32, 236–7, 241
  risks of residualization 236–7
  social 1, 22, 197–8, 208, 212–13, 217, 219
active labour market policies (ALMPs) 27,
    190, 199–200, 204, 206, 218–20
associations 48, 50, 69, 227
Austria 154

Belgium 5, 15, 22, 38–9, 41–2, 44, 49, 51,
    61–3, 66, 68, 70, 72–5, 82, 146, 154,
    158, 165, 223–4, 233
benefits, unemployment 123, 126,
    201, 221
  disincentive/incentive effects of 7–8, 10–13,
    28, 30–1, 34, 105–10, 126, 198, 200
  eligibility for 11, 29, 84, 107, 112, 123,
    127, 129, 203
  financial support 16, 21, 28, 76, 171, 184
  replacement rate/rates 10–13, 28–30,
    106–39
    measurement of 10, 106–8, 111, 116
    women's 12, 124
  social assistance benefits 121, 123, 126,
    197–8, 201–4, 206–9, 210–22, 226,
    233, 252
  social insurance 29, 114, 118, 120–1, 127,
    132, 204, 213, 251

class/social class 13, 31, 46
clubs 41–2, 50–2
compulsion see workfare
criminal activity 67, 76

Democrat party 198
Denmark 4, 7, 11–13, 21–2, 30, 37–42,

44–5, 49–52, 83, 87, 101, 107, 113,
    118–26, 132, 139, 154, 165, 198,
    202, 204–5, 208, 210, 214–16, 219,
    221, 223–4, 229, 251, 259–60
dependency 5, 28, 60, 67, 70, 73, 75, 83,
    201–2, 209, 213, 220, 239, 252
  rational 202
drug dependency 67–8

educational/skill qualifications 74, 97
  educational attainment 14, 31,
    165, 258
  qualification/qualifications 31, 55, 60,
    63–71, 74, 79, 104, 144–5, 151–2,
    157–8, 162, 167, 171, 179–80, 191,
    196, 235
employment:
  irregular see informal economy
  programmes 207, 224–5, 232–6, 241
  policies 193, 200, 257
  /population ratios 143–4
  strategy 257, 260
  subsidized 27, 224–5, 229–30,
    232–6, 241
  trajectories, security of 172, 187
employment commitment 6–9, 26,
    28–9, 81–104
  women's commitment 9, 82–5,
    92–104
employment protection see redundancy
    procedures
  models of 17
European Commission 80, 87, 105, 107,
    112, 196, 199, 213, 243, 245, 262
European Employment Strategy (EES) 25,
    245, 249–50, 252–3, 255–7, 260–2
European social model 244, 254, 259, 262
European tax-benefit model (EUROMOD)
    11, 107, 111, 113, 117–18, 129
European Union 1, 4, 13, 24, 32, 37, 45, 80,
    82, 140, 142–4, 166, 197, 199, 213,
    223, 229, 243–5, 247, 249, 250–62
  1992 Council Recommendations 252
  and macroeconomic dialogue 249–50
  Broad Economic Policy Guidelines
    (BEPGs) 249–50, 258, 260, 262

Printed in the United Kingdom
by Lightning Source UK Ltd.
104756UKS00001B/67